Also by Nigel Parton

The Politics of Child Abuse

Governing the Family

Child Care, Child Protection and the State

Nigel Parton

MACMILLAN

First published 1991 by
THE MACMILLAN PRESS LTD
Houndmills, Basingstoke, Hampshire RG21 2XS
and London
Companies and representatives
throughout the world

ISBN 0–333–54121–9 hardcover
ISBN 0–333–54122–7 paperback

A catalogue record for this book is available
from the British Library.

Printed in Hong Kong

Reprinted 1993

For Rita and Bob

Contents

List of Tables   viii
Preface   ix

1. **Social Work, Social Regulation and the Family**   1
2. **Child Care, Prevention and Partnership**   19
3. **Child Abuse, Authority and Risk**   52
4. **Sexual Abuse, the Cleveland Affair and the
   Private Family**   79
5. **Co-ordination, Management and Social
   Assessment**   116
6. **The Children Act 1989: Reconstructing the
   Consensus**   147
7. **A Contemporary Political Economy of Child
   Protection**   193

Notes   215
Bibliography   225
Index   239

List of Tables

2.1 Number of children removed to a place of
safety during the year April 1 to March 31 in
England 1978–84   35

3.1 Number of children removed to a place of
safety in England, years ending 31 March
1983–8   54

3.2 Child abuse and neglect high-risk checklist   61

3.3 Carlile Report hierarchy of state interventions
in the family   75

Preface

In some respects this study can be read as simply taking further the story and critical analysis first developed in *The Politics of Child Abuse* (1985b). In other ways, however, it is quite different. During the 1980s it seemed that a major shift emerged in the way the state attempted to prevent harm to children living in the family in Britain. Rather than emphasise the dual and sometimes competing concerns of stopping *child abuse* and improving *child care*, increasingly the focus was on a new activity – *child protection*. The 1989 Children Act and the various official guidance to professionals in the wake of the Cleveland inquiry gave expression to a new set of concepts, rules and practices which attempted to overcome the apparent crisis which seemed to characterise the child care system during the period. This could be seen as part of wider changes in state formation and social regulation in Britain in the 1980s illustrated by a series of measures affecting the social services and social policy more generally.

In order to make sense of these changes, a rather different conceptual and analytic toolkit was required therefore. Rather than being centrally concerned with analysing the emergence and impact of the problem of *child abuse* as previously, I am here concerned with, on the one hand, discussing a broader range of legal, regulatory and interventive strategies, while on the other, analysing in some detail the debates, recommendations for reform and the processes of policy change. The book therefore combines both a different conceptual framework and a closer attention to detail in order to explain the emergence of a new discourse focused around notions of child protection and family autonomy.

The book aims to help professionals – particularly social

workers – working in the field, understand the nature of these changes and their impact on both their own role and responsibilities and the experiences of the men, women and children with whom they work. It also aims to provide a case study of the processes of change in social policy and make a contribution to current theoretical debates about the nature of social regulation in contemporary society.

I have accumulated numerous debts in the process of completing the project. Some of the ideas which inform the book first saw the light of day in previous smaller collaborative projects (Parton and Martin 1989; Parton and Parton 1989a, 1989b). Both Norma Martin and Christine Parton will recognise elements of that work here and must also take some responsibility for reawakening my interest and concerns in the area.

However, the opportunity to carry out the research which informs the book and the time to write it arose when I was lucky enough to be awarded a Hallsworth Fellowship during 1989–90. I would therefore like to thank both the Fellowship and the Department of Social Policy and Social Work at Manchester University for welcoming me and providing such a conducive environment for intensive study. Caroline Glendinning and Jean Ashton were crucial in this respect – Caroline for both putting up with me and offering support and Jean for being so good-humoured and meticulous with the typing of what were supposed to be different drafts but in effect were very scrappy bits of paper. Barbara Bys assisted with the typing. Similarly, my long-suffering colleagues in the Social Work section at Huddersfield Polytechnic let me take up the Fellowship at a time of rapid change and severe resource constraint – one suspects, though, they coped better in my absence than if I had been present.

However, numerous others have had an impact on its content via their generous contributions of time and the sharing of their experiences and expertise. I would particularly like to thank Peter Smith and David Hinchliffe for their interest well beyond what could reasonably be hoped for. Discussions with Dennis Allen, Louis Blom-Cooper, Rupert Hughes, Barbara Kahan, Tina Lyons, Christine McKay, Tony Morrison, Neil Patrick, Mary Ryan, Nigel Speight, Jane Tunstill, and Avril

Wilson were all invaluable. Robert Dingwall, Bob Franklin, Nick Frost, Christine Hallett, Jerry Johnstone, Michael King, Mark Philp, Nik Rose and Kevin Stenson all suggested articles and material which I have found most instructive. Finally, I would like to thank Bill Jordan, Jean Packman and Christine Parton for, particularly in the final case, living with the project throughout. Apart from offering generous support and encouragement, they have critically commented on every chapter and generally tried to keep me to the task in hand.

I am very conscious, however, that the particular interpretation I have put on things will vary from those that have been so generous and some may well feel I have missed the mark altogether. It is important to stress more than ever, therefore, that I am completely responsible for what follows.

NIGEL PARTON

1

Social Work, Social Regulation and the Family

Introduction

The Children Act 1989 can be seen as the fruition of heated arguments during the 1980s about how British society should respond to the problems related to child abuse and child care. It was an attempt to address some of the most sensitive and potentially explosive issues concerning the relationship between the child, the family and various state agents. In introducing the Bill for its second reading into the House of Commons on 27 April 1989, David Mellor, the Minister of State at the Department of Health, said:

> As I hope I made clear, we have high ambitions for this Bill. We hope and believe that it will bring order, integration, relevance and a better balance to the law – a better balance not just between the rights and responsibilities of individuals and agencies, but, most vitally, between the need to protect children and the need to enable parents to challenge intervention in the upbringing of their children. Recent well-publicised cases, including the tragic cases of Kimberley Carlile, Doreen Mason and the events in Cleveland in 1987 have graphically shown the consequences of getting that balance wrong. Of course, of itself, legislation cannot stop such tragedies, but we hope that a clear legal framework will help to make more likely clear-eyed judgements by key people involved in child welfare. (*Hansard*, HoC, Vol. 151, No. 94, Col. 1107)

The Act was wide-ranging and concerned with far more than simply child abuse. It attempted to integrate and rationalise

1

legislation in relation to the children in divorce, fostering, adoption, children's homes, delinquency, non-school attendance, as well as where they may be subjected to neglect and abuse. What it addressed at its heart, however, was a problem which had been a major tension for the liberal state since the late nineteenth century, namely: how can we devise a *legal* basis for the power to intervene into the family which does not convert *all* families into clients of the state? Such a problem is posed by the contradictory demands of, on the one hand, ensuring that the family is experienced by its members as autonomous and the primary sphere for rearing children, while on the other recognising there is a need for interventions in some families where they are seen as failing in this primary task and in a context where such laws are supposed to act as the general norms applicable to all.

In this respect, the current arrangements were seen to be failing on both counts. If the tragic deaths of Jasmine Beckford, Kimberley Carlile, Tyra Henry and Doreen Mason had demonstrated that state agents were intervening too little, too late, and hence failing to protect children, the spectre of the Cleveland affair demonstrated that state agents were also intervening too early and too much and hence failing to protect the autonomy of the family. There was a need, therefore, not only to establish a new *balance* between these contradictory demands, but also a new framework whereby this difficult task could be carried out. Such a framework could be resolved only in part by changes in the law. There was also a need for a new set of practices, attitudes and priorities amongst the professionals, particularly social workers, who carried the burden of responsibility in this highly sensitive and emotionally charged area.

The purpose of this book is to assess how this became such a major issue during the 1980s and analyse how the various attempts to respond and resolve it were taken up – and others were not. It is concerned with analysing the main social and political forces that have informed the construction of a new discourse for state interventions in the family and thereby identify the central elements that have been put in place. In the process, we will be in a better position to assess the nature of the changes and the possible implications for those involved, whether they be professionals, parents or children. The book aims, therefore, to provide an insight into three interrelated themes: the nature of modern social work with children and families; the processes whereby elements of the social world become problematised and subject to social policy change; the changes in the form of social regulation of the family in contemporary Britain.

More particularly, we can identify a shift during the 1980s in the relationship between the family and various state agencies for the purposes of preventing harm to children. At its simplest, this can be seen in terms of a move from concerns about *child care* and *child abuse* to ones about *child protection*, where the latter tries to combine attempts to protect children from danger while protecting the privacy of the family from unwarrantable interventions. It is with the understanding of this new discourse, with its central concerns of child protection and the processes whereby it has come about, that this book is concerned.

A Conceptual Framework

Conceptually and methodologically the study has borrowed from the approach(es) developed by Michel Foucault. It is primarily an investigation of the discourse of child protection and the related discourses of social work, medicine and the law. In referring to 'discourses', I am therefore recognising the centrality of language in representing and constituting social reality. However, I am also asserting that there is more at stake than 'mere words'. Discourses are structures of knowledge through which we understand, explain and decide things. They are structures of obligations which establish different responsibilities and authorities for different categories of persons such as parents, children, social workers, doctors, lawyers, and so on. They are impersonal forms, existing independently of any of these persons 'as individuals' (Foucault, 1977b; 1978). They are historical and political frameworks of social organisation that make some social actions possible whilst precluding others. 'A discourse is best understood as a system of possibility for knowledge' (Philp,

1985, p. 69). Foucault's method was to ask what rules permit certain statements to be made; what rules order these statements; what rules allow us to identify some statements as true and some as false; what rules allow the construction of a map, model or classificatory system; what rules allow us to identify certain individuals as authors; and what rules are revealed when an object of discourse is modified or transformed.

In order to understand what is meant by child protection, we need to understand how this differs from concerns and interventions to prevent child abuse and improve child care as previously. More particularly, how do the knowledges and practices derived from law, social work and medicine mesh and interrelate to make such practices possible and how have these interrelationships shifted in the process of identifying child protection as a major issue?

A discourse can be seen as a system of possibility that allows us to produce statements which can be either true or false (Woolgar 1986). It makes possible a field of knowledge. How do we 'know' that a child has been sexually abused when, until recently, both the phenomena of sexual abuse and the practices whereby it could be identified did not exist? How can we calculate that a family is 'safe' enough or a child 'is likely to suffer significant harm'? Both the construction of and frameworks for responding to such questions have undergone not just fine-tuning during the 1980s, but have been placed at the centre of public, political and professional agendas. How did the questions get placed on such agendas and how have the frameworks themselves been constructed? An analysis of discourse in this area will not only outline the significance of changes in language, which themselves signify changes in policy and practice, but will also provide an insight into the nature of contemporary policy and practice itself, how this has come about and for what reasons. What forms of policy and practice have emerged for the purposes of child protection and what types of knowledge should inform this? The study will be limited to analysing how this is represented in 'official' debates, policy documents and guidances rather than the way these are interpreted for the purposes of intervention by practitioners themselves. However, it will outline how the sphere of operations for such practices have been circumscribed and prioritised and in the process, the way new possibilities for practitioners and family members have thereby been opened up.

In attempting to excavate forms of practice, we need to identify the 'conditions of possibility' of the discourse of child protection and demonstrate the 'space' which had to exist for this form of knowledge to develop. The space is both theoretical and practical. It is this space which can be said to provide the rules for the formation of statements, and it is through this space that the discourse is related to social, economic and political factors. For the space itself arises from shifts in these structures.

The 'Disciplinary Society' and the 'Psy Complex'

Foucault's primary objective was to provide a critique of the way modern societies control and discipline their populations by sanctioning the knowledge-claims and practices of the new human sciences – particularly medicine, psychiatry, psychology and criminology – what Ingleby (1985) and Rose (1985) refer to as the 'psy' complex. He argued that these new disciplines legitimated new forms of knowledge and new forms of social regulation which have subverted the classical order of political rule based on sovereignty and right. They instituted new regimes of power exercised through disciplinary mechanisms and the stipulation of norms for human behaviour. The normal family, the healthy child, the perfect wife and the proper man both inform ideas about ourselves and are reproduced and legitimated through the practices of the 'psy' complex. The human sciences define normality both for ourselves and for the purposes of investigation, surveillance and treatment. According to Foucault, during the nineteenth century, these new knowledges increasingly colonised the old powers to such an extent that the more traditional forms of the law and judicial rights have been taken over. No longer are the crucial decisions taken in the courtroom according to the criteria of judicial rights, but in the hospital, the clinic or the welfare office according to criteria of 'normalisation'. Even when decisions are taken in the courtroom, these are increasingly colonised by the 'psy' complex and the criteria of 'normalisation' (Foucault, 1977a).

Disciplinary mechanisms which attempt to normalise, subject the individual to training and require a knowledge of the whole person in their social context and depend on medico-social expertise and judgements for their operation. They depend on direct supervision and surveillance and emphasise the need to effect change in characters, attitudes and behaviours in an individualised way. They are concerned with underlying causes and needs and attempt to contribute to the improvement of those being served as well as social defence. Because the 'psy' professions have an exclusive insight into the problems and the knowledge and techniques required, it is important they have wide discretion to diagnose and treat and thereby normalise.

In comparison, the juridicial emphasises the rule of law whereby those that break the rules will be subjected to a fixed penalty in proportion to the interests violated. There should be just sufficient law to maintain social order and its implementation should be public, accountable and closely delineated by due process and 'evidence'. The individual is deemed responsible for his/her actions so that mitigating circumstances are inadmissable. Once the sentence or penalty has been served, the person returns to a full citizen. There is no attempt to supervise, treat or rehabilitate.

There are three processes involved in discipline: hierarchical surveillance; normalising judgement; and the examination. Hierarchical surveillance provides a non-reciprocal monitoring gaze in which the bearers of power are able to create individual knowledge about human bodies over a continuous basis (Foucault, 1977, pp. 170–6). Normalising judgement involves, unlike juridicial judgement, a continuous discretionary evaluation of conduct in the context of floating standards between positive and negative poles which allows the application of detailed impositions and privileges (Foucault, 1977, pp. 177–83). According to Foucault the examination 'combines the techniques of an observing hierarchy and those of normalising judgement. It is a normalising gaze, a surveillance that makes it possible to qualify, to classify and to punish. It establishes over individuals a visibility through which one differentiates them and judges them' (Foucault, 1977, p. 184). Such a disciplinary mode of power embodies many of the activities of the 'dividing practices' of which medicine and social work are prime examples.

In the same way as Foucault has argued the juridicial has been colonised by the 'psy complex', others have argued that increasingly social problems have been medicalised such that infraction has been seen in terms of sickness rather than morality (Conrad and Schneider, 1980).

According to Foucault, such a shift has fed into major changes in the forms of social regulation. There now seems considerable agreement amongst researchers and social theorists that we can identify three 'master shifts' in contemporary systems of social control: (1) the decline of punishments which inflict physical pain to the body, characteristic of the pre-eighteenth century; (2) the emergence of imprisonment as the pre-eminent penalty for problem populations, isolated from charitable welfare functions, in the nineteenth century; (3) to a gradual movement towards decarceration and a 'dispersal of control' in the twentieth century, where welfare and penalty are increasingly intermeshed (Ignatieff, 1978, 1983; Cohen and Scull, 1983; Garland, 1981; 1985). From the nineteenth century onwards, the primary elements of the 'disciplinary' or 'carceral' society emerged and surveillance, classification, examination, ordering and coding techniques of power began to pervade throughout the social body. No longer was it appropriate to see power as repressive, as power and knowledge were interrelated and power was productive and constituted new practices. Power and knowledge were inseparable and forms of knowledge such as medicine, psychiatry and social work were directly related to the exercise of power, while power itself creates new objects of concern, interventions and knowledge, and thus accumulates new bodies of information (Miller, 1987).

Essentially, Cohen argues that the elements identified by Foucault in the nineteenth century have become even more evident in more recent years: '. . . a gradual expansion and intensification of the system; a dispersal of its mechanisms from more closed to more open sites and a consequent increase in the invisibility of social control and the degree of its penetration into the social body' (Cohen, 1985, pp. 83–4).

A number of dimensions to such changes are identified. While the old institutions – such as the prison – remain, new community-based initiatives are started, thus expanding both the system of social regulation taking in new and more deviants, while intensifying the intervention of the old ones. The visibility, ownership and identity of the social regulation institutions become less clear as the boundaries between them, and between them and the community, become blurred. In the process, the public merges with, and interpenetrates, the private. The family, the school and the community itself are absorbed into and permeated by the newly-developing and pervasive mechanisms of social regulation. Such changes are legitimated on the inevitable failures of the old mechanisms to fulfil their objectives and the system becomes self-perpetuating and justifies itself. With more and more experts brought in with their diffeent knowledges and experience of the social world, the system of classifications to allocate cases and demarcate areas of responsibility becomes of central significance. Cohen, following Foucault, sees the systems of assessment and classification as significant in understanding the internal rationale and self-perpetuating motor of modern systems of social regulation.

> This is not to say that the classification is any sense random. From the foundation of the control system, a single principle has governed every form of classification, screening, selection, diagnosis, prediction, typology and policy. This is the structural principle of binary opposition: how to sort out the good from the bad, the elect from the damned, the sheep from the goats, the amenable from the non-amenable, the treatable from the non-treatable, the good risks from the bad risks, the high prediction scorers from the low prediction scorers; how to know who belongs in the deep end, who in the shallow, and who is hard and who is soft. (Cohen, 1985, p. 86)

If this be the case, a major issue for this study is to identify the emerging systems of classification which characterise child protection work, how these might differ from previous systems, together with the implications for those carrying out the classification and those on the receiving end.

'Governmentality'

In his later work, Foucault argued that the idea of governmentality had increasingly dominated politics since the eight-
eenth century. Governmentality refers to the 'ensemble
formed by the institutions, procedures, analyses and reflections, the calculations and tactics, that allow the exercise of
this very specific albeit complex form of power' (Foucault,
1979, p. 20) and it is the regulation of the population which
has proved its unending concern (Hewitt, 1983). A certain
way of thinking about and approaching problems has dominated, so that modern industrial societies see their task in terms
of the 'calculated supervision, administration and maximisa-
tion of the forces of each and all' (Miller and Rose, 1990, p. 2).
Such an approach does not reduce the exercise of political
power to the actions of the reified sovereign state but draws
attention to the range of mechanisms whereby different
groups seek to regulate the lives of individuals, families and
communities. The analysis of policy suggested by the concept
of government implies that the very existence of a field of
concerns we call 'policy' should itself be treated as in need of
explanation. It highlights the diversity of powers and knowledges entailed in rendering fields practicable and amenable
to intervention (Foucault, 1986). It suggests the analysis of
policy cannot be confined to the study of different agencies, for
a complex and heterogeneous set of conditions make it possible for objects of policy to be problematised, and rendered
amenable to administration. Such an approach, while informed by a quite different theoretical background, bears
close resemblance to that developed by Hall, Land, Parker
and Webb in their study of Change, Choice and Conflict in
Social Policy (1975).[1]

Miller and Rose (1990) suggest that an analysis of policy
should give primary attention to discourse in two respects.
First, policy should be located in discussions about what is
conceived as the proper ends and means of government and
how these are articulated. Second, discourse should be seen as
the technology of thought whereby the particular technical
devices of writing, listing, numbering and computing render
an issue as a knowable, calculable and administrable object.

Knowing an object requires the invention of notational procedure, methods of gathering and presenting information, and
the use of these in ways whereby calculations and judgements
can be made. It is through such procedures that the 'object' of
the family, child care and child abuse are presented in a
particular form and hence made amenable to intervention and
regulation. Language provides the mechanism whereby policies and practices are represented, refined and made amenable to action. If issues or areas of concern are to be
transformed into new areas of government, there must be the
information available – statistics, reports, and so on – such
that it becomes susceptible to evaluation, calculation and
intervention. Similarly, for intervention and action to take
place in relation to the object of concern requires the use of
certain techniques or 'technologies' which provide the particular mechanisms through which the object of concern can
be modified and normalised. Such technologies may appear
quite mundane and refer to the:

> techniques of notation, computation and calculation; procedures of ex-
> amination and assessment; the invention of devices such as surveys and
> presentational forms such as tables; the standardisation of systems for
> training and the inculcation of habits; the inauguration of professional
> specialisms and vocabularies; building designs and architectural forms –
> the list is heterogeneous and is, in principle, unlimited. (Miller and
> Rose, 1990, p. 8)

At this technical level, a diverse range of indirect relations of
regulation and persuasion are put into place for the concerns
to be acted upon. This can have intended and unintended
consequences but has the result of both reinforcing and re-
constituting this new reality and the discourse which both
opens it up and represents it. The various health and welfare
professions which have grown alongside the growth of modern
government can be seen as particularly significant in operating in such spaces and where their claims to truth, scientific
knowledge and technical expertise can become powerful
mechanisms whereby government can be operationalised and
those to be served can be surveyed and acted upon such that it
is experienced as in 'their interests'. The development of the
range of expertise and their respective discourse and techno-

logies are of particular significance for modern government, and develop spheres of influences and claims to disinterested knowledge which provide a range of power(s) in their own right. They have proved particularly significant to enable 'government at a distance' or indirect methods of social regulation to take place. Such a development is of significance if the liberal ideal of maintaining autonomous free individuals who at the same time are, in some way, governed is to he realised.

Government understood in this sense draws attention to the ways in which the conduct of personal life has become a crucial mechanism in the exercise of political power and the active promotion of social well-being. The sphere of government is complex and includes unintended as well as the intended effects of policy. Social work strategies form only a small element within it but provides an important attempt to draw clients and their families into the sphere of government, not through repression, 'but through the promotion of subjectivity, through investments in individual lives, and the forging of alignments between the personal projects of citizens and the images of social order' (Miller and Rose, 1988, p. 172).

Social Work and the 'Tutelary Complex'

The problems identified by David Mellor concerning the relationship between family, state and children, and which lie at the heart of the 1989 Children Act, are however not new. What is new is that the previous forms of intervention and the balance(s) struck between state and family in the upbringing of children seemed to fall into such disrepute. Jacques Donzelot (1980), who draws on Foucault's approach, has analysed the transformations that took place in the late nineteenth century around the emergence of a new set of discourses which were interrelated via their common concern with the family. In doing so, a new site of activity and a new conceptual space was opened up which previously did not exist – what he calls 'the social'. The 'social' developed as a hybrid in the space between the private and the public spheres and produced new relations between the law, administration, medicine, the

school and the family. Central to its emergence was the
incorporation of a range of philanthropists into the judicial
process in respect of children, and the emergence of psychiatry
as a specialism which informed not only judicial decisions but
the practice of the successors to the philanthropists – social
workers. Thus, the subsequent growth and establishment of
social work during the twentieth century was closely interrelated with its increasing centrality to the welfare state,
culminating in the Seebohm reforms in the late 1960s (Clarke,
Langan and Lee, 1980; Clarke, 1988).

The emergence of 'the social' and its central concern with
the family was a positive solution to a major problem posed
for the liberal state (Hirst, 1981; Donzelot, 1988). Namely –
how can the state establish the rights of individual children
while promoting the family as the natural sphere for raising
children and hence not intervening in all families and thus
reducing its autonomy? Philanthropy, and subsequently social
work, developed at a midway point between individual initiative and the all-encompassing state. In effect, it provided a
compromise between the liberal vision of unhindered private
philanthropy, where children would inevitably be subjected to
the ultimate power of parental figures, particularly men, and
the socialist vision of the all-pervasive and all-encompassing
state which would take responsibility for all children's needs
and hence undermine the responsibility of the parental figures
(Dingwall and Eekelaar, 1988). If children were to develop
their full health and sensibilities, this could not be left to the
vagaries of the market and the autonomous patriarchal family.
The emergence of 'the social' was seen as the most appropriate way for the liberal state to maintain its legitimacy while
protecting children. 'For the liberal, however, the unresolved
problem is how child-rearing can be made into a matter of
public concern and its qualities monitored without destroying
the ideal of the family as a counterweight to state power, a
domain of voluntary, self-regulating actions' (Dingwall, Eekelaar and Murray, 1983, pp. 214–15).

Originally, this activity was carried out by philanthropic
voluntary agencies rather than by the state and Donzelot
argues that two techniques were of particular significance in
their relationship with families – what he calls 'moralisation'

and 'normalisation'. 'Moralisation' involved the use of financial and material assistance which was used as a leverage to encourage poor families to overcome their moral failure. It was available primarily for the deserving poor who could demonstrate that their problems arose for reasons beyond their control. 'Normalisation' applied to attempts to spread specific norms of living via education, legislation, or health and involved a response to complaints, invariably from women about men, and hence provided a means of entry into the home. In return for this guidance and moral support, such workers were given an insight into what was happening inside the home and gave a leverage to bring about changes in behaviour and lifestyle. Clearly, however, there were problems if the parents did not co-operate or did not approach the worker in the first place so that the children were left to unbridled parental devices.

In the late nineteenth and early twentieth centuries, symbolised by the 1908 Children Act, we can note the beginning of the absorption of these philanthropic activities into the state. There was to be a much clearer opportunity for statutory intervention if the parents did not co-operate or participate. While moralisation and normalisation were to be the primary form of contact, this was to be framed in legislation which would also give the possibility for coercive intervention. Tutelage, as Donzelot calls it, based on the notion of preventive intervention, would combine a number of elements, though coercive intervention would be used for the exceptional circumstances where the child's situation or the behaviour of the parents had gone below those expected and where the techniques of moralisation and normalisation had failed.

The 'national efficiency' movement defined problems of child welfare in the language of hygiene and individual and public health rather than morality (Eekelaar and Dingwall, 1990, p. 9) but in the process conceptualised the maltreatment of children along with those of maladjustment and delinquency and saw them all as part of the problem of child care for which neglect was the main focus. While concerns during the twentieth century centred increasingly on delinquency, this was seen as arising from severe deprivation in certain 'problem families'.

Not only was the primary anxiety during the 1960s related to delinquency, but the explanation for this and the social response to it was in terms of the unitary family.

The law played two important roles in relation to the 'tutelary complex'. First, medicine and social work were brought into the operation of the law itself. Along with the greater legally-sanctioned tutelary authority over the poor and incompetent family came a greater role for 'psy' knowledges in the decisions of the court. Increasingly, juvenile courts were concerned with the parents' character and the home circumstances rather than merely establishing the 'facts' of an offence against the child. Second, the establishment of the tutelary complex implied no displacement of the rule of law and its primary manifestation, the courts. In effect, the law legitimated the tutelary complex and sanctioned surveillance. Social work agencies were given a new-found authority for their activities and interventions and could approach the court to obtain powers if needed in certain cases. Thus, in addition to legitimating social work activity, the court acted as a back-up to social work when and if required. In effect, the law served as a filter for the failures of normalisation by social work practices to be passed to the more explicitly repressive institutions when necessary. The courts provided social work and other health and welfare apparatuses with both a threat over, and a means of intervention into, families who were deemed to have failed and hence the power to remove the child. In this way, the law and welfare, far from being separate and in opposition, interrelated and meshed.

However, this is not to say that this interrelationship was neat and without its problems, because a characterising feature is that those professionals who operate in the social sphere must have a degree of discretion. The social professionals' diffuse mandate means that they must interpret and use the law selectively as simply one of the options in their wide range of interventions. Perhaps a central irony of the social is that a sphere that is primarily concerned with normalisation should itself be characterised by such normlessness. Social work itself can be characterised as being an 'ambiguous' profession which operates between, and hence has allegiances to, both civil society, in the guise of individuals and families, and the state, in the guise of the court and its 'statutory' responsibilities (Clarke, 1988; Franklin and Parton, 1991). Caught between such potentially conflicting allegiances, it is perhaps not surprising that such practices can be imbued with uncertainty (Pearson, 1975; Satyamurti, 1981).

Such ambiguity and uncertainty captures the central element of social work as it emerged in the late nineteenth century. Social work essentially occupies the space between the respectable and the deviant or dangerous classes, and between those with access to political and speaking rights and those who are excluded. It fulfils an essential mediating role between those who are actually or potentially excluded and the mainstream of society. In the process, it mediates not only between the excluded and state agencies, but crucially between those state agencies themselves. The creation of subjects is essential to such mediation.

> In terms of the relationship which the social worker has with the individual and the state, social work can be seen as 'straddling the split' between subjective states of the individual and their objective statuses. Subjective states maybe characterised for example by pain, suffering, need, love, hate; and objective statuses may be characterised by for example old age, handicap, mental illness, debts, or crime. (Horne, 1987, p. 87)

The social worker faced, on the one hand, with an apparently abusing family or individual, and a juridicial discourse on the other, presents the underlying subjectivity of the abusing family. Social work alludes 'to the underlying character, the hidden depths, the essential good, the authentic and the unalienated' (Philp, 1979, p. 99). In doing so, the social worker produces a picture of the abusing family as a subject which is not immediately visible to the doctor or the court, but which exists as it 'really' or potentially 'is'.

The goal of much social work is to go beyond the 'dividing practices' implied by discipline to the processes, which were of central concern to Foucault in his later work, whereby human beings turn themselves into subjects (Foucault, 1979). In Stenson's terms (1989, p. 18) the concern with discipline shifts towards that of regulation. If discipline is modelled on the gaze and based on the examination, the normalising judgement and hierarchical observation, regulation operates through interiorisation, the confession and talking whereby individuals both take on and express themselves as subjects. If discipline produces knowledge by constituting individuals as objects of scientific discourse, regulation provides knowledge of subjects in their subjectivity. Whereas the former relies on experts drawing on more traditional, objective, positivistic science the latter relies on experts who draw upon interpretive knowledge and use themselves and their insights into relationships as the primary professional tools.

Thus while social work does act as a system of social control, it also speaks on behalf of those it is regulating. To carry out such an essentially ambiguous role, social workers require a degree of professional discretion in the way they carry out their responsibilities. For it to operate successfully in any uncontested way, it is important that it have a supportive social mandate together with an internal professional confidence and coherence. The latter, particularly in the postwar period, was primarily provided by a body of knowledge which borrowed from neo-Freudianism and ego-psychology, while the professional aspirations veered towards the medical professions. What became evident during the 1970s, and even more during the 1980s, was that the space occupied by social work became increasingly contested and that its mandate for work with children and families was subject to a variety of criticisms.

Conclusion

However, having said that this study, both theoretically and methodologically, borrows considerably from that developed by Foucault, that is not to say that I am necessarily in agreement with some central elements of his argument. While it may be that the development of the disciplinary society and the growth of techniques of normalisation usefully characterise the growth of social work with children and families during the twentieth century, this is not necessarily still the case. A central part of my analysis will be to assess how far the recent changes point to the emergence of a new discourse and that this may indicate a fundamental break with the past or at least point it into new territories. More particularly, I will analyse how far it is adequate to see such changes as indicating simply an increasing encroachment of the 'psy' complex on the mechanisms of the law and a further dispersal of discipline. As will become evident, it would seem that not only is the relationship more complex but that, in some respects, the reverse seems to be the case and that in the process, the essential role and function of social work in this area is being reshaped in important respects.

As a number of commentators have argued, it does not necessarily follow that either the dispersal of discipline is inevitable or linear (Bottoms 1983; Nelken 1989) or that such changes are from the top down and not experienced by those on the receiving end as an improvement (Gordon, 1986; Van Krielzen, 1986; Rodger, 1988; Gordon, 1989) as some more recent versions of the approach imply (for example, Lowman, Menzies and Palys, 1987).

In fact the law constitutes the child care system and always has done in the sense that it authoritatively constructs, empowers and regulates the relationships between the agents who perform the child care functions, primarily local authority social workers. As Paul Hirst has commented (1980, p. 92): 'There is no opposition between law and discipline ... without a publicly assigned position and legally defined exclusiveness in the performance of their role, the key institutions and agents of the "disciplinary" region could not function: prisons, psychiatry, medicine, social work and so on'.

Similarly the law is crucial both in determining the increasingly complex division of labour and allocating the respective roles to different agencies and professionals engaged in child care practices. In the process, it accommodates competing professional interests and establishes a hierarchy of professional authority in key areas of decision-making. Local authority social workers fulfil and embody many of the statutory duties of the child care system. Since their incorporation in the state, social workers have been constituted as the executive element of the child care system. However, I will be arguing that the way social workers have carried out these duties has increasingly been criticised and is now being subject to significant change. More particularly, we can identify two areas of particular significance. First, while the changes introduced do not seriously threaten the significance of social work in the child care field, and in many ways its role is legitimated further, it certainly seems that it is to be subject to closer scrutiny, increased review and greater accountability to the court on the one hand and parents and, to a lesser extent, children on the other. In effect, the space occupied by social work between the state and the private family is being refashioned such that professional discretion is being curtailed in some areas but extended in others. Secondly, the relationships and hierarchies of authority between the different agencies and professionals in key areas of decision-making is being modified. If in the past child abuse has been seen as essentially a medico-social problem, where the expertise of the doctor has been seen as focal, increasingly it has been seen as a socio-legal problem, where legal expertise takes pre-eminence. It is in this context that a preoccupation with child protection takes on a new significance and the focus of social work with children and families emerges in a different form.

2

Child Care, Prevention and Partnership

Introduction

The 1970s was a decade of significant change for social work with children and families. It opened amid important organisational change and considerable optimism about what could be achieved. The Seebohm Report (Seebohm, 1968), together with the Local Authority Social Services Act (1970) which followed, established the personal social services as a central element of state welfare provision. It very much reflected the interests of the social work lobby (Hall, 1976; Cooper, 1983; White, 1991) and aimed to establish

> a new local authority department, providing a community based and family oriented service, which will be available to all. This new department will, we believe, reach far beyond the discovery and rescue of social casualties. (Seebohm, 1968, para. 2)

Its rationale was a concern with the family and to a lesser extent the community. Rather than wait until families reached a point of dependence, disintegration and despair, the role of the new service was to be supportive and preventive. It was to build on the apparently good practices developed in the child care service but given a broader remit.

The establishment of the child care service in England and Wales in the postwar period coincided with the growth of

19

social intervention, culminating in the establishment of the welfare state. In many respects, the legitimation and growth of state social work in Britain was interrelated with, and dependent upon, the postwar consensus and the nationalisation of the welfare state during the 1950s, 1960s and early 1970s.

The consensus which underpinned the growth of child care social work during this period had a number of dimensions. It was assumed that the interests of the social worker, and hence the state, were similar to, if not the same as, the clients they were trying to help. It was essentially a benign, but paternalist, relationship. Interventions in the family were not conceived of as a potential source of antagonism between social workers and individual family members. Not only was it assumed that many problems had their genesis within the family, but that their resolution resided there as well. Individual family members did not have an identity or set of interests distinct from, or in opposition to, the family as a whole. A pre-eminence was put on the importance of the 'blood-tie' between parent and child so that the family was seen as a unitary social good and the social worker's primary task was to support it. When it was felt that a family required modification, this should be on the basis of the normalising techniques of counselling, help and advice. Coercive interventions were not seen as appropriate and should be reserved for the exceptional. The emphasis was on *child care* and working *with* the whole *family*.

Both the political consensus of the period and social work itself were imbued with a degree of optimism which believed that measured and significant changes could be made to the lives of families, communities and society more generally, via the judicious use of state interventions. The optimism was reinforced by the assumption that such changes could be brought about without seriously undermining any significant group in society. They were in everyone's interests and everyone would benefit, though some more than others.

A central plank in the postwar reconstruction was the belief that a positive and supportive approach to the family was required so that the state and the family should work in partnership to ensure that children were provided with the appropriate conditions in which to develop. The 1948 Children Act gave expression to this approach. Heywood (1978, p. 148) argued that the legislation was passed 'in a fresh and hopeful' atmosphere.

The welfare state, based on the Beveridge Plan, aimed to take responsibility for individual and family needs in the general areas of health, education and income maintenance, while Keynesian-type interventions in the economic sphere would maintain gradual economic growth together with full employment. In this context, the role of the child care service was residual but based on a positive and optimistic view of the family. The Act legitimated a professional model of social work to replace the administratively patterned approach that had been the hallmark of the Poor Law and Public Assistance. In the process, local authority social workers were to be given considerable discretion and control over the way they provided the service and carried out their duties with children and families.

However, it is important to recognise what the reality of the child care service may have meant for many of the families who were on the receiving end. For while the priority may have been on preventative work, this was developing from a very low base-line and was consequently very rudimentary and virtually non-existent in many areas (see Packman 1981). Similarly, whatever the professional rhetoric may have suggested, it is unlikely that many children or parents would have experienced the service as working in partnership or consultation. It is just as likely that the power and authority of the service went unchallenged through desperation, fear or deference to those who knew better. One consequence may well have been that, while a high proportion of children went into care 'voluntarily' with the 'agreement' of the parents, the reality for a proportion may well have been that they had little choice and were presented with a *fait accompli*. This is not to underestimate, however, the belief held by many that the overall philosophy and approach was a good one and that there was not widespread optimism about the potential of the service.

The optimism which infected the attitudes of child care social workers throughout the 1950s and 1960s was reflected in the confidence of the rest of the society in their ability to effect change in families through their therapeutic and counselling skills (Packman, 1981; Halmos, 1965). During this period, there was similarly an increased recognition, as reflected in the 1963 Children and Young Persons Act, of the importance of material factors in the genesis, or at least exaggeration, of inter-personal problems and that preventative interventions could play a significant part in both averting the admission of children into care and preventing delinquency which was the main concern at the time. Support of and interventions in the family as a whole were seen as having important positive consequences for children. Such interventions were not seen particularly as a source of 'real' antagonism between social workers and their clients, whether children or parents. Interventions which had therapeutic intentions necessarily had therapeutic outcomes and it was social workers who had the essential knowledge required and thereby knew what was best for all concerned. In the process, therapy and counselling appeared to provide the core of practice, while the law simply provided the context for the work. When more coercive aspects were drawn upon, these were primarily conceptualised as a tool for fulfilling these more significant therapeutic ambitions.

Such an approach was evident in the early work of the NSPCC Battered Child Research Unit in London, where the crucial factor for the social worker was not to establish whether the law had been broken and whether the parents were guilty or innocent. The main objective was to form a 'consistent, trusting, professional relationship' (Okell and Butcher, 1969, p. 9). Intervention was to be based on a careful psycho-social diagnosis and should provide a 'transfusion of mothering . . . in the hope they will identify with us and eventually interject a less punitive self-image' (Court, 1969, p. 15). The major feature of such a 'nurturing model' was an emphasis on intrapsychic and social factors, particularly emotional and social deprivations, as determining family relationships. History was seen to dominate, therapy was restitutive and parental maturation, or rather maternal maturation, was the goal. The social workers assumed that parents were essentially powerless to change their situation and hence accepted much of the responsibility on the parents' behalf for bringing about improvements: 'The emphasis was on acceptance and provision, whilst the need for control and the establishment of limits to behaviour was undervalued' (Dale *et al.*, 1986, p. 9). Not only were the courts and the legal system seen as secondary and as simply providing the mandate for such therapeutic interventions, but also the police were seen as marginal and a potential source of difficulty. 'Since our main emphasis was to be on treatment and rehabilitation, we felt that we would prefer that they (the police) were not involved in our families, as we did not believe they had a therapeutic role to play in battered baby cases' (Baher *et al.*, 1986 p. 106). Notions of normalisation dominated both the theory and practice of child care with children and families. Quickly, however, this optimism was dented and a range of different criticisms of social work with children and families were articulated.

The Seeds of Discontent

The Expenditure Committee of the Social Services Sub-Committee (1975) expressed a series of concerns about the contribution and efficacy of social services in caring for and controlling deprived and delinquent children under the auspices of the Children and Young Persons Act 1969. Similar anxieties had been expressed by magistrates, the police and the youth services.

Within social work a number of significant commentators felt that the good, if patchy, practices established in the old Children's Departments (see Packman, 1981) had been lost or at best dissipated, resulting in a decline in standards for children and families.

In 1973, Tony Rampton, then Chairman, and Jane Rowe, then Director, of the Association of British Adoption Agencies (ABAA) (subsequently to become The British Agencies for Adoption and Fostering (BAAF)) expressed to the National Children's Bureau (NCB) worries about the quality of public care for children who were separated from their families. Similar concerns were felt by several of the Bureau's member organisations. As a result, the NCB, with financial assistance from The Gulbenkian Foundation, established a working party, chaired by Roy Parker:[1] 'to consider the care, welfare and education of children separated from their families for recurrent or long periods'.

It was claimed that: many children were staying in residential homes when they could be better placed in foster homes or adopted; with more support and help a substantial number of children could be restored earlier to their parents; by providing timely and appropriate services much long-term separation of children from their parents could be prevented. The working party was also 'aware that the standards of services for protecting and caring for children have been called seriously into question by the suffering and death of children like Maria Colwell' (Parker 1980, p. 59). The working party concluded that while the claims were exaggerated, they were also justified and there was room for improvement.[2] The report placed a particular emphasis on the importance of prevention at all stages of intervention in both preventing children coming into care but also in seeing care itself is an element in a preventative strategy to reduce family breakdown and child distress.

The NCB working party study was the first attempt to analyse some of the emerging concerns about child care practice. However, these quickly became evident elsewhere. By 1978, the DHSS was becoming alarmed about child care policy and practice, particularly the alleged indifference of social service departments to parents' and children's rights (see Morris *et al.*, 1980; Holman, 1976; Fletcher, 1979) – symbolised by the establishment of the Family Rights Group, Justice for Children and the Children's Legal Centre in the mid to late 1970s. There were, however, a number of elements to this alarm.

First, and more generally, a range of different research studies suggested that some of the claims on which the growth of social work had been based during the 1960s and early 1970s were open to criticism. American studies suggested that long-term, unfocused work with families made them worse rather than better and that planned, short-term goal-orientated work was more effective (Reid and Shyne 1969; Fischer,

1978). In Britain, research at the NSPCC showed that anxious, unfocused 'monitoring' of families in which child abuse was suspected seemed to increase the risk of abuse and that clearer, more purposeful work was required (Skinner and Castle, 1969; Baher *et al.*, 1976). Also research cast doubt on the ethics and utility of giving financial help for preventive purposes. They were usually given for small items for which people could claim from the supplementary benefits system (Heywood and Allen, 1971; Jackson and Valencia, 1979; Hill and Laing, 1979). Not only did social workers discriminate against the neediest clients but were likely to make payments conditional on changes in behaviour (Handler, 1973). Individual rights were being sacrificed in the guise of welfare.

Second, there was the growth in the number of children in care for, despite the apparent rhetoric related to prevention, the number of children in care went up inexorably throughout the decade from 87 000 or 6.5 per 1000 under 18 in 1971 to 100 200 or 7.8 per 1000 under 18 in 1980 (Packman, 1986, p. 3; Parton, 1985a). Third was the increase in the use of compulsory powers by social services departments at the expense of voluntary child care arrangements (Packman, 1986, p. 4; Parton 1985a) so that the proportion in care not subject to a court order or parental rights resolution declined from 41 per cent in 1972 to 25 per cent in 1980. There was also evidence of a big increase in the use of Place of Safety Orders. Fourth, the enormous variability in the rates of children in care (together with the use of voluntary and compulsory powers) which could be fifteen-fold indicated 'a degree of variability in practice that requires explanation and may, indeed, be unacceptable' (Packman, 1986, p. 5).

Fifth, the number of children staying in long-term care was increasing for no apparent good reason. It appeared that those who remained in care for any significant period experienced diminishing contact with their parents and subsequently had problems when leaving care in adolescence (Millham *et al.*, 1986, p. 4).

Sixth, a number of public enquiries into deaths of children, a number of whom had been in care but were living at home, highlighted the difficult decisions in child care more generally. 'The overall impression of practice given by the reports is one of much good work interspersed with numerous omissions, mistakes and misjudgements by different workers at different times' (DHSS, 1982, p. 69).

Together these concerns raised serious questions about the capability of social service departments to fulfil the expectations made of them. Pervading such concerns were more fundamental value issues related to the relationship between state and family; the importance of the 'natural' family, the blood-tie and psychological parenting; and how far the law should intervene to mediate and transfer parental rights (Fox, 1982).

DHSS and ESRC were prompted to fund a number of research studies between 1978 and 1982 which looked at the factors influencing a child's entry to care (Packman, 1986) and length of stay in care (Vernon and Fruin 1986), together with more specific research looking at children's homes (Berridge 1985), foster care (Rowe *et al.*, 1984), children leaving care (Stein and Carey, 1986), the experience of children, parents and social workers (Fisher *et al.*, 1986), child care reviews (Sinclair, 1984), the problems of long-term cases and maintaining links with the family (Millham *et al.*, 1986). There were also supporting studies which looked at social workers and solicitors in child care cases (Hilgendorf, 1983), the assumption by local authorities of parental rights and duties (Adcock *et al.*, 1983) and on the implementation of Section 56 of the Children Act 1975 (Stevenson and Smith, unpublished).

Three of the studies were closely related and reflected the central concerns of the research initiative: Jean Packman (1986) examined the processes of decision-making when children came into care; Judy Vernon and David Fruin (1986) at the NCB looked at the factors and decisions influencing the length of time a child remained in care; while Spencer Millham and his colleagues at Dartington studies the problems of children in longer-term care maintaining links with their families. The central theme in all three being the nature of, influences upon and implications of social work decision-making in child care (DHSS, 1985). The studies were to have a strategic significance in the late 1970s and early 1980s. Not only did they represent a significant research investment, signifying how seriously the concerns were being considered, their timing was to prove politically important. Much of the fieldwork was carried out in the early 1980s – just prior to, or at the time of, the House of Commons Social Services Committee 1982–4. Some of the research was to provide not only insights into the child care system, it was also to provide important 'evidence' to substantiate some of the hunches and themes which the Committee considered.

Throughout we can identify certain institutions, individuals and relationships as significant in framing the concerns, in particular the NCB and Roy Parker and in some respects also the BAAF. Roy Parker, who had been a central figure in the Seebohm Committee, chaired the NCB working party committee. He also served on the DHSS Children's Research Liaison Group Committee during the late 1970s when the initiative for the research was made. A close and mutually supportive group of child care academics, researchers and professionals, who identified with the good social work practices of the previous children's departments, could be seen to have a number of important connections and some degree of influence during this period. What began to emerge was that the way the problems and their resolution were conceived showed a certain consistency and consensus between the research and the report of the House of Commons Social Services Committee (Short Report).

The Short Report

In July 1982, the all-party Social Services Committee of the House of Commons (1984) decided to undertake an inquiry into children in care chaired by the Labour MP Renee Short. It held twenty-one sessions for oral evidence, read nearly two hundred written submissions and visited local authorities in England and Wales, together with brief visits to Denmark and the Netherlands. It identified three reasons for the inquiry: (1) the continuing and growing debate about the rights of children and the rights of parents, and the extent to which it is practicable to defend one without infringing the other; (2) the growing dissatisfaction with the balance between the courts and local authorities in decision-making about children; and (3) the marked swing away from residential care towards foster care (para. 13). The first two were to prove central throughout the 1980s. The problems focused on the appropriate relationship, rights and responsibilities of parents and the state in relation to children and hence the appropriate balance and sphere of influence between courts and social services departments in mediating these, particularly when disputes arise.

The Committee was serviced by three professional advisors, all of whom helped substantially in the drafting of the final report. This is not unusual as MPs have a range of conflicting demands on their time. The advisors not only had a long-standing 'professional' interest in the issues but they also provided an element of consistency and continuity. Barbara Kahan had been Children's Officer for Oxfordshire (regarded in the 1960s as one of the most progressive child care departments – see Packman, 1981) and Deputy Chief Inspector, Home Office Children's Department, and Assistant Director Social Work Service, DHSS; Denis Allen had been a Children's Officer and subsequently Director of Social Services in East Sussex throughout the 1970s and hence at the centre of the Maria Colwell Inquiry; and Diana Rawstron, former secretary to the BAAF Legal Group, was the legal advisor.

The report felt that recent disagreement on the respective rights of the child, parents and the state had led to 'a new and disturbing stridency in the advocacy of these rights on behalf of one group or another' (para. 15) which centred particularly on parental access to children in care and parental rights resolutions. However, it argued that such rights had no absolute validity but were derived from the exercise of responsibilites. 'If more consideration were given to the respective *responsibilities* of state, parents and child, the issues might be seen in more positive and less divisive terms' (para. 15, my emphasis). While parents do not own children, they do, in the context of the family, have the primary *responsibility* for rearing them. The role of the state should be circumscribed and secondary.

> The state has an overriding responsibility to protect children and ensure satisfaction of their basic needs if those caring for them are failing to do

so. In the exercise of that responsibility, the greatest caution has to be exercised. State intervention is a last resort. The state can never be a substitute for real parents. But when it is necessary, our communal responsibility to protect children must outweight everything. (para. 16)

This last resort, protective function was fundamental. For it to work, however, parents had to be given the fullest opportunity for fulfilling their caring role whether their children were in or out of care. State agencies, social workers in particular, should support parents and encourage a reciprocal, participatory and benign relationship. While the Report gave pre-eminence to the family, in the way that children's departments and welfare state provisions more generally had in the postwar period (Rustin, 1979), it also recognised that children had interests of their own, for:

The growing conviction that children have, or should have, enforceable rights as individuals, even within a general tradition of liberal paternalism, can be expected to have a major impact on the whole field of child care over years to come. (para. 18)

Throughout, however, it emphasised the essential *connection* between *children*, their *families* and the *circumstances* in which they lived. The balance it constructed was dependent on this interconnected and interrelated relationship. While the *focus* was the child, this was framed in an almost ecological conceptualisation of children, families and their social circumstances (Bronfenbrenner, 1979). In particular, it saw an essential relationship between poverty, deprivation and child care such that children reared in the disadvantaged sections of society were at most risk of coming into care. This social democratic notion posited a positive role for welfare intervention to compensate for the ravages of the market so that the primary aim for the child care services should be support and prevention. This could not be fulfilled by social service departments alone and was crucially dependent on other services such as housing, education and income maintenance. In this it recognised a factor demonstrated in the research (see particularly Packman, 1986) that children in care came almost exclusively from the poor. More particularly it emphasised that 'unsupported families', of which the growth of single-parent households was the prime example, combined the twin dangers of social isolation and a lack of material and financial resources and put children at risk of not just coming into care but staying in care for a long time.

It therefore stressed the need for prioritising prevention. In doing so, however, it recognised the need for a fine balance and the danger of undermining the family, which was by far the most beneficial arena for rearing children. This was particularly so in relation to local authority care which:

> If used too widely and too easily, the family structure on which society rests can be endangered and parental rights put at risk; if too sparingly, children will not receive the protection to which they are entitled. (para. 26)

Following the research (see below), the report tried to move away from a negative conception of prevention, as simply being 'preventing a child coming into care', to a more positive one where care itself could be part of the preventive strategy. Not only might care prevent unnecessary suffering but also the ultimate collapse of a family when used in a timely and planned way. It identified a number of elements to developing such a preventive strategy. First, by overcoming Local Authority departmental demarcations and improving inter- and intra-departmental co-ordination. Second, by improving the organisational commitment to prevention by raising its profile explicitly in the same way as fostering and adoption had been via specialist workers, teams, procedures, etc. Third, by exploring family centres which were seen as a promising development in 'intensive social work' (para. 35) with a complete family unit. Fourth, and more fundamentally, a clearer understanding and operationalisation of preventive work in order to clarify 'where preventive effort should be concentrated or how' (para. 34).

It made a number of more general comments and recommendations: that the long-term rate of Supplementary Benefits should be extended to unemployed families with children; that the preventive remit should be broadened to stimulate a more imaginative approach and the use of cash assistance in particular, in line with Scottish legislation; a re-examination of the liaison and co-operation between social service departments and social security; the provision of easier and more flexible access to day-care, particularly for children 'at risk' of coming into care; a more constructive use of child minders.

The emphasis on prevention was the fundamental base for developing sensitive, supportive and participative services where the interests of the child in the context of the family could be provided for. In order to further clarify the different interests and responsibilities of the child, parents and state, two other elements were stressed. First, the crucial importance of *planning* within the time limits of children. This had been a major preoccupation of BAAF for some years and was given prominence in *Children Who Wait* (Rowe and Lambert, 1973). It has been a major theme for the Social Services Inspectorate throughout the 1980s (SSI, 1989). The committee recommended that authorities 'consider extending the practice of written statements of policy to all individual institutions and all other units of service provision within their child care network' (para. 233). Lack of clarity about goals was seen as the reason why many children drifted into care and was a central function of management. The use of written contracts was encouraged as a means of avoiding confusion for all concerned. Judicial reviews of children in care were not recommended, though the committee proposed that Care Orders be three-year time-limited, thus giving the courts a limited power of review (para. 80). Similarly the committee noted the expansion of the use of wardship and hoped that the changes would reserve its use for 'rare and exceptional cases' (para. 82).

This linked to the second central area for change given prominence in the report – the relationship between, and the responsibilities of, the courts, the law and social services. Here it noted considerable confusion, inconsistency and vagueness. It recommended that the law be rationalised. The courts should make decisions where significant issues concerning long-term care, rights and responsibilities are concerned, while social services departments should take day-to-day decisions about the care of children. It was not appropriate that the courts should become involved in day-to-day decisions except in exceptional circumstances, as in wardship.

Similarly it was not appropriate that the social services department should have the power to make decisions which had consequences for individuals' rights, whether of parent or child, and their long-term future without these being made accountable to an independent arbiter, the courts, and where the different parties had an opportunity to put their case:

> The general principle on which we have based our consideration of the correct balance between the need for justice and the welfare interests of children is that the courts should make long-term decisions impinging directly on the rights and duties of children or their parents, and that the local authority or other welfare agency should make decisions on matters which, although they may be of equal or greater importance, are not susceptible to clear and unambiguous resolution. It is then a question of defining into which category each class of decision falls. (para. 67)

However, there must be the maximum possible protection for the rights and interests of all parties within both the welfare and justice systems for 'that principle is more important than delineating an artificial boundary between the two systems (para. 67). Thus while there should be a clear separation of function and responsibility, there should also be closer involvement and accountability between the two. It was not a question of either a justice or a welfare model, as the arguments around delinquency had previously suggested (Von Hirsh, 1976; Taylor *et al.*, 1980; Hudson, 1987), but a clarification of the responsibilities of each and the lines of accountability between the two.

The welfare element of the child care system itself was predominantly administrative rather than juridical in that internal decisions were made by local authority officers at various levels in the bureaucracy drawing on their professional expertise both individually and in groups, for example in reviews and case conferences. While the report did not envisage a major increase in the role of the courts via judicial review, it was important to improve the complaints and appeals procedures.

In order to reconstruct the justice/welfare spheres, however, it was argued that the process of court decision-making and the environment in which it took place should be less legalistic. The procedures should be more 'inquisitorial' rather than 'adversarial' and it recommended that:

> the written notice of proceedings should be more informative as to the grounds on which proceedings are being taken, and that there should be the maximum possible advance disclosure of each party's case. We also recommend that there should be a procedure for discovery of documents, and for the admission of written evidence where the parties agree. (para. 96)

The report was keen to find a balance between accountability, justice and informalism and felt that 'the introduction of a family court system could offer the possibility of a significantly better deal for children and families' (para. 101). It noted two entries into care which gave particular cause for concern: Parental Rights Resolutions and Place of Safety Orders.

Under Section 3 of the 1980 Children Act (Section 2 of the 1948 Children Act) a local authority could assume full parental rights of children who came into care with the 'voluntary' agreement of their parents (Section 2 of the 1980 Children Act or Section 1 of the 1948 Children Act). It was an administrative decision taken within the local authority and only if the parents object did the case go before a court. The committee found there were no exact figures on how many resolutions were passed each year and evidence suggested variation between 3000 per annum (oral evidence of Mr Bill Utting, Director of the Social Work Service, 24 November 1982, DHSS) and 5000 per annum (memorandum submitted by the Association of Metropolitan Authorities, 19 January 1983). This lack of clarity regarding the statistics suggested an area of practice where the lines of accountability and the nature of decision-making may themselves be vague. What was known was that 17 500 children in care were subject to such a resolution, representing almost half those received into care on a 'voluntary' basis or around one-fifth of the total in care population.

The report noted that the power was a relic of the Poor Law (Harding 1989) and felt its likely increase in usage related to the recent emphasis on 'permanency planning' (see Parton, 1985a) in social services where legislative control of children, who had been in care for any length of time, was taken to make decisive decisions for their future. However, the National Council for One Parent Families (NCOPF) published a report (NCOPF 1982) critical of its use. It argued that they were being abused, that parents were not kept informed and had no way of influencing the decision and that it was wrong in principle that such a decision should be made by administrative fiat rather than in full court where due process and justice could be seen to be done. While the committee concluded that such powers were not being abused (Adcock *et al.*, 1983) and that the amendment to the Health and Social Security and Social Services Amendment Act 1983 (which ended the possibility of parents signing away their rights to object to such a transfer in advance) was an improvement, they did recommend that the transfer of parental rights should only be undertaken by a court. It was important to clarify and separate out, as well as make accountable, the role and responsibilities of social services and the courts.

The other area of particular concern was Place of Safety Orders. These dated back to the 1870 Infant Life Protection Acts and were legal mechanisms for removing a child or young person from a situation of risk to 'a safe place'. A place of safety was defined in Section 107(1) of the Children and Young Persons Act 1933 as a community home, police station, hospital, surgery or other suitable place, the occupier of which was willing temporarily to receive the child or young person.

While there were a number of statutory provisions which empowered such a removal, the most important was that embodied in Section 28(1) of the Children and Young Persons Act 1969. Under that Section, any person could apply to a magistrate for authority to detain a child or young person and take him/her to a place of safety; in practice this was normally done by local authority social workers, officers of the NSPCC and, sometimes, the police. The magistrate had to be satisfied that *the applicant* had reasonable cause to believe that grounds exist for a care order under the Act as set out in Section 1(2)-(e), that is, neglect, ill-treatment, moral danger, beyond control of parent, not receiving full-time education. Under the order, the child or young person could be detained for up to twenty-eight days or less as specified. The application was *ex parte* and the order was not appealable and could not be

Table 2.1   *Number of children removed to a place to safety during the year*
April 1 to March 31 in England 1978–1984

Year	Aged under 5	5–16	16+	Total
1977–8	2101	3117	253	5471
1978–79 (excludes Wandsworth, no figures available)	2335	3109	261	5705
1979–80	2556	3788	269	6613
1980–81	2390	3513	309	6212
1981–82	2550	3400	301	6251
1982–83	2390	3027	309	5726
1983–84	2162	2731	314	5207

SOURCE: DHSS, Children in Care of Local Authorities Statistics.

renewed. They were primarily intended to ensure that children at risk of abuse or neglect or beyond control could be removed from immediate danger until a decision was made as to their long-term future.

The committee expressed three interrelated concerns. First, available statistics suggested the use of POSOs had increased dramatically over the previous decade. For example, official statistics showed an increase from 204 in force on 31 March, 1972 to 759 in force on 31 March, 1976. Since 1977 figures were published for orders made within each year. These figures indicated a further increase until the end of the decade followed by a slight decrease (see Table 2.1).

Second, however, they were concerned that the figures were incomplete and did not reflect the real numbers involved. This incompleteness reflected the vague unaccountable nature of the process.

Third, while there was insufficient evidence to determine whether or not place of safety procedures and orders were being abused, they felt 'there are good grounds for anxiety' (para. 124).

These anxieties arose from three main sources. First, the informal knowledge of the professional advisors suggested important changes had been taking place. Second, a number of those giving evidence were categorical. Representatives of the Magistrates Association (HOC, Vol. III, paras. 2152–

2160) said that Place of Safety Orders were being used increasingly as a means of starting care proceedings rather than as an emergency measure. One magistrate from Wales estimated this was so in 90 per cent of the cases while their chairperson estimated it at 50 per cent.

Third, however, the committee's anxiety was substantiated by 'a cogent memorandum based on [Packman's] recent research which suggested that some practice represented an abuse or misinterpretation of the powers given by statute' (para. 123). Jean Packman was a well-respected social work researcher whose previous detailed empirical work (Packman 1968) was well-received by researchers, social workers and civil servants at the DHSS. She had previously worked in Oxfordshire and was close to one of the professional advisors to the committee, Barbara Kahan. Her memorandum drew upon her research on decision-making funded by DHSS (Packman, 1986). Such comments, then, did not emanate from a particular interest or pressure group but a 'disinterested', professional and highly respected source.

Jean Packman's memorandum commented that the manner in which a child was removed under a POSO was 'the most traumatic mode of admission to public child care that exists and can, perhaps, best be compared with the compulsory removal of adults into mental hospitals. The trauma of such a removal is – or should be – a measure of the gravity of concern for the "safety" of the child'.

In her research based in two authorities, POSOs were made in approximately a *third* of all cases where a decision to admit a child into care was taken. In 49 per cent of the admitted cases, a POSO had actually been considered as an option before the final legal route was chosen. The memorandum noted by way of comparison that compulsory admissions to mental hospitals had amounted to between 12 per cent and 15 per cent of all admissions and this proportion was seen as unacceptably high, leading to the greater restrictions on compulsion in the 1983 Mental Health Act.

The memorandum noted that the proportion of admissions via a POSO differed in the two authorities (27 per cent and 38 per cent) and that a substantial minority were initiated by the police (and not just a social worker). The researchers were concerned by both these findings and the reliability of national statistics which seemed to underestimate the use of POSOs.

The age range of the children involved was very wide with only 30 per cent under five years old and actual or suspected neglect or abuse was a prime factor in the decision to take a POSO in only 24 per cent of the cases. Jean Packman argued in her memorandum that the findings

> suggest that the POSO is far from being used primarily as an emergency measure for the very young child in physical danger and that issues of 'control' over the unruly child are to the fore in many cases. Whilst this may be 'legal' by reference to the 'beyond control' ground in care proceedings, it is in marked contrast to the situation before the 1969 Act when (impressionistically, at least) POSOs were rarely used, and then generally in cases where a child was believed to be at extreme physical risk.

Because of the crisis nature of the POSO, 91 per cent of the placements were unplanned. Similarly, parents rarely accompanied the child and in 67 per cent there were restrictions on visiting the child in the placement. 'Not surprisingly, some parents recalled such admissions with anger and distress. The terms "Gestapo", "SS" and even "1984" were used by a few parents to describe the atmosphere of a POSO and at least one family spoke bitterly of the removal of their son, in handcuffs'.

Further, the intention to apply for a POSO was sometimes present well prior to its actually being applied for. Professionals were waiting for the right moment. It seemed that taking 'control' was an important element. The fact that more than 50 per cent of the children were returned to their families (25 per cent without any statutory supervision) within six months, and 25 per cent spent less than a week away from home, suggested to the researchers that 'safety' was not the prime reason for many POSOs. They felt the law was being abused in spirit, if not the letter.

Two further comments are important regarding the memorandum. First, the policy and practice it outlined seemed distant from the preventive, community based 'family' model espoused in the Seebohm Report and prided so much in the good practice of the children's departments. It epitomised the committee's worst fears about what was wrong. But, second, images of conflict, breaking up families and removing children in the guise of the Gestapo and the SS closely pre-figured those that were to explode into the public domain in mid-1987 via the media. At this moment, however, in 1982–4, they were images tucked away amidst the evidence to one parliamentary committee and amongst the concerns of a few researchers, professionals and pressure groups. Clearly, however, the message was disturbing.

The memorandum did not suggest how the problems could be overcome. This was left to others. The committee heard that a number of magistrates would only grant an order for eight days or until the next sitting of the juvenile court. In evidence, the Law Society emphasised that 'on or before the expiry of forty-eight hours or, if a weekend or bank holiday supervenes, as soon as practicable thereafter, the Place of Safety Order should be reviewed by a full juvenile court and at that review the child should be legally represented' (Memorandum submitted by the Law Society, 16 March 1983, para. 5). In comparison, however, the Association of Directors of Social Services argued that any major reduction in the length of time for a POSO would provide 'a totally impracticable time in which to carry out the consultations with schools and other people whom it might be quite proper for us to interview before coming to a view about a child's future' (evidence of ADSS, 20 April 1983, para. 2595). ADSS would not support a change in the law. Similarly, the NSPCC felt that in order to avoid delays via a series of interim care orders, the POSO should automatically last twenty-eight days but should be followed by a final full court decision (evidence of the NSPCC, 26 January 1983, para. 844).

There was very wide variation here in possible resolutions to the problem. The parliamentary committee responded with two recommendations. First, the need for more detailed research on POSOs (para. 129) and second 'that all Place of Safety Orders should have to be confirmed or otherwise by a court within a week of their original grant' (para. 130). This was the first time that the issue had officially been experienced as a problem requiring change. Clearly the committee felt the need to tighten and reduce the length of time for the orders and hence their potential usage. The memorandum from Jean

Packman, together with the evidence from the Magistrates Association and the Law Society, had been significant.

The Short Report was well received in all quarters and seen as a good basis from which to proceed. One of its prime recommendations – that the DHSS 'establish as soon as possible a Working Party on Child Care Law' (para. 119) – was quickly responded to in an attempt to produce a simplified and coherent body of law.

Social Work Decisions in Child Care

As we have seen, the work of the Short Committee was taking place when a range of research studies funded by the DHSS and ESRC were coming to fruition. These were of importance in providing both a detailed insight and critical appraisal of the workings of the child care system, particularly in terms of social work decision-making. Implicit and sometimes explicit in these studies were ideas about how policy and practice could be improved. The Short Report, together with the research studies, provided the two main pillars for the framing of the Review of Child Care Law (DHSS, 1985a). In effect, DHSS 'used the research as an information base in policy revision' (DHSS, 1985b, p. 1).

A high priority was put on gauging the validity of the research and disseminating its findings. A practitioner group was formed to consider the relevance of the findings and how these could be brought to the attention of policy makers, managers, practitioners and educators. The group met during the winter of 1984–5. Jane Rowe, who was by then Research Project Director of BAAF, offered to draft a research summary and overview to aid this process and crystallise the findings and their implications (this was subsequently published as DHSS, 1985).

It is important to note a comment by Jane Rowe (1989, p. 39) on the background and perspectives of the researchers for 'all are believers in the value of social work, indeed many are former practitioners. They are sensitive to the difficulties of a young profession. When they are critical, it is in no way to "rubbish" social work but because they set high standards for it. I think we need to take their criticisms very seriously'. Not only their criticisms but their proposals for change.

The research covered forty-nine local authorities and over 2000 children. The consistency of the findings was seen as so remarkable that a member of the practitioner group came up with a comment which seems to have spoken for many – 'reading these reports is like looking out of different windows and seeing the same view' (Rowe, 1987, p. 2).

The research found that the admission of children into care often took place in an atmosphere of crisis where more than a third of the decisions to admit were taken within the previous twenty-four hours and more than half within the previous week. As a consequence, the admission process was found to reinforce rather than reduce the trauma of separation so that 'long established patterns of good child care practice (for example pre-placement visits) . . . were honoured more in the breach than the observance' (DHSS, 1985b p. 7).

The increasing use of compulsory powers, such as Place of Safety Orders, often led to poor planning, more trouble maintaining links between children and their families and parents often being distressed and angry, making for poor future relationships with the social workers. 'From several of these reports, a picture builds up of social workers responding to pressure for admission to care and, in the process, often putting parents through hoops in which they were almost forced to threaten abuse or abandonment to prove their need for help' (Rowe 1989, p. 40). When the children were admitted to care their experience was often one of frequent changes of placement, loss of links with family and diminishing social work support.

For all these deficiencies, however, the research showed that the overall outcome maybe quite positive – particularly with short-term care. Similarly, when parents felt their problems and wishes had been understood this was valued highly as was getting straight answers, being kept informed, and having a social worker who was honest, reliable and had an ability to 'get alongside people' (Rowe, 1989). However, parents whose children stayed in care for more than a brief period invariably felt pushed aside and devalued. The research showed how easy it was for misperceptions and misunderstandings between social workers, parents, children and others to begin and then grow rapidly. There was also evidence about the poor quality of assessments and reports.

A number of central themes were identified. Virtually all the social workers viewed care negatively, seeing it as a last resort and a failure on the part of both themselves and parents. As a consequence, care was rarely seen as a service, was invariably used in a crisis and added to feelings of stigma and passivity. However, the researchers also referred to the potentialities of using short-term care as a preventive measure in a positive and planned way. It was important, therefore, not to see care as a unitary concept but to be clear about its purpose.

Throughout, the increasing use of – but potentially negative effects of – compulsion was evident. It was clear that there was a lack of clarity regarding when to decide upon a compulsory or voluntary route into care and that social workers often failed to draw on a serious knowledge base when making decisions. The researchers stressed the gap and hence the need to consult, inform and work *with* parents; drawing on the help of the wider family when possible; and understanding the importance of the parents' response to separation. All suggested an approach whereby social workers and parents worked together in a more negotiated, open and participative manner.

The studies also highlighted the possibly inherent tension created in trying to provide an individualised professional service in the context of a large bureaucracy. It was noted how difficult it was for a bureaucracy in effect as a 'good parent' and how important it was to try and personalise the care for the social workers as well as the parents and children.

Finally it was clear that social workers were powerful people in respect of child care decision-making: the power to admit or not; to control access and visiting; to decide when placements should begin and end. Paradoxically, however, the social workers experienced themselves as powerless. They felt they were at the bottom of their hierarchy; lacking in resources; in the hands of courts and other agencies; and battered by clients' needs and demands. As a consequence, 'the prevailing picture of drift, passivity and lack of planning is pervasive and clearly not conducive to child welfare' (DHSS, 1985b, p. 18).

As the DHSS summary document commented, 'the implications of these research studies are profound and far-reaching' (DHSS, 1985b, p. 21). It was also recognised that many of the difficulties were beyond the power of social services departments to change. Much of the pressure came from social and economic factors and the inherent stresses arising from large local government bureaucracies.

The most urgent needs 'appear to be shifts in attitude and priorities, increased understanding, more sensitive perception of clients' feelings by social workers and of social workers' feelings by managers' (DHSS, 1985b, p. 22). According to Jane Rowe 'the single most important implication from the research is the need to achieve a dramatic improvement in the support provided for field and residential social workers. Their morale must be at an all-time low at present' (Rowe, 1989, p. 46).

Perhaps most significantly the research demonstrated that the situation was serious because the gap identified between aims and achievements was 'distressingly wide' (DHSS, 1985b, p. 22). It was a situation that required a response. Perhaps if the law could be rationalised, social workers and courts would be clearer on their boundaries and responsibilities and mutual trust would improve. In the process, the morale and confidence of social workers, who were seen as focal to the operation of the child care system, would improve.

The Review of Child Care Law

Ministers quickly established an inter-departmental working party in response to the Short Report recommendations in July 1984: 'to make proposals and set out options for codification and amendment of child care law' (DHSS, 1985a, para. 1.1).

The working party consisted of officials from DHSS (from the Child Care Division, the Social Services Inspectorate and the Solicitors Branch), the Home Office, the Lord Chancellor's Department and a Law Commissioner. 'The working party based their review on the report of the Select Committee, evidence given to the Committee and other relevant material which included the considerable body of research which already exists in relation to child care, and research especially commissioned by the working party from the University of Bristol' (DHSS, 1985a, para. 1.5). While there was criticism that it did not include a professional social worker (see, for example, Jones, 1985, p. 2), considerable attempts were made to consult via the circulation of twelve interim discussion papers in January and March 1985. These were provided by a legal team from the Law Commission headed by Brenda Hoggett, the Commissioner for Family Law and gave a social work perspective to set the law in context.[3] Over sixty organisations and individuals responded to these papers (see DHSS. 1985a, Annex B). The working party also visited Scotland to observe the children's hearing system, met a number of organisations informally, and visited several courts. A further stage of consultation took place following the publication of the Review in September 1985 and comments on it were requested by 15 January 1986. A great amount of time, resources and expertise were invested by senior civil servants, their advisors and the various individuals and organisations who responded. It indicated that the issues were being taken seriously.

The Review followed the lead of the Short Report in wanting to clarify the responsibilities, boundaries and lines of accountability between the family, social services departments and courts, for:

> an examination of child care law needs to go well beyond the legal framework under which courts make decisions on the care of children. Local authorities provide a spectrum of support and care to children in need, and their families, with graduated steps involving increasing restrictions in the interests of the child over a parent's free exercise of parental responsibilities. It is important that each step is clearly separate, has the appropriate legal rules and procedures attached to it and that the rights and responsibilities of all parties are clearly defined. This is not so at present. (DHSS, 1985c, para. 2.2)

Three themes informed the recommendations for change: (1) the desirability of involving as far as appropriate the parents and the child in decisions about services provided for them; (2) that parents rather than the child were usually the true respondents in care proceedings; and (3) that in care proceedings the aim was to get the right result for the children and that the form of procedure should be directed to this (para. 2.1). However, the report was very conscious of the inherent difficulties for 'it is pertinent to remember that the first test of Solomon's wisdom was a dispute over the custody of a child' (para. 2.35).

In the light of this sanguine comment, the Review made explicit its basic principles. While recognising that parents and children may have different interests, it argued that in the vast majority of families, including those who may be in need of social services, 'this distinction does not exist' (para. 2.8). The interests of children are hence best served in their families while the interests of their parents are best served 'by allowing them to undertake their *natural* and *legal responsibility* to care for their *own* children' (para. 2.8, my emphasis). The focus should be 'to enable and assist parents to discharge those responsibilities'. Even where the child cannot remain at home, the emphasis should be on maintaining family links 'to care for the child in *partnership* with rather than in opposition to his parents, and to work towards his return to them' (para. 2.8, my emphasis).

It also argued, however, that some parents would be unable to exercise these responsibilities for the good of their children and that action would be needed to remove them. However, the process whereby such action 'is taken must give *fair protection* to the interests of parents, fairer protection than is given by the present procedures' (para. 2.9, my emphasis). The recommendations on 'Emergency and Care Proceedings' were therefore designed to achieve a procedure 'which is fair, and seen to be fair, to all sides' (para. 2.9). These recommendations included: the advance disclosure of the authority's case; party status and rights of appeal; abolishing the administrative procedure for assuming parental rights for children already in care.

Central to that process were the grounds whereby 'the state in the shape of the local authority, may be permitted to intervene in family life for the good of the children' (para.

2.10). In this respect, if a 'best interests' test was used, the state would be permitted to intervene whenever it could be demonstrated that alternative arrangements would serve the child's welfare better than those offered by the parents. 'But "the child is not the child of the state" and it is important in a free society to maintain the rich diversity of lifestyles which is secured by permitting families a large measure of autonomy in the way in which they bring up their children' (para. 6). Thus, following the Short Report, the Review took the view:

> that the 'best interests' of the child should continue to predominate in issues between private individuals but that the state should only be able to compulsorily intervene where the child *is being or is at risk of being harmed if it does not.* (para. 2.15, my emphasis)

The Review followed the Short Report's guiding principle that the court should determine the major issues concerning the rights and duties of children, their parents and the local authority, while the local authority should be responsible for the day-to-day management of the case once a child was in care.

What emerged was not simply a new set of teminology, but a new set of concepts which aimed to reframe and reconstruct the role, philosophy and practices of the child care system and its relationship with the courts. In this respect, it clearly drew upon both the Short Report and the research on social work decision-making.

> In particular we see 'prevention' more positively as family support, 'rehabilitation' as return to a family, and 'care' as to be distinguished more sharply between voluntary arrangements made in partnership with parents, which might be called 'shared care', and compulsory arrangements under a court order, a 'parental responsibility order' or similar, which transfers parental responsibilities to the local authority. This status of 'shared care' should we believe be seen as a support service to the family by the local authority and not as necessarily implying parental inadequacy. (para. 2.3)

Not only was voluntary care to be more clearly distinguished from compulsory care but it was to be called *shared care* in an attempt to reflect the principle of partnership which was to lie at its core. It was hoped in the process that it would not be associated with images of inadequacy and stigma but would be experienced by both professionals and families as a support *service*. From now on there would, in effect, be two quite distinct systems of the child care system – shared care and compulsory care – with different aims, philosophies and practices.

The old terms such as 'care', 'rehabilitation' and 'prevention' were all put in inverted commas, thus enhancing their dubious status, while those elements which were to replace them such as return to a family; family support; voluntary arrangements made in partnership with parents; and compulsory arrangements were not. This emphasised their natural, taken-for-granted status as reflecting the world as it really was. 'Shared care' was also in inverted commas, suggesting its possible temporary status. As the Review argued, 'terminology is important' (para. 3). It demonstrated not just new ways of signifying the world, but new ways of seeing, constructing and constituting it.

Thus the Review aimed to dispel the notion of 'care' which was seen as stigmatising and associated with inadequate parents, as well as with a lack of parental involvement. Instead, the emphasis was upon partnership between local authorities and parents wherever possible. Three forms of care were envisaged: respite care; shared care; and compulsory committal to care by the court.

Respite care, which was only available for handicapped children, would provide a short break for parents for up to one month or a cumulative total of three months in any twelve. It would be flexible and free of detailed regulation since it would be essentially outside the care framework. The parent would retain the main responsibility for the child whilst the local authority would be responsible for the adequacy and supervision of the placement.

Shared care aimed to bring about greater involvement by natural parents in the care of the child whilst at the same time enabling local authorities to make sure that the child's welfare was safeguarded. Where a child had been in shared care for over six months, local authorities would continue to be able to require up to twenty-eight days' notice for the purpose of a phased return home. In every other case, where an authority felt it necessary to retain a child, compulsory power via a court order should be sought as parental rights resolutions were to be abolished.

The Review also wanted to define the parents' responsibilities following a compulsory order in order to involve parents more than hitherto. Three principles should guide local authorities when planning for children in their care: (*a*) they would continue to safeguard the child and to promote their development; (*b*) the child's interests and the need to ascertain his or her wishes and feelings would be given priority; (*c*) parents should be involved in the child's care wherever practical.

The Review recommended that there should be a single procedure and a single composite ground under which local authorities could intervene compulsorily. In its view, intervention:

> is justified only where it is demonstrated that the child is suffering or is likely to *suffer harm* to his health, development or wellbeing as a result of the care available to him falling below a reasonable standard or his being beyond parental control. Further, no order should be made unless it is likely to be effective in the sense of being the best means available to the court, including making no order at all, of safeguarding and promoting the child's welfare. (paras. 3.28, 3.29, my emphasis)

The Review also recommended a widening of the local authority duty to investigate whenever it received information suggesting there were grounds for compulsory proceedings. 'We see scope for widening this duty to cover any child feared to be *at risk* and for requiring the authority to make sufficient enquiries to enable them to decide what action, if any, to take' (para. 3.18, my emphasis).

Following the Short Report, and in line with its general approach, the Review recommended significant changes to Place of Safety Orders which were to be renamed Emergency Protection Orders. The findings of Jean Packman were generally substantiated by a subsequent research project commissioned by the Review (see DHSS 1985a, Annex C and Dartington Research Unit 1985). While the Review took the view that their use should be restricted to emergency situations, 'intervention should be possible to protect the child where *risk* is continual as well as imminent' (para. 13.9, my emphasis). However, it would be the *magistrate* rather than the *applicant* who should be satisfied that 'there is reasonable cause to believe that such harm is likely to the child' (para. 13.10). The order would last for a maximum of eight days and it was envisaged that parents would be informed that an order had been made, together with the child's address, provided this was in the child's interests. The Review recomended a general tightening up of the procedures surrounding Emergency Protection Orders. For example, evidence should be given on oath; written statements in support of an application should be provided at the hearing, or within twelve hours of the order being made; magistrates should record in writing the reasons for making an order and these should later be given to the parents, the child and the local authority, if they were not the applicants. The parents would also be given information concerning their right to seek legal advice. We can see here a real attempt to curb the discretionary power of the social worker and increase due process.

With regard to the court proceedings themselves, it was recommended that parents be made full parties, and that other relatives, such as grandparents, be able to participate as the court directed.

Care proceedings would resemble civil proceedings relating to the custody or the upbringing of a child much more closely than previously. It wanted to establish a framework where the interests of all those involved would be recognised, was more flexible and less accusatorial. All the allegations and evidence should be disclosed before the hearing so that the decisions reached would be both better informed and better protect the rights and interests of both parents and children. It was hoped that cases could be dealt with more speedily.

However, the Review was not convinced by the argument that any changes to the substantive law and procedure could only be effective in the context of the introduction of a Family Court System: 'on the contrary we can see some logic in a prior consideration of the law' (para. 2.30). In this respect, the Review departed from the Short Report. This issue was to surface again with some force during the passage of the Children Bill in 1989.

Finally, the Review envisaged considerable modification to Supervision Orders. The Review, following the Short Report, was concerned about the small number of cases where a

Supervision Order was made. In 1983, there were about 1400 Supervision Orders made in care proceedings compared with about 3000 Care Orders.It was felt these might be used more if they have greater powers not only over the child but over the parent as well and might be of particular utility if used instead of a Care Order where the local authority intended to return the child home on trial if a Care Order was made. Whereas currently they could only impose conditions upon the child rather than the parent, and hence were seen as ineffective, it was recommended that the court should have power to impose requirements on parents, provided they consented. The following conditions were outlined: (*a*) to keep the supervisor informed of any change of address and of the child's whereabouts; (*b*) to allow the supervisor to see the child in the home and to assess the child's welfare needs and condition; (*c*) to allow the child to be medically examined; (*d*) to comply with any directions from the supervisor regarding attendance for a medical examination, medical or psychiatric treatment or participation in particular activities; (*e*) (subject to certain safeguards) to permit the child to receive medical or psychiatric treatment; and (*f*) to comply with the supervisor's directions regarding the child's education.

The Review made a real attempt to extend the range of options to the court to situations where whilst the allegation or concern had been proved, removal of the child was not required. We can see a real attempt to 'normalise' family relations and provide a degree of protection to the child. It gave more power to the social worker than would be provided under voluntary surveillance or monitoring. However, discretion was not unbridled and that which was available was with the court. The only effective discretion for the social worker was to return the case to court for discharge or variation to a Care Order. Their dependence on the power of the court was evident.

Conclusions

I have analysed in some detail the development of official ideas about how to reform the child care system in Britain in the first half of the 1980s. In particular, the NCB working party, the decision-making in child care research and the Short Report all informed the Review of Child Care Law in 1985. The role of researchers was significant as were a number of influential social work figures who were concerned that the good practices of the old child care departments had been lost in the rapid changes following the reorganisation of social services departments. It was as if there was a serious attempt being made to reconstitute the original thinking behind the child care departments but modified for the changed social and political realities of the 1980s. This was clearly argued by Fisher *et al.* (1986):

> We are convinced that the philosophy which was originally intended to predominate in the postwar UK child legislation – namely that the work of public agencies was to provide supportive services to families, part of which could include admission to care as a means ultimately of preserving family relationships in the long run – has been lost from practice. This loss is both accidental, in the sense of resulting from neglect and omission, and deliberate, in the sense that current social policy is founded on myths and misinformation about family life which tend to polarise the public and private care of children. In our view, this philosophy of *partnership* with clients, in which the primary caring role of the family is reasserted but effectively *supplemented* by public services, must be reintroduced into national policy and practice. The 'good society' must, in our view, treat those in need of child care services as fellow citizens rather than as 'inadequate' parents or children. (pp. 124–5, original emphasis)

The principles of partnership, family support, shared care, respite care, maintaining links and return to family, were all given pre-eminence. Not only did such principles relate to the professionalised model of good child care but took cognisance of the complaints relating to the use of compulsion and arbitrary power, particularly in relation to parental rights resolutions and Place of Safety Orders. In this respect, pressure from the Magistrates' Association and the Law Society stressed the need for greater justice, due process and openness. Increasingly, then, the recommendations for change began to separate out the compulsory and voluntary systems of care, where the latter was reframed as shared and respite care. While the primary concern of the former was the protection of the individual, both the welfare of the child and the interests of the parents, the concern of the latter was extending partnership, support and working alongside parents and children. Throughout, the family was seen as the place to rear children and should be reinforced as far as possible.

There was a real attempt to clarify the accountability of the child care system. Primarily, this accountability was to the parents and to a lesser extent the children. It was also to the courts, however. In this respect, considerable efforts were put into clarifying the boundaries, responsibilities and relationships between the welfare and court elements of the state child care system. The principles, policies and practices of the voluntaristic elements of the child care system were to dominate and hence construct the framework. The compulsory elements were to be recast and reserved for the few who could not be accommodated.

3

Child Abuse, Authority and Risk

Perhaps the major factor which contributed to concern about child care policy and practice during the 1970s arose from a series of child abuse inquiries. The Maria Colwell Inquiry (Secretary of State, 1974) signalled the beginning of modern political, public and professional interest in child abuse (see Parton, 1979, 1981). Public inquiries proved crucial providing the impetus for introducing new administrative and management procedures for identifying and managing the problem (Parton, 1985b, Chapter 5) and exposing both the professionals and agencies more generally to media scrutiny and usually opprobrium (see Franklin and Parton, 1991). However, it seemed that intense public and media reaction to child abuse declined after it reached its peak in the mid-1970s (Hartley, 1985). The mid-1980s saw this quickly change, however, with the inquiry into the death of Jasmine Beckford chaired by Mr Louis Blom-Cooper QC.[1] It appeared just at the time when the review of child care law and the decision-making in child care research were coming to a conclusion. However, its perceptions and explanations of the nature of the problems to be addressed were somewhat different as were many of its recommendations for change in child care policy and practice.

The Beckford Inquiry proved a powerful event which was to make a significant impact upon thinking and responses to child abuse, particularly amongst social workers. The panel of inquiry was established on 28 March 1985 and reported on 4 December 1985. It inquired into the events leading up to, and the circumstances surrounding, the death of Jasmine Beckford. However, the report proved far more than simply an inquiry into a single case. In its 450 pages and sixty-eight recommendations, it raised general issues about the conduct of the four main agencies involved – social work, health, education and the courts – and made far-reaching recommendations for change. In that respect it went much further and received greater publicity than any of the other inquiries published since the Maria Colwell Report. It was welcomed at the time as 'a watershed in the handling of child abuse in Britain' (Laurance, 1985, p. 408) and as affording 'an opportunity, even a turning point. The cost of having to absorb the harsh criticisms and to learn the lessons has been Jasmine Beckford's life. Nothing else is too high a price to pay' (*Community Care*, Comment 1985, p. 1).

Its impact on *child care* policy and practice can be gauged from the comments of the public inquiry into the events in Cleveland two years later.

> The publication of the Jasmine Beckford Report and the publicity which surrounded it, prompted the Social Services Department further to review its *child care* strategy. The Director of Social Services regarded the report 'as an absolutely vital document to study and resolved that, if at all possible, Cleveland Social Services would learn from the unfortunate instances made elsewhere and ensure that we did not make similar mistakes which could result in children being unavoidably abused'. (Secretary of State, 1988, para. 4.13, my emphasis)

John Chant, the Social Services Assessor on the Cleveland Inquiry panel felt that: 'the climate created by Louis Blom-Cooper's reports and the publicity which surrounded them played a significant part in the events which took place in Cleveland' (Chant, 1988, p. 16).

More generally, this change in 'climate' can be gauged from the sudden up-turn in the use nationally of the Place of Safety Order, following the Beckford Inquiry and the publication of its report in December 1985. While in 1985 the number of children removed to a place of safety in England was 5305 (0.47 per thousand population), by 1987 this had increased to 8055 (0.73 per thousand population) to decline slightly in 1988. (See Table 3.1.)

Clearly, therefore, we need to understand what the Beck-

Table 3.1   *Number of children removed to a place of safety in England, years ending 31 March 1983–8, by age group*
(Figures in parenthesis represent the rate per thousand of the population)

Year	Aged under 5	5–15	16+	Total
1983	2390 (0.83)	3027 (0.42)	309 (0.20)	5726 (0.49)
1984	2162 (0.73)	2731 (0.39)	314 (0.20)	5207 (0.45)
1985	2119 (0.72)	2893 (0.42)	293 (0.19)	5305 (0.47)
1986	3037 (1.02)	3770 (0.56)	384 (0.26)	7191 (0.65)
1987	3383 (1.13)	4243 (0.64)	429 (0.29)	8055 (0.73)
1988	3162 (1.04)	4221 (0.63)	397 (0.28)	7780 (0.71)

SOURCE: DHSS, Children in Care of Local Authority Statistics.

ford Report was saying about child abuse and social work with children and families more generally, together with its arguments and recommendations for change.

Jasmine Beckford: A Child in Trust

From the outset, the report made it explicit that the inquiry team interpreted their remit in a far more extensive way than a strict reading of their terms of reference might indicate. A number of interrelated themes can be identified which together can be seen to characterise the report in terms of what it said about: the relationship between social work practice, statutory responsibilities and the law; the attitudes of social workers, particularly towards children and families; the social work skills needed in work with children; and the assumptions that were made about child abuse and the role of social workers.

A major focus of the report was to locate social work in its statutory context. Rather than the law being simply an important area of knowledge that social workers should be familiar with – along with other areas of knowledge – it was seen as fundamental and hence providing the social charter for modern social work:

> we are strongly of the view that social work can, in fact, be defined *only* in terms of the functions required of its practitioners by their employing agency operating within a statutory framework. (London Borough of Brent, 1985, p. 12, original emphasis)

In effect, social work activity was the functioning of one area of the law in practice. The crucial and overriding element that transformed a range of methods, skills and activities into social work was the law. The implication was clear. Because social workers failed to understand this crucial element, they failed to appreciate their role and functions and the full import of their responsibilities.

The picture presented was one of social workers going about their work but crucially unaware of their statutory mandate: 'Jasmine thus became the victim of persistent disfunctioning social work while the law demanded, above all, her protection' (p. 127). It was thus recommended that the local authority legal department, the police and the prosecuting service be included in the decision-making, so that when crucial decisions were made, particularly when returning a child home, these should only be made after full legal consultation in the multi-disciplinary case conference. Similarly, lawyers were seen as the pre-eminent and crucial profession within local government because 'the truth is that the law is part and parcel of the functions of every department' (p. 153). Social work practice was perceived and evaluated via a legal gaze so that social workers became little more than local government officers who only existed in and through a framework of statute.

This emphasis on the law was not simply concerned with social workers' technical knowledge of the statutes but aimed to change attitudes within social work and the direction of social work with children and families.

Social workers' approach to families was seen as being infused with a 'rule of optimism' and that this was misplaced. In essence, 'the rule of optimism' meant that the most favourable interpretation was put upon the behaviour of the parents and that anything that may question this was discounted or redefined. While the concept was in part derived from the work of Dingwall *et al.* (1983) it was stripped from the social and organisational context within which it was first located and was reduced to individual attitudes and behaviour (see Dingwall 1986).

This tendency in practitioners was attributed to two devices – 'cultural relativism' and 'natural love'. By cultural relativism was meant the assumption that all cultures were equally valid in formulating human relationships. Thus members of one culture, such as white middle-class social workers, as in the Beckford case, had no right to criticise members of another culture, for example black working-class parents, as with the Beckford family, by using their own standards of judgement. Natural love referred to the belief that the relationship between a parent and a child was instinctual and grounded in human nature.

In assuming that all parents must love their children it became very difficult to interpret any evidence that may question that natural bond and hence suggest the child may not be being cared for adequately. The net result of these two devices was that social workers accepted parents' accounts of events without question. The 'rule of optimism' was seen to be at play throughout the case of Jasmine Beckford. The social worker was 'fobbed off with implausible excuses on almost every occasion of her visiting the house about the whereabouts of Jasmine' (p. 85), for the last ten months of her life and which led the judge to describe her behaviour 'with ample justification' as being 'naive almost beyond belief'. Similarly, 'as soon as the social workers thought they saw the first signs of improved conduct on the part of Morris Beckford and Beverley Lorrington an *overwhelming optimism* took hold' (p. 127, my emphasis).

As a consequence, the social workers failed to put into practice their statutory responsibilities for the child and failed to use the authority in their work that was crucial in fulfilling these responsibilities. However, the report argued that these factors identified in the Beckford case were not uncharacteristic of social work practice generally.

> We fear that their attitude in regarding the parents of children in care as the clients, rather than the children in their own right, may be widespread among social workers . . . We have listened to a number of social workers and expert witnesses, and in each case we have detected this attitude which is the negation of any authoritarian role in the enforcement of Care Orders. (p. 294)

While recognising that social workers often walked a tightrope between issues of care and control and between responsibilities to the client and society, the report was in no doubt as to where social workers' ultimate responsibility lay. It was argued that the social workers' role was to carry out the law and use the authority invested in them.

The resolution of many practice dilemmas in terms of the 'rule of optimism' resulted from the ethos of social work on the one hand and the nature of the problems social workers faced on the other, and to sustain their own morale they exaggerated progress where there may have been none. To overcome this loss of objectivity, a particular responsibility was put on the social worker's supervisor, whose role was to be aware of the attitudes of the social worker towards the case and to correct, if necessary, the way in which they affect her handling of it. It was crucial for the supervisor to counteract any potential distortions of judgement.

The overriding solution, however, was to change the attitudes which informed practice so that social workers became more realistic in their view of human nature and did not assume they could bring about major change in the situations and families they dealt with. The report argued that the tragedy occurred not because the child abuse system was particularly misplaced or lacking, but because the professionals' attitudes were inappropriate.

The report took for granted what had become the dominant model for defining, conceptualising and explaining child abuse – what I have called elsewhere 'the disease model' (Parton, 1985b; but see also Dingwall, 1986; Parton, 1989). The model first articulated by Henry Kempe (Kempe *et al.* 1962) was taken on in its entirety:

> As long ago as the landmark article of 1962 by Dr Kempe and his American colleagues, the battered child syndrome, it was noted that although the knowledge of psychiatric factors in child abuse was limited, they were probably of prime importance in the 'pathogenesis of the disorder'. The authors thought that parents who inflict abuse on their children do not necessarily have psychopathic or sociopathic personalities or come from some borderline socio-economic groups, although most publicised cases have fallen into one of those categories. But they averred that in most cases some defect in character structure was probably present . . . As one member of the Denver programme under Dr Kempe observed in 1976, child abuse is 'a disease whose carrier is the parent and whose victim is the child' (Child Protection Report 1976). (pp. 87–8)

The model was used for evaluating the work done with the Beckford family and constructed a framework for dealing with such cases in the future. A body of knowledge was presented as fact and scientifically proven. If every practitioner learnt and applied this knowledge, child abuse could be identified, predicted and prevented. It was the failure of the social workers in being aware of and applying this knowledge which let down Jasmine Beckford so crucially.

It was assumed that child abuse was an illness of sufficient unity to be put into a diagnostic category in its own right and that the pathology resided primarily in the parents but manifested itself in the relationship with the child. While allowing that in some cases it may be an expression of family stress, it was psychological or interpersonal family factors which were of prime importance in the aetiology. There was a defect in the character structure or personality which, perhaps in the presence of added stress, gave rise to physical expression. The orientation thus viewed the causes of child abuse as residing with the parents and started by asking the question, 'what type of individual or family would harm their children?' In the process the way the problem should be responded to was in terms of individualised identification, prediction and treatment. The primary purpose of research was to discover the characteristics and symptoms that differentiated the abusing family from the normal and the central task for the practitioner was to be aware of these 'known characteristics of child abuse' (London Borough of Brent, 1985, p. 100) so that they could identify and predict actual and potential abuse in their practice.

At various points in the report the characteristics of the Beckford family were demonstrated to be consistent with the research findings of what constituted an abusing family. But at each point the social workers failed to recognise the signs and, hence, failed to recognise that this was a 'high risk' case. The main characteristics of the case which were seen to identify it so clearly as one of child abuse were:

1. That the injuries that led to the original Place of Safety Order and, subsequent Care Orders in August 1981 demonstrated, according to 'radiological opinion', to be part of a longer history of injuries rather than a one-off incident (p. 68).

2. That the child's physical growth and development improved significantly while living with foster parents between September 1981 and April 1982 only to slip back following the return home. Dr Leonard Taitz, an expert witness, was quoted to support the finding that 'recent research indicates that where children show substantial catch-up growth in foster homes it is doubtful whether early return to the actual parents is appropriate' (p. 73).

3. Morris Beckford was stepfather to Jasmine Beckford. While his name appeared on the birth certificate it was established in the inquiry that he was not the natural father. This was never found out by the social workers and they assumed he was the natural father throughout their involvement. This was an example of where 'the rule of optimism' encouraged an accepting and naive approach with dire consequences because 'a step-parent has a higher statistical average of battering his or her child' (p. 84).

4. On 4 November 1982, Beverley Lorrington admitted to Ms Wahlstrom, the social worker, that she was extremely unhappy in her relationship with Morris Beckford. However, this point was not mentioned at the case conference just five days later when the decision was made to remove both children from the child abuse register. This was seen as another important sign being missed as 'parental disharmony is a major indicator of risk of child abuse' (p. 118).

5. The birth of the youngest child, Chantelle Beckford, on 11 December 1983, provided another stress within the family as it would for any parent (mother) caring for three children under four. 'Yet they did not for one moment recognise what this event meant in terms of the additional risk to Jasmine or Louise or, indeed, to the new baby' (p. 122).

6. However, throughout, there was one set of factors which was seen as crucial for identifying 'the psychopathology of child abuse' (p. 86), and these factors were known from the outset:

> Morris Beckford had undergone a horrendous experience as a cruelly beaten child at the hands of both parents. Beverley Lorrington too had described an unhappy childhood, running away from home after school-leaving age. There was also the bald statement

that both Morris and Beverley had attended a special school for ESN children, run by Brent Education Authority. Yet none of these pointers to a cycle of deprivation, predictive of child abuse, was ever followed up. (p. 86)

The 'cycle of violence' whereby parents who abuse their children were themselves abused in childhood was accepted as received wisdom. It was seen as a major factor in both explaining the problem and identifying high risk or dangerous situations. This was a major characteristic predictive of future abuse in the Beckford case which was missed.

The evidence given to the inquiry by Professor Cyril Greenland proved important in outlining this model of child abuse and the characteristics associated with it. He had been involved in trying to refine methods for predicting dangerous behaviour for many years. While this had previously been in relation to the dangerous mentally ill and the violent offender (Greenland, 1978, 1980a), in more recent years he had been studying child abuse or, as he called it, 'lethal family situations' (Greenland, 1980b, 1986a, 1986b, 1987). Much of his evidence has been published since as part of a larger study (1987). This provides a full, if confusing, account of his approach, research and recommendations. It is notable that in certain passages the report bears a very close resemblance to Greenland's book, particularly when the former is discussing the importance of the law to practice and 'high risk' situations.

While Greenland made reference to social factors such as unemployment, poverty, poor housing and 'underfunded, poorly staffed and overworked social services agencies' in contributing to child abuse, they were reduced to contextual issues or as simply associated with certain families. His central focus, and hence his strategies for intervention, were based upon the practitioner's ability to predict high risk and thus isolate the dangerous. In the process, prevention became defined as 'the identification and management of high-risk cases' (Greenland, 1987, p. 26). He had been refining a high-risk checklist for some years and subsequently applied it, retrospectively, to 168 cases of death from child abuse and neglect in North America and Britain. Two sets of factors were itemised – in relation to the parents and to the child.

Table 3.2   *Child abuse and neglect high-risk checklist*

Parents	Child
1. Previously abused/neglected as a child	1. Was previously abused or neglected
2. Age twenty years or less at birth of first child	2. Under five years of age at the time or abuse or neglect
3. Single parent/separated; partner not biological parent	3. Premature or low birthweight
4. History of abuse/neglect or deprivation	4. Now underweight
5. Socially isolated – frequent moves – poor housing	5. Birth defect – chronic illness – developmental lag
6. Poverty – unemployed/ unskilled worker; inadequate education	6. Prolonged separation from mother
7. Abuses alcohol and/or drugs	7. Cries frequently – difficult to comfort
8. History of criminal assaultive behaviour and/or suicide attempts	8. Difficulties in feeding and elimination
9. Pregnant – post partum – or chronic illness	9. Adopted, foster- or step-child

SOURCE: Greenland 1987, Appendix, pp. 185–7.

While 'high risk' was never defined, either by Greenland or by the Beckford Report, the checklist was seen to have a particular utility as 'a score of over half of the completed items in either section appears to be associated with high risk' (Greenland, 1987, p. 97). Similarly, while Greenland said that the checklist had never been rigorously tested *prospectively* and hence did not have any 'demonstrated predictive value' (1987, p. 98), he went on to argue that 'it may provide a means of reaching consensus among interdisciplinary teams concerned with the assessment of risk' (p. 98).

Thus at the heart of the Greenland approach and the Beckford Inquiry was an assumption that the best way of responding to the problem of child abuse was to identify the high-risk case (see Parton and Parton 1989a, 1989b). In response to the question 'can high-risk situations be identified in advance in order to prevent child abuse and neglect deaths?' Greenland responded in a way which was quoted authoritatively and almost verbatim in the Beckford Report (London Borough of Brent, p. 289).

> A cautious yes, in many cases. Since over 80 per cent of the UK and over 60 per cent of the Ontario victims had been previously injured, it seems prudent to classify all cases of non-accidental injuries to young children as high-risk cases. (1987, pp. 178–9)

He commented that, in addition, almost half of these cases were stunted in growth. However, not only is there a problem as to what this leaves out, but both the research itself and the policy and practice implications which it suggested have come in for severe criticism (see Dingwall, 1989; Parton and Parton, 1989b; Parton 1989). What is important is that it legitimated and apparently provided the evidence for an approach to child abuse crucially dependent upon 'predictive techniques of dangerousness' (London Borough of Brent, 1985, p. 289).

According to the Beckford Report, the ability to identify and predict abuse and therefore prevent *it* before *it* happens was central to what all those involved in the child abuse system should be doing. By applying this science of child abuse, the children concerned could be protected and for some children this clearly meant being removed from home permanently. Quoting Henry Kempe the report commented that: 'if a child is not safe at home, he cannot be protected by casework' (p. 288). Thus, once a 'high-risk' child was identified, attempts to maintain the child at home or to rehabilitate once removed were foolhardy.

A major failure in the Beckford case was that the social workers were unaware of the facts of child abuse so that when they came across them they did not recognise the significance. More particularly, the *medical* prevention of neglect via the use of 'centile chart' growth rates was ignored. Again, this was not something particular to the social workers in this one case but typical of the lack of knowledge amongst social workers generally. This was a major shortcoming which the inquiry team saw themselves being able to publicise. Commenting on the failure of the Area Officer, Mr Bishop, who chaired the initial case conference, to recognise some of these factors the report said:

> he now appreciates that the combination of a physically abused child's abnormally low weight, understimulation and the general lack of competent parenting are the indicia of predictive child abuse. *His failure to appreciate that at the time is no more than a commentary on the absence of knowledge about child abuse generally among social workers. The yawning gap in that knowledge should now be filled by the publicity given to this case during the public hearings and, we trust, by the publication of our report.* (p. 83, my emphasis)

If social workers improved their 'knowledge' of child abuse high-risk factors and became less reticent in using the authority that their statutory responsibilities invested in them, children would be protected and scarce resources would be directed to where they would be most effective.

> Society should sanction, in 'high-risk' cases, the removal of such children for an appreciable time. Such a policy, we calculate, might save many of the lives of the forty to fifty children who die at the hands of their parents every year, and at the same time would concentrate scarce and costly resources of Social Services Departments to the 'grey areas' of cases where something more than supervision, and something less than long-term removal, is indicated. (p. 289)

Not only was the child the primary client, but 'to treat the parents as the clients is fatally to misdirect the efforts of what is, in essence, *a child protection service*' (p. 294, my emphasis). The report was very critical of the loss of the specialist skills and knowledge which it thought had been lost since the Seebohm reorganisation. However, rather than attempt to resurrect the professionalised child care service, with its emphasis on working with the whole family in a partnership, a much more prescribed role was implied which concentrated on identifying 'high risk' and using authority to protect children. More wide-ranging attempts at prevention were seen as a waste of resources.

As Ashley Wroe (1988) has demonstrated, not only did the case thrust the issue of child abuse and the (in)competencies and nature of social work back into the media, but the statements of certain primary definers were crucial in structuring the form this took. Legal discourse, whether of the judge at the original trial or via the report itself was dominant. The newspaper reports of the trial aroused a considerable volume of media disquiet, together with political discussion both within Brent and Parliament itself. In the course of sentencing Beverley Lorrington at the Central Criminal Court on 28 March 1985, Judge Pigot remarked that the social worker had shown 'a naivete almost beyond belief'. This received tremendous media exposure. The early weeks of the public inquiry were also widely covered.

Similarly, the publication of the report on 4 December 1985 received massive publicity. However, Wroe comments that the newspapers reflected the conclusions of the report 'in a surprisingly balanced way' (Wroe, 1988, p. 24). The inquiry conclusion that Jasmine's death was 'both a predictable and preventible homicide' (p. 287) received wide coverage and social work and social services were presented in a negative and sometimes extremely negative light (Wroe, 1988, p. 30). Social workers came across as essentially 'naive', 'gullible', 'incompetent (and negligent)', 'barely trained (and training misguided anyway)', and 'powerful, heartless bureaucrats' (Wroe, 1988, pp. 26–28). These may seem contradictory. How can social workers appear as powerful while failing so blatantly to fulfil their statutory obligations to protect Jasmine?

The early press coverage of the case was closely related to the statements and anger of the foster parents, Mr and Mrs Probert, from whom Jasmine had been removed only to suffer in her 'natural' home. The wishes and views of the foster parents, who did not feel such a move was in Jasmine's interests, were seen to be discounted with horrendous consequences by the social workers. Mrs Probert's view that 'social workers have got too much power' was given wide coverage. As Wroe demonstrates, a number of sections of the press felt this was another example of too much power vested in social workers:

> 'Social welfare should cease to be a paper empire, a mandarinate' (*Telegraph* leader, 4 December). The power of social workers as agents of state intervention, tearing children away from caring and undervalued foster parents, came through (*Mail*, 29 March, 'torn from love'; leader – 'is it something in the unfeeling arrogance of local bureaucracy that can dull the intelligence and humanity of social workers?') (Wroe, 1988, p. 28)

Social workers had far too much discretionary and unaccountable power which they used almost by default. In effect, social workers did not fully understand their statutory role and the real authority that goes with that. In doing so, not only did they fail to protect children, Jasmine, and face up to dangerous, cruel parents, Morris Beckford and Beverley Lorrington, but they also removed children, in this case Jasmine again, from a loving and caring family, the foster parents Mr and Mrs Probert. This failure was particularly evident as the child in question was on a Care Order.[2] As the Beckford concluded:

> We think in fact we have identified and isolated one fundamental aspect of professional response to child abuse that has been overlooked or discarded by modern social work training and practice. It is that the making of a Care Order invests Social Services with pervasive parental powers. By such a judicial act society expects that a child at risk from abuse by its parents will be protected by Social Services personnel exercising parental powers effectively and authoritatively on behalf of society. Such a child is a child in trust. (p. 297)

These comments were directed to cases where the grounds for a Care Order had been proven in court and where, therefore, the child was in the care of the local authority. An important fact which was to be lost amidst the overall message that social workers should be effective, authoritative, and use their statutory powers in order to protect the child in high-risk situations.

Three Place of Safety Orders figured in the course of the Beckford case and this was used as an opportunity by the inquiry team to discuss at some length (Chapter 27) their views on the growing controversy about POSOs. This seems surprising as these decisions did not materially affect the outcome of the case. More particularly, the discussions and the recommendations that go with it could be seen to go against the main body of the report which was critical of social workers' failure to use the law in order to protect Jasmine. Three issues were addressed in the light of the criticisms of POSOs in the DHSS research, the Review of Child Care Law and the Short Report (p. 256).

First, the report argued that while there was no right of appeal against a POSO, 'we regard it as axiomatic that a parent or child could apply to the court for setting aside the order. We do not know of any such case, but we think that the right to do so should be specifically stated in any future legislation' (p. 256). Further, the report argued that the grounds should be as precise as possible and should not refer to future or imminent danger which was not seen as sufficiently stringent. 'We recommend that the criterion for the Place of Safety Order should be the applicant 'has reasonable cause to believe that there is a real and present danger to the health or well-being of the child' (p. 256).

Second, it was argued that 'twenty-eight days is too long a period for a child to be removed from his parents, without the issue of removing being tested judicially – at a court hearing in which the parents and, if appropriate, the child can challenge the order by making representation to the juvenile court' (p. 257). They noted that a number of organisations, including the Magistrates Association, had been recommending a reduction in length to eight days but 'we would go further. We recommend that Section 28(1) of the 1969 Act be amended to fix the limit at seventy-two hours or where there is no relevant juvenile court sitting within the next seventy-two hours, up to a maximum of eight days, beginning with the date of authorisation' (p. 257).

Third, they suggested POSOs were often granted inappropriately when the child was already in a place of safety such as a hospital. The only situation where a social worker would be entitled to apply in such circumstances 'is where there are grounds for believing that the parents might remove the child from the hospital, thus placing the child in danger' (p. 257). Thus the report recommended 'that social workers and magistrates should respectively apply for, and grant applications only where there is present and real danger to the health and wellbeing of the child. Short of that test for a Place of Safety Order, social workers should be directed to initiate care proceedings' (p. 258).

These recommendations provided a much more narrowly defined set of criteria for both the application for and use of POSOs. It is inappropriate, therefore, to simply see the Beckford Report as being only concerned with trying to increase the interventive practices of social workers into families and encouraging them to use whatever statutory powers were at their disposal. While I agree with much of Robert Dingwall's critical analysis of the report, I think he is in danger of misinterpreting this element. He – and in some respects myself (Parton, 1986) – argues that 'the effective aspiration of the panel is to reverse the dominant decision rule in child care, that parents should receive the benefit of any genuine doubt or uncertainty' (Dingwall, 1986, p. 494) and further that:

> Blom-Cooper and his colleagues may disclaim any intention to make all children 'children of the state' but that is the net effect of their critiques of social work practice. Social workers would become a family police, operating in a vastly more coercive fashion. (p. 503)

The Beckford Report argued that when a child was removed from its parents, this should be via a full court hearing and that social workers should be seen to be clearly accountable to, and provide full evidence to, the court. Wherever there was a need for emergency social work intervention, this should be narrowly and strictly defined. However, once the case had been proven, the child was then 'in trust' to the local authority under the auspices of a Care Order. At this point the natural parents forego their rights.

However, in the context of the general emphasis of the report, it was not surprising that these more obviously juridicial elements got lost. Certainly the way the message was refracted through the media gave these themes little prominence. It is ironic indeed that Cleveland Social Services, which 'went into Beckford in a lot of detail and set up systems to prevent it happening here' (Bishop, 1988, p. 12), should be the subject of a public inquiry two years later where the use of Place of Safety Orders would be a central issue. The recommendations of the Beckford Report would, in theory, have provided a much narrower space where they could have been used. However, the implications of this were rarely given prominence in the public, political and professional fall-out from the Beckford Inquiry and its subsequent report.

Tyra Henry: Whose Child?

Many of the major issues at the centre of the Beckford Report also came through one of the other major child abuse inquiries of this period – that into the death of Tyra Henry (London Borough of Lambeth, 1987). Again, Tyra was on a Care Order but returned home primarily into the care of her grandmother on the agreement that under no circumstances should she be allowed into the care of her father who had been convicted of severe cruelty against her older brother. The plan broke down and Tyra died after severe attacks from her father.

The report was critical of social work misjudgements and the failure to take the Care Order seriously. It was argued that essentially the social workers failed to recognise they were the child's parents and therefore did not fulfil their statutory responsibilities.

The answer to administrative errors and professional misjudgements lay in increasing legal accountability, for the report argued that social work was naive about its statutory role. The report felt the social worker's approach was:

> symptomatic of a perennial problem of 'style' in social work – to find the appropriate balance between representing officialdom and befriending people in real difficulties. (p. 21).

The major vehicle for ensuring 'the right balance between friendliness and authority' (p. 110) and avoiding 'an inappropriate and damaging measure of collusion' (p. 111) was via the use of 'interventionist and challenging supervision' (p. 114). The team leader function in social services was again seen as vital, as was the careful use of contracts with clients in insuring that social workers carried out these 'policing' functions.

Kimberley Carlile: A Child in Mind

Similar failures were illustrated by the third major inquiry of the period into the death of Kimberley Carlile (London

Borough of Greenwich, 1987). Kimberley's death, however, posed a central problem. Not only was she neither under the supervision or care of the social services department but the inquiry concluded that the department did not really have available to it the legal mechanisms whereby she could have been protected. There was a gap in the law which was reinforced by problems in the child abuse system itself. While the social worker was again subjected to unbridled media attack (Ruddock, 1991) and his interventions came in for criticism in the report, these other issues were given prominence in a way they had not been previously. The legal loophole was to prove a major focus of concern during the passage of the Children Bill during 1989, while some of the problems posed for the child abuse system were addressed in government circulars and guidelines in 1988.

The chair of the inquiry was again Mr Louis Blom-Cooper and while the report does carry similar characteristics to the Beckford Report, it was not so confident that we had the knowledge to prevent further such tragedies occurring. While social work was again found wanting, the blame was neither as categorical nor the professionals seen as so pathologically inept.

Kimberley Carlile died aged four and a half on 8 June 1986 as a result of 'traumatic subdural haemorrhage caused by an injury to the left temple, consistent with having been caused by a blow, such as a kick' (London Borough of Greenwich, 1987, p. x). She had also been subjected to starvation, bruising and burning. Nigel Hall, her step-father, was convicted of her murder and sentenced to life imprisonment. Mrs Pauline Carlile, her mother, was convicted of causing grievous bodily harm and sentenced to twelve years' imprisonment. The inquiry was set up on 28 May 1987 and reported on 11 December 1987.

The family had been known to Greenwich SSD since October 1985, after the children, who had been in the voluntary care of Wirral SSD, had been discharged from care to live with their mother, who had recently set up home in London with Nigel Hall. However, he rejected the Social Services Department's offer of help. In January 1986, there were allegations at school that Darren, Kimberley's older brother, had been thrown across the room by Hall. These were referred to social services and the school and the health visitor were asked to 'monitor' the situation.

On Friday 7 March 1986, an anonymous telephone call to social services alleged a 'little girl being beaten' who 'cries pitifully'. Two social workers visited immediately but did not see Kimberley. During the following week, the family were contacted by both social services and the health visitor. The Senior Social Worker, Martin Ruddock, who met the family, did not feel the situation nor Kimberley's demeanour gave great cause for concern. Because of a severe shortage of staff he kept the case open to himself and tried to co-ordinate the efforts of the other agencies. He made a final visit to the home on 14 April 1986 but Hall, who was particularly belligerent, would not let him into the house. Kimberley was never seen alive again by any welfare professional.

As with the Beckford and Henry cases, the welfare professionals were seen to have failed to identify the 'psycho-pathology of the Carlile family' (p. 106) and be sensitive to the 'indices of child abuse' (p. 107). However, the report was far more equivocal about the utility of much research for practice:

> These 'predisposing' factors may act as warning signs, but they will not predict abuse in any particular case. We remain far from a knowledge of what causes a caretaker to kill his or her child. And without a cause we are unlikely to find a remedy, remembering that all the available evidence points to multiple causal factors. (p. 134)

Similarly, there was a recognition of the social context of child protection work and that unless society was prepared to support greater intervention by the welfare agencies, some children were always likely to die:

> Society, rightly in our opinion, is not prepared to tolerate too heavy-handed disruptions to family life, and expects careful judgement to be exercised in deciding on the appropriate action to be taken in any particular case. This more flexible approach offers some security to families. But, given that human judgement is fallible, society must tolerate occasional failure. Staff who follow up suspicions of child abuse are not creating these risks. They are inheriting the risks, and are accepting them on our behalf. (p. 136)

The report was also exercised as to why a series of inquiries had come up with the same recommendations but still children died. The report argued that the problem lay with the child abuse system itself.

> Mr Ruddock failed in a number of respects and on a number of occasions to protect a child manifestly at risk of abuse. But did the multi-disciplinary child abuse system, developed over the last fifteen years, in some sense fail Mr Ruddock? (p. 209)

The report felt it did and made two alternative suggestions for giving it a proper overhaul, for: 'we are trapped by the historical organisation whereby we divide *child care* from *child health*. That doesn't make a lot of sense in *child protection*' (p. 13, my emphasis).

It argued that the first way was to entrust the management of the system to one authority either by establishing one child protection authority employing all the staff and doing the work, or by assigning to one authority the overall responsibility for the child protection service and giving it power to require the assistance of professionals working in other agencies. While such a change would have the advantage of clarity, it would have the disadvantage of separating child protection from child care and child health and would also cut across existing organisational and professional heirarchies.

The second suggestion was seen as more feasible. This would require that overall responsibility for the *management* of the system would be shared. In order to overcome problems of too many agencies, lack of accountability and vagueness, a governing body, appointed by the contributing agencies, could be given executive powers – unlike Area Review Committees. The role of Area Review Committees was seen as ill-defined, unfunded and without real authority. As a result, Social Services were left with the responsibility without any mechanisms for getting other agencies to act when they do not wish to. It left both children and social workers exposed.

The other major issue addressed in the report was perhaps even more fundamental:

> At the heart of our Inquiry have been the acute problems that social workers constantly face in the course of *investigating allegations* of child abuse.

> Mindful of the dilemma facing social workers, between the duty to pay full respect to family life and to observe scrupulously the rights of parents to bring up their own children without unnecessary interference from authority, and the duty to protect children from risk of abuse by their parents, we have paid particular attention to the fine balance that needs always to be maintained between the two. Here we are not considering the consequences that flow from a Care Order, in which a child is in trust to a local authority to protect the child, even, if necessary, by overriding the rights of natural parents. Here *we are at the crossroads of competing social policies* — parental rights and the interests of children. (p. 144, my emphasis)

No suitable legal mechanism had been available for either gaining access to Kimberley or ensuring she had a medical examination. The social workers believed, confirmed by the legal section, that they could not use a POSO because without a medical examination, or at least a good look at the child, they had no grounds for applying for one. They were further discouraged by the 'good advice' that a POSO did not confer power to authorise a medical examination anyway. The report argued that the social workers could not therefore be criticised for failing to apply for a POSO in such circumstances.

Under Section 40 of the Children and Young Persons Act 1933, any person could lay information on oath to a magistrate if they believed that 'any child or young person had been or was being assaulted, ill-treated or neglected in a manner likely to cause unnecessary suffering to health'. If satisfied, the magistrate could issue a *warrant* empowering a police officer to enter premises, by force if need be, to seek the child and, if the suspicions were confirmed, then remove the child for up to twenty-eight days as specified in the warrant. Additional authority could also be given for a doctor to accompany the officer executing the warrant. If no evidence of harm was found, there was then no power to remove the child. In effect, the power was less drastic than the POSO. Again, however, it did not give the power to medically examine the child. Expert evidence to the inquiry suggested that the warrant was rarely used and little known, prompting a circular memorandum from the Chief Social Services Inspector at the DHSS at the end of June 1987 to all Directors of Social Services reminding them of it. Certainly, the social workers in Kimberley's case were unfamiliar with it.

Application could possibly have been made to make Kimberley a Ward of Court specifically to carry out a medical examination or, finally, the police could have invoked their power under the Police and Criminal Evidence Act 1984, Section 17(1), to enter and search premises without a warrant for the purpose of saving life or limb in the case of dire emergencies where gross physical abuse was imminently threatened or taking place.

The Report concluded that the law was inadequate and overly complex and made a professional level of competence difficult to achieve. It wanted to see a 'significant shift' towards the interests of children and that 'armed with new and clearly defined powers' (p. 145) social workers would begin to carry out their tasks with greater confidence. The relationship with parents

> would soon become one in which the persuasive power will supersede the coercive power. In short, there should be less reliance on strict enforcement of law and more on promoting predilection among parents for protection of their children. (p. 145)

It made five proposals for change 'in an ascending order of interference with parental rights' (p. 149).

First, a right of entry to premises similar to that for approved social workers under the Mental Health Act 1983, to be given to suitably qualified social workers of at least two years standing designated as child care officers. The right would exist where the child was in care, under a supervision order and, following a process of consultation, where there was suspicion of child abuse. The parent would be entitled to be present at any interview or examination.

Second, the report recommended, for the first time, a developmental assessment for a child under the age of five. It was felt to be just the type or order that would have been appropriate for Kimberley's situation. 'Its prime virtue would be that it would partake of none of the coercive nature of a removal and detention of a child from the child's parents and home' (p. 154). The applicant (social workers, health visitors or medical practitioners) would simply have to satisfy the magistrate that s/he believed that the health, safety or welfare of the child may be at risk, coupled with a single refusal to produce the child on request for such examination. The order would be served on the parent by the police and failure to comply would lead inevitably to an Emergency Protection Order or Section 40 Warrant CYP Act 1933. If the examination did disclose child abuse, either the health authority or social services would then be under a duty to apply for an EPO and call a case conference with a view to applying for a Care Order. The Child Assessment Order was a new order, designed as broader, more interventive and more preventive in intent but much less draconian than either the old POSO or the new EPO.[3]

Third, it was recommended to keep the Section 40 Warrant under the 1933 CYP Act but amended so that the magistrate was empowered to authorise a medical practitioner to conduct a medical examination.

Fourth, the report supported the much more stringent criteria for removal to a place of safety proposed in the White Paper for the new Emergency Protection Order (EPO) to replace the Place of Safety Order (POSO) and its length reduced to eight days. However, because the EPO was still seen as a draconian measure, it was strongly recommended that as soon as parents were notified of the making of the order they should have an immediate right to apply to the court for a review of the grounds – in contrast to the White Paper proposals which would only give parents the right to challenge an application for a seven-day extension beyond the initial eight-day order. This was consistent with what had been recommended and argued in the Beckford Report.

Finally, the report recommended there should still be available the police officer's right of entry without warrant under Section 17(1)(e), Police and Criminal Evidence Act 1984 to save life or limb.

Diagrammatically, then, five different ways of intervening in the family to protect children were recommended which ascended as shown in Table 3.3.

Conclusions

The mid-1980s witnessed a resurgence of widespread concern about child abuse tragedies. Many of the issues given promin-

Table 3.3   *Carlile Report hierarchy of state interventions in the family*

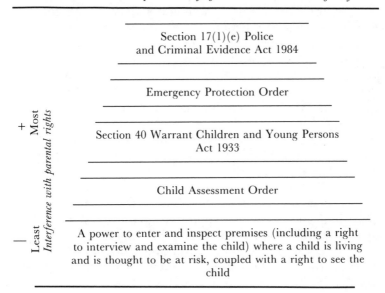

Section 17(1)(e) Police and Criminal Evidence Act 1984
Emergency Protection Order
Section 40 Warrant Children and Young Persons Act 1933
Child Assessment Order
A power to enter and inspect premises (including a right to interview and examine the child) where a child is living and is thought to be at risk, coupled with a right to see the child

+ Most — Least Interference with parental rights

ence originally in the case of Maria Colwell and numerous other since were underlined via the deaths of Jasmine Beckford, Tyra Henry and Kimberley Carlile. While there had been moves throughout the first half of the decade to reorganise the child care system and reform the law, it was cases of child abuse which dominated public, political and in many ways professional perceptions of what the problems were. Social workers were seen as too naive and sentimental with parents, failing to concentrate on the interests of the children and to use the statutory authority invested in them. They failed to understand and use the knowledge that it was assumed we had about child abuse. These messages were particularly evident in the Beckford and Henry inquiries and the way they were refracted via the media. In both cases, the children were in the care of the local authority.

The case of Kimberley Carlile, however, was rather different. Not only was she not in care but the report felt that both the child abuse system and the law had failed the social worker(s) in their primary task. Both were therefore seen as in need of major reform. The report also recognised that the tasks of child protection in a liberal state were fraught with difficulty and contradiction. Even so, and for all the respect shown to the central professionals, at the end of the day the primary blame/responsibility for Kimberley's death was seen to reside with Martin Ruddock, the senior social worker carrying the case. 'We conclude that Kimberley Carlile's death was avoidable through the intervention of the welfare agencies' (pp. 216–17). And that 'bad practices are bad practices under whatever circumstances pertaining at the time. At most, the bad practitioners may plead mitigation of their culpability' (p. 218).

As Hallett (1989) has pointed out, child abuse inquiries almost inevitably go about their business in a 'common-sense quasi-judicial' way which apportions blame in an individual-ised way. They have done little to challenge 'taken-for-granted' assumptions about child abuse or professional cul-pability. Individual social work practitioners and social work practice itself always appears in a poor light.

> Child-abuse inquiries by their very nature highlight, for the most part, mistakes, omissions, errors of judgement and the shortcomings of systems and individuals. A great deal of good social work practice goes on unnoticed, unacknowledged and unpraised. (Hutchinson, 1986, p. 181)

In effect, the legal or juridicial discourse is the lens through which social work is judged and found wanting. Social work in form and effect is stripped from its day-to-day context and ambiguity for the purposes of judging its efficacy in certain cases which have been seen to go dreadfully wrong.

> Among the most important issues left large unaddressed by this process are the paradigms surrounding the social construction of child abuse as a social problem, the dominant modes of response to child protection in a liberal democracy, and the issue of resources. (Hallett, 1989, pp. 139–40)

The Kimberley Carlile Report provided a fascinating example of the double-bind that social services and social workers could be put in because of this failure to seriously address resources. In one way, the report went into some detail (Chapter 11) about the pressures and shortfalls in resources and recognised the range of competing demands made upon departments. However, it argued that:

> we insist that within Social Services expenditure the protection of children must be a priority, because of the nature of the work and the consequences it has for the kind of society we live in. We do this in full awareness that reports on various other client groups, and other services, will be pressing their claims. However, for us to urge anything less would be to fail Kimberley, and children at future risk. (London Borough of Greenwich, 1987, p. 72)

It made no attempt to spell out the implications or cost, financial and human, for such a priority because:

> it is beyond our terms of reference and beyond what can reasonably be considered relevant to what happened to Kimberley to go into these complex calculations in detail. (London Borough of Greenwich, 1987, p. 67)

The report argued that resources were not material for what happened to Kimberley because 'resources were available in this case. Kimberley had a health visitor and a social worker' (p. 65). Yet it was doubtful whether Kimberley could be said to have had a social worker. Martin Ruddock, as the senior, was trying to cover the case until further staff were available and in post. When an inquiry sets about its task in such individualised and legalistic ways it will always find an individual – usually the front-line worker – to hold responsible. It has considerable difficulty addressing, and holding responsible, wider issues. Even when these are identified, the child abuse system and the law in this case, they are not given the same significance when, at the end of the day, the ultimate responsibility/blame for a child's death has to be identified.[4]

It is perhaps not surprising, therefore, if day-to-day social work policy and practice should respond to possible cases of child abuse in a manner which attempted to keep risk to a minimum and which interpreted its statutory mandate in a conservative and defensive way in order to avoid a public furore arising where children die at the hands of their parents and where social workers are seen as culpable. Such an approach to children and families seemed in sharp contrast to that outlined in the Short Report, the research on decision-making in child care and the Review of Child Care Law. It was as if there were two competing agendas or paradigms for practice and it was the one symbolised by the child abuse inquiries which was dominant. Such a clash of perspectives was to be one of the elements which fed into the Cleveland 'affair' in mid-1987.

4

Sexual Abuse, the Cleveland Affair and the Private Family

Well in advance of the publication of the Carlile and Henry Reports in December 1987, a new and quite different child abuse scandal exploded into the public domain. The Cleveland affair, as it has often been called, represented quite different anxieties. If previous inquiries demonstrated that welfare professionals, particularly social workers, failed to protect the lives and interests of children and intervened too little too late into the private family, the concerns focused around Cleveland seemed to demonstrate that professionals, this time paediatricians as well as social workers, failed to recognise the rights of parents and intervened too soon and in a too heavy-handed way into the family. While this was to prove the major theme running throughout Cleveland, it also touched a range of other personal and political sensitivities related to sexuality, intimacy, gender and professional power and knowledge. For the first time, the concerns were articulated via sexual abuse.

The inquiry was to superimpose a set of new priorities upon those articulated via the previous inquiries. Not only was it by far the most expensive – estimates put the cost in excess of five million pounds – but it was to dominate media and political debate in a way that caught many unawares.

The Seeds of Discontent and Conflict

In June 1987, a local newspaper in Cleveland began to

publish stories concerning a large number of confused and angry parents who claimed that their children had been taken from them by local authority social workers on the basis of disputed diagnoses of sexual abuse made by two paediatricians, Dr Marietta Higgs and Dr Geoffrey Wyatt. The *Daily Mail* ran the story on 23 June 1987 with the front-page headline 'Hand Over Your Children, Council Orders Parents of 200 Youngsters', and within days 'Cleveland' had become a national scandal, with the various professional combatants, together with the parents, receiving massive television, radio and newspaper exposure.

The local Member of Parliament, Stuart Bell, took up the parents' cause and heavily criticised the actions of the paediatricians and social workers, and claimed the parents had been subjected to a massive injustice. His intervention in Parliament raised the temperature about the issue. On the 29 June, he put down a Private Notice Question asking the Minister of State for Health, Mr Tony Newton, to make a statement. The Minister said that he awaited a report from the Regional Health Authority and while it was 'extremely important that if there appears to be a case of child abuse, it should be carefully and sensitively investigated. If the current investigations confirm suggestions that there have been significant failings in achieving this in Cleveland, the Government will be ready to institute an inquiry' (*Hansard*, HoC, 29 June 1987, Col. 255).

Mr Bell responded by saying that while he was as 'anxious and determined as anyone to protect children from the infamies of child abuse', there was 'a question mark over the future of 204 children taken into care in Cleveland since May'. He alleged that Dr Marietta Higgs, a consultant paediatrician, and Mrs Sue Richardson of Cleveland Social Services [the child abuse consultant] '*colluded* and *conspired* to keep the police out of the allegations of sexual abuse whereby Dr Higgs made the diagnosis, a social worker made out a Place of Safety Order and a Justice of the Peace signed it without the intervention of the police, other agencies or any counselling procedures or corroboration' (*Hansard*, HoC, 29 June 1987, Col. 255, my emphasis).

Tim Devlin (MP, Stockton South) asked the Minister if he

was aware that children 'are being collected from their beds at two o'clock in the morning by social workers? Does not my Honourable Friend see a clear parallel with the activities of another body which carried the initials SS?' (*Hansard*, HoC, 29 June 1987, Col. 257).

Such comments provided excellent ammunition for the media. For example, the *Daily Mirror*, quoting Tim Devlin, said 'there is a clear parallel with the earlier activities of another body which carries the initials SS' (30 June 1987) and the *Daily Mail* said that 'social workers act like dictators and their powers are awesome' (15 July 1987). As in previous inquiries, the media provided the impetus for establishing the inquiry. It identified and constructed the central issues which required a response and thereby marginalised others. In effect, it played the major role in publicly defining the agenda. However, it was not completely independent in this. Certain primary definers received a sympathetic and expansive exposure of their views (see Parton, 1985b, pp. 85–97). Stuart Bell and the parents played this role initially but subsequently different professionals, who were actively involved in the drama, entered the fray (see Nava, 1988; Franklin, 1989; Illsley, 1989; Franklin and Parton, 1991; Aldridge, 1990).

A number of themes were set in play from the outset which were to dominate the ensuing debate which was 'the Cleveland affair'. First, the image of the authoritarian state which was out of control and unwarrantably and insensitively interfering in the lives of families – both children and parents. Second, that the parents – by implication all of them – were innocent. Third, that various state agencies and professionals were not in unison. Not only were there significant differences in approach and interpretation *between* professions, particularly paediatricians, social workers and the police, but there were important differences *within* the professions. This was most evident in the medical profession, where there were heated disputes between the two paediatricians and the police surgeon and subsequently other sexual abuse medical 'experts'.

Perhaps the most unusual dimension was that paediatricians and social workers were constructed as the insensitive representatives of the authoritarian state which posed a fundamental attack on family life, while the police were seen as the defenders of civil liberties or, more properly, the protectors of parental rights.

Stuart Bell followed up his claims with a press conference on 6 July where he accused Cleveland Social Services officials of manufacturing the recent increase in sexual abuse as 'a put-up job, part of the *empire building* strategy of social services' (*Guardian*, 7 July 1987, p. 1, my emphasis). He cited an internal report by Cleveland Social Services in June which had led to an extra £86 000 being allocated for recruitment. The appeal for extra staff had relied heavily on the fact that since May 113 children had been the subject of Care Orders – eighty-three on the grounds of risk of sexual abuse, compared with forty-nine Orders because of suspected sexual abuse in the whole of the previous year.

On 9 July, Tony Newton announced to MPs that having studied the reports from the regional health authority and the social services inspectorate, together with the material supplied by Stuart Bell and Tim Devlin, he was setting up 'a full inquiry into the arrangements for dealing with suspected cases of child abuse in Cleveland in recent months. Therefore, we propose to establish a statutory inquiry headed by a High Court judge. The judge will be assisted by a panel of three assessors: one with medical experience, one with social services experience and one with experience of police work'.[1]

He also drew attention to a judgement published the previous day from the European Court of Human Rights upholding five applications from the United Kingdom complaining about the lack of parental access to children in care.[2] The Minister concluded that he would be studying the judgement in detail. 'In *framing* legislation, we shall also wish to take account of the lessons of Cleveland and the other inquiries to which I have referred, but our aim will be to bring such legislation forward at the earliest practicable opportunity' (*Hansard*, HoC, 9 July 1987, Col. 527, my emphasis).

While Michael Meacher, the Labour (Opposition) social services spokesperson, welcomed the announcement, he was concerned that a judicial inquiry of this sort would be too narrow to achieve a 'national consensus'. 'Above all, will the Minister accept that a national consensus does not yet exist, either on the critieria for identifying child sexual and physical abuse or on the interprofessional procedures to be followed when such cases are suspected? Will he acknowledge that, until such a consensus has been created, no reliable statistics of the national incidence of child abuse can be attempted, and the conflict between paediatricians and police surgeons that we have seen in Cleveland will not be resolved?' (*Hansard*, HoC, 9 July 1987, Cols. 52–28). It was to the establishment of a new set of checks and balances whereby mutual trust between professionals and their publics and thus the construction of a new consensus that the Inquiry was to be concerned. To do so, however, it first needed to account for what had been going on in Cleveland. The inquiry was headed by Mrs Justice Butler-Sloss[3] and lasted seventy-four days, starting on 11 August 1987 and ending on 29 January 1988. It heard evidence in private session for eight days, all of it given by parents, and thereafter was in public, except when evidence was heard which would identify a particular family.

The Inquiry

The primary purpose of the inquiry was to judge and begin to resolve the competing claims, perspectives and practices that were in evidence in Cleveland. The problems to be addressed were summarised in a *New Society* leader (3 July):

> In the field of sex abuse there are very delicate balances to be struck. There is the danger of missing the signs against the danger of misdiagnosis. There is the danger inherent in the sudden removal of a child against the danger of leaving her or him in an abusing family. There is the danger of morbid and voyeuristic publicity against the danger of cover-up. (*New Society* 1987, p. 3)

While these issues had been evident in attempts to tackle child abuse generally, they were starkly illustrated in sexual abuse. The inquiry saw its task as addressing how sexual abuse should be *managed*. What it did not do was attempt to assess either how big the problem was or even how many of the children in Cleveland had been abused.[4]

> It has been impossible from the evidence provided to the Inquiry to
> arrive at any consensus or obtain any reliable figures of the general
> prevalence of sexual abuse of children in the country or in Cleveland ...
> we are strongly of the opinion that great caution should be exercised at
> the present time in accepting percentages as to the prevalence and
> incidence of sexual abuse. (Secretary of State, 1988, pp. 4–5)

Similarly:

> There are some issues of importance upon which we did not receive
> evidence and which we have not addressed. These include specifically the
> nature of abusers and the reasons for sexual abuse of children; the
> effectiveness and appropriateness of the strategies used once the problem
> has been identified; and the response of society and the agencies to those
> who abuse. (p. 245)

The report was almost exclusively concerned with the *processes* of investigation and how different state agencies and professionals judge and relate to both each other, children and parents when there were allegations or suspicions of child sexual abuse. The central issue was 'the difficulties of recognition of sexual abuse of children and the threshold of suspicion at which action was to be taken' (p. 11). Not only were there differing claims as to what constituted recognition and the threshold of suspicion but also disputes about the form investigation and intervention should take.

Before analysing the nature of these disputes and how the inquiry attempted to judge and weigh them, it is important to outline the recent history of, and responses to, sexual abuse. For there were distinctive features associated with sexual abuse which fed into the arguments in Cleveland.

The Discovery and Nature of Sexual Abuse

In the late 1970s, the sexual abuse of children was a growing national concern in the USA and the number of reported cases was increasing considerably (Finkelhor, 1984). The growth of professional and public concern was much slower in Britain. A major reason put forward which many were to argue was at play in Cleveland, was widespread avoidance and denial both among the public and the professionals themselves.

Research studies and case reports had been available in Britain for some time. Greenland (1958) and Wells (1958) had published material on child sexual abuse and a study by Gibbons and Prince (1963) of eighty-two child victims of sex offences included recommendations for legal reforms. McGeorge (1964) reported on 400 children who had been sexually assaulted and Farn (1975) wrote a detailed article for police surgeons in which he reviewed the laws on sexual assaults of children and outlined procedures for medical examination. Editorials also appeared in the *British Medical Journal* (1961, 1972) and a brief commentary in the *Police Surgeon Supplement* (Williams, 1978). However, according to Mrazek, Lynch and Bentovim: 'Despite these attempts to enlighten the professional community, no further efforts were made to determine the incidence of child sexual abuse or provide specialised treatment services for the children and families' (1981, p. 48). By 1980, however, they felt the climate was changing. Influenced by developments in the USA, there was more open discussion of the issue, the Government and the NSPCC were becoming more involved and a review on the subject was published (Mrazek *et al.* 1980). Concluding their survey of the development of the recognition of child sexual abuse in Britain, Mrazek *et al.* (1981) identified a series of questions which would need to be addressed, and which were to be at the heart of the Cleveland Inquiry:

> The criteria for making the necessary judgements often will not be explicit but may be intertwined with broader values, beliefs, and practices of the county and/or subculture of that society. Regardless of the outcome, the questions are very similar. Should child sexual abuse be included within the child abuse spectrum? How should it be defined for legal and therapeutic purposes? How can the law be balanced so the child and family, the perpetrator, and society as a whole can be protected? What services can be provided with client-receptiveness, cost effectiveness, and outcome taken into consideration? How can reliable and valid information be obtained on incidence, individual and family prognosis, availability of treatment resources, treatment effectiveness, and long-term outcome? What professional organisation(s) should assume primary responsibility for investigation of suspected cases, treatment, professional, and public education, and long-term case co-ordination? (1981, p. 49)

Both Dr Arnon Bentovim (a child and family psychiatrist at the Hospital for Sick Children, Great Ormond Street) and Dr Margaret Lynch (Community Paediatrician at Guy's Hospital) proved important and energetic figures in the early 1980s in drawing attention to, and helping to frame the issue of, child sexual abuse. Both were members of the British Association for the Study and Prevention of Child Abuse and Neglect sub-committee on child sexual abuse, which in July 1981 published a booklet on child sexual abuse (BASPCAN, 1981). The booklet discussed the characteristics of families where it may occur, together with an outline for its assessment and management. The approach was developed from the model for responding to physical abuse and neglect and saw sexual abuse as a manifestation of problematic family dynamics and relationships. The booklet was primarily concerned with raising awareness amongst professionals. Clearly, however, it felt a therapeutic response was the most appropriate and subsumed the juridicial within the therapeutic for 'decisions about legal proceedings should be taken *in the context* of a general therapeutic approach' (BASPCAN, 1981, my emphasis).

The ideas were further developed under the auspices of a CIBA Foundation study group. The purpose of the group was to examine *scientific* and *medical* subjects that were of public concern. The subject of child sexual abuse was thought to be suitable for this approach and at the suggestion of Arnon Bentovim the first meeting was held in December 1981. The group acknowledged their debt to the late Henry Kempe (CIBA, 1984, p. x) who was influential in bringing the issue of child abuse into the public domain (see Parton, 1985b, ch. 3) and who played a major role in ensuring the problem was conceptualised within a medical-disease frame of reference. Henry and Ruth Kempe gave a seminar on child sexual abuse at the CIBA Foundation in early 1981. The study group was a direct result of that seminar.

The group claimed that there had been a 'considerable upsurge of interest both in recognising sexual abuse of children and in clarifying how and when to get help in dealing with the problem' (CIBA, 1984, p. xix) and pointed to the distribution of 11 000 copies of the 1981 BASPCAN pamphlet, the steady demand for workshops and lectures, and the growth of TV, radio, magazine and newspaper interest as evidence. The group met seventeen times in two and a half years and the ensuing book provided 'guidance about what actions may be taken by the different groups of professionals involved in the management of sexually abused children and their families – the victims, the perpetrators, and the close family and friends' (CIBA, 1984, p. xi). The professions represented in the study group were psychiatry, paediatrics, general practice, the social services, the probation service, teaching and youth work, the law, and the police.[5]

The book very much developed the policy and practice framework outlined in the BASPCAN (1981) pamphlet.

> We hope that the interest in the problem now being shown by many professionals and volunteers will result in *therapeutic* action that will in turn encourage those caught in the dilemma to come forward for help. *A multi-disciplinary approach that combines control with therapy* will go some way towards reducing the sexual abuse that persists in the community, largely because of fear of punishment. (CIBA, 1984, p. xii, my emphasis)

The book was keen to integrate sexual abuse into the mainstream of child abuse and neglect because 'sexual abuse, which is potentially damaging but not life threatening, was being dealt with by police investigation and prosecution with little in the way of therapeutic child care or protective work, and limited inter-professional co-operation' (CIBA, 1984, p. xvii).

However, there were also dimensions which differentiated it from other forms of abuse related to the secrecy that shrouded it and the problems of diagnosing and identifying it. *'Sexual abuse occurs in secret, is kept a secret by the family and is being kept a secret by society's attitudes and taboos'* (CIBA, 1984, p. xx, original emphasis). Sexual abuse, unlike physical abuse, often presented itself in a veiled way. While some children may have obvious genital injuries or conditions requiring medical care (venereal disease or pregnancy), relatively few showed such clear clinical features. It was an essentially medical-health problem but for which the traditional medical technologies, practices and knowledges appeared at a loss.

The book stated that recognition in many cases depended

on professionals being responsive to certain physical and behavioural indicators and outlined what these might be, together with certain patterns of family characteristics which were associated with it. It recognised the importance of verbal 'disclosures' of the abuse which may come from any family member but, because of the secrecy, may well involve interviewing young children about the specific allegations of abuse. Not only may this require giving the child the time and space to communicate in a climate of trust but developing strategies whereby the influence exerted by adult family members on the child 'not to tell' could be resisted.

While there were fundamental differences in theory and practice between such a family dysfunctional model of child sexual abuse and feminist perspectives, this was one area where there was an element of agreement. For the feminist perspective, the abuse of power is an essential feature of sexual abuse (Dominelli, 1989). Unlike the family dysfunctional approach which attempts to ensure that those affected by the abusing relationship assume their traditional roles as child, mother and father, a feminist approach stresses the concept of male power as both a central explanation and focus of intervention (Parton, C. 1989). Unlike physical abuse and neglect, the women's movement, drawing upon its wider experiences of male abuse of women and rape, played a much more active role in drawing attention to the problem of child sexual abuse. It stressed that such abuse was perpetrated almost exclusively by men and reflected not only the inferior position of children within the family but also the power and predatory attitudes of men. As a consequence, the priority in child abuse policy and practice should be to protect children from the more extreme manifestations of male power (Nelson, 1987). In the short term, it was argued that extreme forms of abuse merited an extreme response and that power should be used to compensate for the powerlessness of children in order to protect their interests. What is important to note was that such an approach emphasised the necessity in sexual abuse work for professionals to use their power, both professional and legal, on behalf of the child. While the more traditional dysfunctional approach developed from a sympathetic position towards the family generally in trying to correct and rehabilitate families wherever possible, it was also clear that its priorities were to stop the abuse.

Sexual abuse, perhaps more than other forms of abuse, required practitioners to use their power on behalf of the child and should not collude with any of the parties – particularly one or both parents. Such an approach has similarities to that outlined in the Beckford, Henry and Carlile Reports. Legal and therapeutic interventions were seen as interrelated whether at the investigative or treatment stages. 'It does not aim at legal and punitive actions although it may need legal measures to back up treatment and will use temporary separation of family members if this is helpful' (CIBA, 1984, p. 30). Such an approach was developed in America as 'therapeutic control', whereby the potential for change was seen to lie in the firm therapeutic opportunities provided by a firm statutory mandate (see, for example, Sgroi, 1982).

In order to overcome the problem of secrecy and the inadequacy of traditional clinical techniques, Arnon Bentovim and his colleagues at Great Ormond Street Clinic developed the use of anatomically correct dolls in structured interviews to help young people 'disclose' and talk about what had happened to them. During the 1980s, they made considerable efforts to overcome some of the problems of secrecy and power which lay at the heart of child sexual abuse work.

In outline, the child was interviewed by a psychiatric social worker and sometimes a doctor. During the course of the interview, use was made of the anatomically correct dolls to encourage the child to demonstrate behaviour which they were unable to describe in words. Since children were often reluctant to talk, the interviewer applied a degree of coaxing on the child to overcome this resistance. The encouragement may involve leading or hypothetical questions to enable the child to make statements against another family member. Such pressure was necessary to match the trauma which the child had suffered. A transcript of the interview was taken, together with a video-recording. The interviewer started from the premise of wanting to believe the child. The approach was originally used to deal with cases where abuse had been proven so that it functioned as a form of therapy to enable the child to recover. However, it was also developed as an aid to initial diagnosis. The techniques received much publicity within professional circles as perhaps one of the few that was available to respond to the particular problems associated with child sexual abuse (see Bentovim *et al.*, 1988).

However, the approach evoked considerable scepticism in the legal sphere when it was used as evidence in court. In 1986, it was subject to considerable judicial criticism (see Special Issue of *Family Law Review*, 1987, No. 1).

> There is an 'interface', as it has been described, between the needs of clinical therapeutic methods and the needs of the courts in legal proceedings. In doing what has been found so far to be best to meet the needs of the former, methods may be necessary which defeat or do not best meet the needs of the latter. (Latey, J. in Re M (A Minor) (Child Abuse Evidence) (1987) *Family Law Reports*, p. 293)

In the light of criticisms, the Great Ormond Street team subsequently modified their techniques so that the structure of interviews were more flexible, though the underlying assumptions and general approach remained the same (Douglas and Willmore, 1987; Woodcroft 1988; Glaser, 1989; Crewdson and Martin, 1989). It seemed to offer to professionals in the context of an increasing awareness of child sexual abuse a set of techniques which could significantly improve the possibilities of initial investigation.

The other main advance in the medical sphere was developed by two paediatricians in Leeds – Jane Wynne and Christopher Hobbs. Their approach was not only more in tune with traditional clinical practice, as it focused on *physical signs* of abuse, but it opened up a previously almost unrecognised dimension to the problem (Hobbs and Wynne, 1986). They argued that inspection of the anus via the reflex anal dilatation technique was an important element of the physical diagnosis and that 'buggery in infancy and early childhood is the next major aspect of child abuse to which the whole array of multi-disciplinary research should be directed' (Hobbs and Wynne, 1986). The article gave rise to heated debate in the letters column of *The Lancet* about the efficacy of the technique which was to pre-figure the explosion of medical argument in Cleveland (see Roberts, 1986; Hey *et al.*, 1987; Clayden, 1987).

However, it raised awareness that there may be physical signs to sexual abuse which were analogous to physical abuse and neglect. In the process, the doctor, particularly the paediatrician, was placed at the centre of attempts to identify and diagnose. As Hobbs and Wynne commented: 'the doctor's role is to diagnose the abuse and notify to other agencies with responsibility for the protection of children. The skills required to do this are in doctors' hands and others await our willingness and commitment to act on behalf of the children who are being abused' (Hobbs and Wynne, 1986, p. 796).

The 1980s, therefore, witnessed the development of two quite different developments in *medical* technologies for identifying sexual abuse, both of which underlined the role and expertise of doctors. Each reflected the traditional techniques for monitoring and hence constituting physical and sexual aspects of ill-health. As David Armstrong has argued:

> The key difference between techniques which monitor (and thereby constitute) the body and techniques which monitor (and similarly constitute) sexuality is that one is primarily a technology of seeing, the other of listening and the latter is perhaps best exemplified by the confession. (Armstrong, 1987, p. 71)

Childwatch

Late 1986 also witnessed a quite new departure in the publicity of child abuse via the 'Childwatch' programme and the launch of 'ChildLine'. Childwatch was a major BBC-1 programme which was broadcast at peak viewing time on Sunday 30 October 1986 between 8.30 and 11.00 p.m. and was watched by an estimated 16.5 million people (Koshal, unpublished, quoted in La Fontaine, 1990, p. 3). It was presented by Esther Rantzen, a well-known television celebrity who had fronted the long-established consumer affairs programme, 'That's Life', for many years. A similar publicity/campaigning approach had been taken previously in the 'Crimewatch' and 'Drugwatch' programmes.

> The Childwatch team felt that the isolated tragic cases that made headlines, the occasional child discovered dead behind locked doors,

produced public shock and anger, but few lessons were learnt. If as seemed likely there were many more undiscovered cases of child abuse, should we not try to discover them? Even more important, should we not be learning ways of preventing such cases, of finding and supporting the families at risk, and where necessary intervening to rescue the children in danger? How and why does child abuse occur? (Rantzen, 1987, p. 8).

The programme's aims were remarkably similar to the child rescue movements of the late nineteenth century (Gordon, 1989; Ferguson, 1990) but refashioned and repackaged for the high technological society of the late 1980s.

The first part was aimed at a family audience and encouraged children to disclose to adults incidents of abuse. It also launched 'ChildLine', the first national freephone helpline for children in trouble or danger.[6] 'Speak to someone who cares' was the keynote message and the freephone telephone number was given out at regular intervals.

The second part provided an examination of the phenomenon of child abuse based on specially commissioned research (McCron and Carter, 1987) which consisted of two survey-based research exercises. The first was a self-completion postal survey of a self-selected sample of people who volunteered to provide information about their childhood experiences of abuse. Of 3000 questionnaires returned, 2530 were analysed for presentation on the programme. Ninety per cent of the respondents reported sexual abuse, 56 per cent described physical violence and 38 per cent described neglect. Almost half the sample experienced both sexual abuse and physical violence. Of respondents who experienced neglect, 70 per cent said their mothers were responsible. Almost half blamed their fathers. Of those who experienced physical violence, 53 per cent said their fathers were responsible and 35 per cent said their mothers. The main perpetrators of sexual abuse were fathers (40 per cent). In a smaller number of cases, uncles, brothers, step-fathers and friends of the family were responsible (between 10–15 per cent in each case). Two central messages were underlined, therefore, in the programme: first, sexual abuse was a much bigger problem than many realised and constituted perhaps the largest unrecognised aspect of child abuse; second the perpetrators were rarely strangers but were usually adult males close to the child; nine-tenths of respondents were victims of abuse within the family circle (BBC, 1986).

In parallel with this, a second nationally representative survey of adults aged sixteen and over was undertaken in order to provide a contextual basis for the volunteer survey. Two thousand and forty-one adults were interviewed in their own home. Nine per cent claimed to have suffered abuse consisting of 3 per cent physical, 5 per cent emotional, 1 per cent neglect and 3 per cent sexual. Extrapolating from this, 1.2 million children would have suffered some form of abuse by the time they reached adulthood of which 400 000 would be sexually abused. There would be about four million of the adult population who had been abused as children (BBC, 1987).

The programme was a significant intervention into the issue of child abuse, particularly in relation to sexual abuse. It provided a novel mix of the media personality and new technology (Howarth, 1991). Its timing in late 1986 served both to raise public awareness but also disturb many previously untouched sensitivities. In attempting to bring such previously private troubles into the public domain, there was the potential for unintended consequences.

> ChildLine has to combat public ignorance of child abuse and its extent but without causing an overreaction. Some people believe that the kind of publicity used at its launch – the image of a potential threat at every domestic hearth, a monster lurking in every dad – played a part in the backlash by press and public against what has happened in Cleveland. (Laurance, 1987, p. 11)

The Parents

According to the Cleveland Report, 'the crisis in Cleveland came to public knowledge as a result of the *complaints* of parents about the *allegations* of sexual abuse' (p. 36, my emphasis). This was the first time that a parents' lobby had played any significant role in constructing a public inquiry into child abuse. This was helped by having a spokesperson, the Reverend Michael Wright (and subsequently Stuart Bell) who was able to translate their concerns to the media. They were also helped by the fact that a few years earlier a small support/campaign group had been formed which had been attempting to publicise the issues which were to be at play in Cleveland. Not only was the group able to provide support and guidance to the Cleveland parents, but it was able to articulate their concerns and claims in a clear and persuasive way.

Parents Against INjustice (PAIN) was launched by Sue and Steve Amphlett in July 1985 after they had been accused of injuring one of their own children and found themselves in the 'child abuse system'. Mrs Amphlett subsequently became the group's director and ensured that its message was heard. In the first eighteen months of operation, they had articles in numerous journals (including *She, Woman, New Society, Nursing Times, Community Care, Social Work Today, Mail on Sunday* and the *Sunday Telegraph*, see PAIN Newsletter No. 1, January 1987) and also appeared on numerous radio and TV programmes including a BBC-2 Open Space programme, 'Innocents at Risk' (17 March 1986). In the early days, they were completely dependent upon personal resources and small donations.

According to its publicity material, PAIN was founded by parents 'who are innocent of child abuse or neglect, but have nevertheless found themselves involved in child abuse and care procedures ... the group recognises and supports the necessity for well-defined procedures, but is concerned that reaction to recent well-publicised cases of child abuse will lead to an increasing number of parents being wrongly accused'.

> *The group believes that the same procedures and errors of judgement that are responsible for the victimisation of innocent parents and children are also responsible for the failure to detect and prevent genuine cases of abuse.*

While PAIN agreed that children were abused, it argued that child abuse procedures and professional judgements caught completely innocent *families* in a web which they had no way of getting out of.

Its principle objectives were : (1) to campaign for reform in child abuse and care procedures with accepted and enforceable codes of practice; (2) to ensure that the principles of *natural justice* were given due regard within the procedures; (3) to encourage public debate on the *rights* of parents, children and families and on child abuse issues; and (4) to offer support and advice and act as a referral helpline to parents *unjustly* accused of child abuse.

Initially, their work was in the area of physical abuse and neglect – particularly what was described as brittle bones disease (Sharron, 1987) – but increasingly the focus became sexual abuse. The claims, criticisms and recommendations of the parents at the Cleveland inquiry reflected many of those previously articulated by PAIN.

Mrs Amphlett, in her evidence to the inquiry, argued that: there was insufficient emphasis on the child *within* the family setting and until child abuse was established, the emphasis should be on the *protection* and *preservation of family life*; there was a need to *protect* children from misguided and over-zealous professionals; a full *assessment* of the family was necessary, and more parental involvement in investigation and decision-making; parents should attend case conferences and have the opportunity to correct *misconceptions*; and social workers should retain a degree of independence from the medical opinion (Secretary of State 1988, p. 162, my emphasis). Some of her other comments were that in many cases parents were not interviewed by social workers; parents had more confidence in police interviewing than social workers; while parents did not want to subject their children to unnecessary medical examinations, it was important that they have a right to a second opinion; parents felt powerless with social workers; many solicitors were inexperienced in child care so that parents received poor advice; and to remove children on the balance of probabilities was an infringement of civil liberties (Secretary of State, 1988, p. 162).

In Cleveland, the report said that many of the parents were critical of the two paediatricians – that the medical examinations were brief, took place at difficult times, they were kept waiting, they experienced resistance when second opinions were requested, and consent was not sought for examinations. More generally, they were critical of the insensitive way in which they were treated and that neither they nor their children were listened to or believed. As a consequence, the original problem they had gone to hospital for was either ignored or left untreated.

'Social Services, inevitably perhaps because they were dealing with dissatisfied and unhappy parents, shared with the doctors the main thrust of the parents' complaints' (Secretary of State, 1988, p. 40). Parental complaints again referred to the way they were treated and generally excluded but were specifically critical of the use of Place of Safety Orders and the restrictions of access once the Place of Safety Order was in operation. They were not properly informed of information and decisions, were not included in case conferences and a number were unhappy with the 'disclosure work' being carried out. There were few complaints about the police, but overall the parents felt isolated and lacking in support. The report commented that 'whether the parents were abusers, possible abusers or ordinary people caught up in the result of a misdiagnosis, this situation of isolation and lack of support, was a most worrying feature of the Cleveland crisis' (p. 46) and that:

> the criticism of parents about their contacts with social workers during 1987, was understandable and much of it justified. It must however be seen in the context and climate in which social work practice took place at that time. (Secretary of State, 1988, p. 84)

Social Work Practice

As we noted in the previous chapter, Cleveland Social Services department had taken very seriously the implications of the Beckford Report. This took place in a department where the report considered that already 'child care practice traditionally relied upon the use of statutory-based interventions and on Place of Safety Orders' (p. 57) anyway. Such an approach was given added legitimacy in the more specific concerns related to sexual abuse where:

> The Place of Safety Order appeared to be used to control parental access and in order to facilitate disclosure interviews with children. There was a high level of concern that if parents had open access to children, pressure would be brought to bear on the child not to tell what had been happening. (p. 66)

The report quoted Sue Richardson as saying sexual abuse was 'essentially a misuse of power by an adult against a child. So in any investigation the adult concerned is likely to continue to misuse and exploit the power and it is difficult to carry out an effective investigation unless you are proceeding from an authoritative base'. She felt 'the policy of investigating sexual abuse by family co-operation is a bit of a myth' (p. 81).

In judging whether the child had been abused, the report considered that Dr Higgs' and Dr Wyatt's diagnosis were accepted unquestioningly. Little of the differences of opinion between the paediatricians and the local police surgeon and, more significantly, the debate on the use of the reflex anal dilatation tests in *The Lancet*, were allowed to query this. An apparently 'high-risk' situation should be responded to by firm action.

This was formalised, *de facto*, as departmental policy in a memorandum from the Director of Social Services on 29 May which directed the exclusion of police surgeons from examining children referred to social services for reasons of sexual abuse. The key role in medical diagnosis was accorded to the consultant paediatrician and that 'where the consultant paediatrician is of the opinion that there is medical evidence of sexual abuse, an immediate Place of Safety Order should be taken to protect the child's interests during investigation'. It stressed the importance of obtaining a disclosure from the child, and the need to restrict access to parents[7] (p. 64). The approach was supported by the two paediatricians who 'praised the department for reacting so *firmly* to the diagnosis of sex abuse ... and hoped the *strong* response would continue' (p. 69, my emphasis).

The net result was that the social work practitioners were given no room for manoeuvre. Social work in any independent sense was squeezed by its own departmental managerial directions on the one hand and clear, and apparently legitimate, medical diagnosis on the other. *Medical diagnosis* not only dominated and prescribed *social assessment* but it predetermined the form any social work response would take.

Local policy and practice also failed to recognise the need for a legal input. 'A noticeable shortcoming in the arrangements was the lack of a legal representative even in complex cases' (p. 57). So while social workers may have been fulfilling the roles prescribed for them by their bureaucracy and the medical profession, there was a failure by all concerned to recognise that this was an essentially statutory role, particularly where a Place of Safety Order was being used. Constrained social interventions dominated unbridled from any juridicial input:

> Often in suspending belief, social workers fell into the trap of suspending all critical appraisal and without their general skills in assessment being properly utilised, saw their task narrowly as securing the protection of the child. It was not a helpful approach. *Ultimately children can only be protected on the basis of evidence that can be tested in court. The need was for a broadly based assessment against which the conclusions based on the physical signs could be tested.* (p. 73, my emphasis)

What came through was a failure on behalf of the social workers to recognise that the social work task in relation to child protection was ultimately circumscribed by law and accountable to the court rather than circumscribed by medicine and accountable to the hospital. Social workers in any independent fashion failed to mediate between medicine and the law or the hospital and the court such that the latter in each case (medicine and the hospital) dominated what was constituted to be sexual abuse for the purposes of intervening in the family.

The failure to recognise this crucial legal context was also evident in the emphasis given to 'disclosure work'. 'The basis upon which any information obtained in this way could be used as evidence in court proceedings was not generally understood' (p. 74). Throughout the report, the doubtful status of 'disclosure work' was underlined by always putting it in inverted commas. Inherent in the concept was the assumption that abuse had occurred but was simply hidden and shrouded from discovery. 'The "alternative possibility", namely that the child has no sexual abuse to disclose, is not considered as a viable option' (p. 206).

The report concluded that 'there was strong focus on the needs of the child in isolation from the family and this was a common pattern. Social workers concentrated their efforts on the immediate need to protect the child rather than an assessment of the family' (p. 75). Yet this social-family assessment was *the* central responsibility of social workers and was crucial to judging the level of risk to a child.

This lack of basic understanding 'of the unique features of each family as a family meant that parents felt alienated by what they saw as an apparent lack of willingness to understand their point of view'. A central part of social assessment, and hence of social work practice, was to recognise and respond to the subjective realities of clients. Social workers were experts in the subject located in its social-family context (Philp, 1979; Horne, 1987, 1990). The recognition of the subject, however, was not to take the side of the client (parent) but acted to transform, integrate and mediate as part of professionalised social assessment. It was concerned with objectifying the subject but was different to the response in Cleveland where parents' subjective realities had been denied.

The report considered the emphasis should be on encouraging co-operation with parents, as children were best cared for when proper plans were made and this was not possible when a Place of Safety Order was made. 'They must not, however, constitute a reason for leaving a child in a situation where he is at *high risk* of further abuse or violence. If that is the social workers's *considered view*, then their duty must guide them to apply for a Place of Safety Order' (p. 213, my emphasis). Responding to child sexual abuse, in particular, was best managed in a 'planned and considered way. Responding on an emergency basis is rarely required and is not likely to be helpful' (p. 213). However, the distinction between the high-risk case requiring an emergency response and others requiring a planned and considered response was not easy and required expert *judgement*. 'In each case the task is to make an initial *assessment* of the problem, determine the *degree of risk* to the child, liaise with other agencies and formulate the first steps in intervention, if intervention is thought to be necessary' (p. 214, my emphasis).

The social-family assessment was essential to the social work task. The main elements of such an assessment were outlined to the inquiry by David Jones, General Secretary of the British Association of Social Workers, and himself an experienced social worker previously with the NSPCC.

> The broad principles outlined by Henry Kempe in making an assessment
> of the family should still apply. It was necessary to assess the family by
> looking at the parents individually, the parents' relationship, the vulner-
> ability of the child, the child's situation in the family, the family's social
> situation, their contacts with the extended family etc. as well as
> considering and recording the family's perspective of events, which set
> the referral in motion. (p. 214)

However, the level of knowledge within social work to fulfil
these tasks was relatively underdeveloped. It was felt that
training had lapsed far behind the demands made of social
workers in the context of sexual abuse and that this was a
factor in Cleveland:

> If the level of suspicion is high but the assessment cursory it is likely that
> many innocent families will be damaged by false accusations. If the skills
> of assessment are excellent but the level of suspicion or awareness is low
> than children will go on being damaged. (p. 225)

Training to improve assessment to improve judgements was
vital.

In order to improve the quality of assessments in difficult
cases, the report recommended the establishment of Specialist
Assessment Teams (p. 249) consisting of an approved medical
practitioner, a senior social worker and a police officer. Not
only would it improve the quality of assessment, but also
enhance the mechanisms for inter-agency work. For it was
also similarly important for agencies to work together within
a clear framework so that not only would intervention be
successful in securing the welfare of the child but also in
respecting parents' rights. The social assessment and clear
inter-agency work were crucial for ensuring that both the
interests of the child and the rights of parents were protected.

Sexual Abuse as Child Health

The Cleveland Inquiry was untypical of previous child abuse
inquiries in that it was concerned not just with social work
practices but medical practices. For the first time, medical
practitioners – particularly paediatricians and to some extent

police surgeons – their knowledge base and their claims to expertise were put under the microscope. In the process, basic assumptions and alternative conceptions about the nature of the problem and the best way of responding were subjected to detailed analysis.

The medical profession had played a central role in discovering and subsequently legitimating child abuse as a public problem and conceptualising it in an essentially medical discourse (Parton, 1985b). Child abuse was seen as a problem of public health which should be notified (Parton, 1989). However, the nature of sexual abuse posed particular difficulties for the traditional expertise and clinical practices of medicine. This was a particular challenge for the branch of medicine whose *raison d'être* was children – paediatricians (see Armstrong, 1983, ch. 3). Developments in the early/mid-1980s, however, suggested that medicine could reclaim its central significance. The work at Great Ormond Street outlined new techniques that could be applied while the articles by Hobbs and Wynne suggested that the more traditional clinical approaches to the physical diagnosis of the body could play a central part. Commenting on her visit to a seminar in Leeds, where she was introduced to the work of Dr Wynne in June 1986, Dr Higgs said:

> I think I realised for the first time the numbers of children that could be involved in this problem, the importance of the medical examination. (Secretary of State, 1988, p. 131)

The approach of the paediatricians in Cleveland was characterised in the report as: (*a*) being almost exclusively child-centred, (*b*) believing sexual abuse was a much larger problem than previously thought and was subject to considerable social, professional and parental denial and (*c*) essentially a health, as opposed to a legal or social, problem.

At numerous points in the report, Dr Higgs and Dr Wyatt were quoted as saying they saw sexual abuse as '*the most important aspect of child health*' (p. 128, my emphasis). As with any health problem, particularly when it may be of epidemic proportions, the paediatricians saw themselves as having a professional responsibility to diagnose and for which they had a particular, but not exclusive, faith in the use of the reflex anal dilatation test. 'Their belief in the validity of the con- clusions from the physical signs led them into over confidence in the diagnosis' (p. 145).

Once sexual abuse had been diagnosed, the emphasis in the management of the case was on separating the child from the family so that the child could be protected and further assess- ment, particularly in the form of disclosure work, could be done. Place of Safety Orders were seen as important for both to take place. The medical discourse became professionally dominant. Dr Higgs' 'enthusiasm and authority placed her in the position of professional leadership' (p. 144) so that social workers were given little space for independence.

The legal discourse was also marginalised. The report noted her lack of experience of court proceedings and that 'she lacked appreciation of the *importance* of the *forensic element* in her work' (p. 144, my emphasis). This failure was underlined on numerous occasions. Recording and note-taking take on a quite different significance for court work rather than health work. While Dr Wyatt

> probably regarded the notes he was making in other cases as sufficient for his own use in managing his patients *it is unfortunate that he did not take steps to inform himself of the purpose to which they would be put and the crucial part they might play in court proceedings.* (p. 151, my emphasis)

This failure was even more evident when the report com- mented that:

> Although Dr Higgs did not consider the provision of reports for legal purposes as her highest priority, in matters concerning the children, the preparation of a medical report may be crucial to the police investigation and other court proceedings. *We would suggest that if a doctor does not understand the importance of the report for the Police then he or she should leave the recognition and management of child sexual abuse to others.* (p. 141, my emphasis)

In essence, the assessment, investigation and subsequent intervention into cases of sexual abuse was seen by the report as a legal matter and while medical 'evidence' may be important to this process, it was secondary and subservient to legal discourses. As a consequence, it was crucial to separate out the evaluative from the therapeutic and to recognise that social as well as medical evidence was as, if not more, valid to this process.

The status of medical knowledge and practice was further undermined by the considerable controversy *within* the medical profession as to the validity and utility of its expertise. The report was conscious of the debate within *The Lancet* arising from the Hobbs and Wynne article in 1986 concerning how far the reflex anal dilatation test could diagnose sexual abuse. While the report concluded that the test was never used on its own to diagnose sexual abuse – originally a major concern in criticism levelled by the media – the lack of consensus both within the profession generally, and evident in Cleveland in the severe disagreement between the paediatricians and the police surgeons, about the *significance* of the test, brought medical expertise into serious question.

The inquiry heard the views of several medical practitioners on the question and concluded: 'the evidence is that the sign of anal dilatation is abnormal and suspicious and requires further investigation. It is not in itself evidence of anal abuse' (p. 193).

What emerged was that the anal muscles 'operated in a complex system', controlled in part automatically, in part by learned subconscious behaviour and in part consciously and that this was *'not altogether understood by the experts'* (p. 190, my emphasis). Further, it was not known to what extent it occurred in normal individuals, whether it occurred in certain physiological states or whether it occurred in certain disease states. Thus, while the medical experts agreed that anal dilatation might follow anal abuse, there was considerable disagreement as to the other circumstances in which it might occur (pp. 190–3). Similarly, the 'value of digital examination in anal abuse of children remains *a matter of medical controversy'* (p. 193, my emphasis).

Medical knowledge in the area was so undeveloped that there was no agreement on the use of terms and definitions. This failure was particularly exposed under the gaze of legal demands:

> One problem which beset the Inquiry and provided ammunition for cross-examination was the lack of agreed medical terms to describe the

signs observed . . . not only were there differences in the words used to describe what was seen, but we had the feeling that on some occasions at least medical practitioners examining within a short period of each other either did not *see* or *did not elicit* the same clinical signs. (p. 183, my emphasis)

The major criticism of the paediatricians was not concerned with whether they correctly or incorrectly diagnosed sexual abuse. In fact, as the report said, it did not see its function 'to evaluate the accuracy of any diagnosis' (p. 183). The problem was that medical knowledge and practices were themselves fundamentally flawed. Hence the major criticism of Dr Higgs was her unshakeable confidence in the ability of medical knowledge and medical practices, including the use of reflex anal dilatation, to identify child sexual abuse.

In the current state of knowledge she was unwise to come to a firm conclusion rather than a strong suspicion on physical signs alone . . . to give a firm diagnosis of sexual abuse without other grounds of suspicion, no prior allegation or complaint by adult or child and no social family history was to risk the upheaval of the family and the child without the assurance that the diagnosis would be substantiated. *She lacked appreciation of the importance of the forensic element of her work, and the need to justify her conclusions at case conference, care proceedings and/or in the criminal courts.* (p. 144, my emphasis)

It was this failure to (*a*) recognise the contested state of medical knowledge and (*b*) the essentially subservient nature of medicine to the law in this area which lay at the heart of the Cleveland affair. These failures were then reflected in, and made worse by, the way parents and children were treated. There was never any question that Dr Higgs and Dr Wyatt were acting in anything but good faith and were certainly not waging an attack on family life, empire building or colluding and conspiring with Mrs Sue Richardson as alleged by Stuart Bell MP. Similarly, there was no question that the state, via the paediatricians, had embarked on an arbitrary and routine investigation of children for sexual abuse whenever they were presented to them and for whatever reasons:

We are entirely satisfied that there has been at no time routine screening of sexual abuse and that the paediatricians in Cleveland have only examined children when in their professional judgement there was cause to do so. (p. 194)

For the inquiry to have concluded otherwise *would have* suggested a fundamental attack on family life and an unwarranted and unaccountable encroachment of paediatricians under the auspices of the state.

However, as Lord Justice Butler-Sloss has commented since, the inquiry took the view that until the medical profession could resolve its disputes about medical evidence, particularly in relation to the significance of the physical signs of sexual abuse, such evidence should 'remain off stage' (Butler-Sloss, 1988). Until that time, the report clearly approved of the advice, outlined in a letter from Professor John Forfar, President of the British Paediatric Association, to Dr Higgs on the way paediatricians should develop their role and approach their task:

> The regulation of medical practice is achieved best when it is accomplished within the medical profession. New stances based on a new awareness of clinical signs, or new significances being attached to them, require first to be established within the profession. This takes some time and requires persuasion and scientific evidence of validity, based on the accepted method of communication to professional journals or scientific meetings. It is the dedicated research worker and the pioneering enthusiast who so often changes medicine for the better and uncover deficiencies in medical practice and understanding. *In the end however, any new development has to be fitted into the complex jig-saw which constitutes balanced medical practice.* As well as the benefits, the possible adverse effects of any revision of accepted practices have to be taken into account. Child sexual abuse is a very serious matter which we as paediatricians must seek to eliminate, but removal of children from their parents and forced institutionalism is another very serious matter. The values which different paediatricians and child psychiatrists will attach to these will vary. Perhaps, more importantly, any mistake in pursuing correction of one will cause the other. (p. 203, my emphasis)

Such a balance was reinforced by the context of economic and resource realities, for Dr Higgs and Dr Wyatt had gone about their task of diagnosing illness without having cognisance of the need to prioritise.

> She did not recognise the place of priorities and the inadequacy of the resources in Cleveland to meet the crisis. If intervention was to take place

> on the scale implied by her practice she shared with others a responsibil-
> ity to ensure that the resources necessary to meet the needs of the
> children were avilable. (p. 145)

Responsible medical practice was not simply a question of
identifying and treating illness but had to recognise an
essential balance between both conflicting values and diverse
priorities. Most particularly in the area of child sexual abuse,
until medical expertise had developed further, it should take a
relatively small part in the responsibility for diagnosis/
assessment and throughout should recognise its secondary
role to legal demands. In Cleveland, 'the medical diagnosis
assumed a central and determining role in the management of
the child and the family' (p. 243) and compromised the work
of the social workers and the police. Such a situation needed to
be avoided in future.

The Agencies of Law

While the report did argue that the police, and police
surgeons, had to take some responsibility for the collapse of
inter-agency co-operation in Cleveland, this was not given
such a high public profile. One of the more striking features of
the whole affair was the comparatively little attention paid by
the media to the law enforcement agencies in Cleveland. Bea
Campbell has since argued that the police were *the* major
contributors to the crisis, primarily in their failure to take
seriously the diagnoses of sexual abuse and their inability to
work with intelligent and articulate women – Dr Higgs and
Mrs Richardson. She argued that this resulted from the
essentially sexist attitudes of officers and the patriarchal
nature of the police force itself (Campbell 1988).

However, the report also expressed concern that magistrates failed to assert any independence and were far too ready
to accede to the applications for Place of Safety Orders on the
mere say-so of social workers. One hundred and twenty-five
children during the period were diagnosed as sexually abused
and ninety-one of them were the subject of Place of Safety
Orders. All but one application was made *ex parte*. None was

refused by the magistrates. Something over half the applications were heard by a single magistrate at home during the hours when the magistrates' court was sitting.

According to Louis Blom-Cooper:

> These bald facts disclose a disquieting situation. The main conclusion must be that the magistrates acted as rubber-stamps to applications to remove and detain children on the say-so of social workers. They do not appear to have exercised the judicial function which was laid upon them by S28 of the 1969 Children and Young Persons Act. Perhaps the most worrying aspect of this indiscriminate grant of a powerful order affecting the rights of parents and children is that no magistrate appears to have understood the emergency nature of the Place of Safety Order. (Blom-Cooper, 1988, p. 492)

The Cleveland Report reminded magistrates that their central responsibility in granting an Order was a 'discretionary *judicial* act' (p. 227, my emphasis) and that the granting of an Order for the purposes of disclosure work was an improper application of the law. The magistrates allowed themselves to be dominated by paediatricians and social workers when the lines of accountability and responsibility should have been the reverse.

A New Legal Framework

A major theme running through the report was that as a consequence of the breakdown in inter-agency co-operation and the heated arguments between the various adults, the children themselves may have been overlooked. However: 'Parents alone (except possibly in wardship) have inherent rights and obligations in respect of a child. All rights and obligations in respect of children exercised by others arise either from authority given expressly or by implication, or by express statutory provision' (p. 227). This emphasis on parental rights was given wide-ranging and practical significance for (p. 246):

(*a*)   Parents should be given the same courtesy as the family of any other referred child and applied to all aspects of the investigation into the suspicion of child sexual abuse.

(*b*)   Parents should be properly and clearly informed and, where appropriate, consulted at each stage of the investigation by the professionals dealing with the child whether medical, police or social worker. They were entitled to know what was going on and to be helped to understand the steps that were taken and where appropriate should be given the opportunity to participate in case conferences.

(*c*)   Social Services should confirm all the important decisions to parents in writing and should give parents the opportunity to consult lawyers to advise them.

(*d*)   Parents should always be advised of their rights to appeal or complaint in relation to any decision made about them or their children.

(*e*)   Social Services should also seek to provide support to the family during the investigation and parents should not be left isolated and bewildered.

While the report emphasised giving children a voice in decisions made on their behalf, precise and practical recommendations were not evident, so that Lyon and de Cruz have commented that 'it seems we are back again to treating the child as an object of concern rather than a person if we fail to give him access to the same rights as those possessed by his parents' (1988, p. 377).

The report was concerned that measures that were designed 'to meet circumstances which threaten the life or safety of a child should not be regarded routinely as the first stage of authoritative intervention' (p. 228). The recommendations for changes in the law were framed explicitly in terms of the White Paper in the hope of increasing its chances of getting onto the statute book. Overall, it supported the emerging consensus on the need for a changing set of checks and balances and rationalisation of the law, together with clearer lines of accountability between the court and social and health professionals. Its recommendations, however, varied in detail to those from previous reports. Its recommendations for legal change can be summarised in terms of substantive changes in the law and procedural reforms.

The report welcomed the replacement of POSOs with

Emergency Protection Orders (EPOs) as proposed in the White Paper (DHSS 1987) on 'the law on child care and family services' published in January 1987 following the Review of Child Care Law. The new Order would include a legislative formula which attempted to spell out when intervention was appropriate: the test was to ascertain whether there was reasonable cause to believe that damage to the child's health or wellbeing was likely unless s/he was immediately removed to a place of protection. While the report acknowledged that *ex parte* Orders were essential in cases of physical assault and threatened removal of a child from hospital, significantly it considered the attendance of parents before the Justices as 'desirable' in other cases. This amounted to a rejection of the view expressed in the Carlile Report (London Borough of Greenwich 1987, p. 147) that prior notice might jeopardize the child's safety. The report also recommended that application for an Order should be made to a full bench in court hours, and only to a single magistrate where a court was not sitting. Following the White Paper, the report recommended that EPOs should be for eight days with possible extension, via the court, to fifteen days.

During the initial period of the EPO, neither the White Paper nor the Cleveland Report envisaged the possibility of the parents or child contesting the Order. Only an extension would be susceptible to legal challenge. Yet, as we have seen, in both the Beckford and Carlile Reports it was argued that fairness required the right to an immediate 'appeal', by way of an application to set aside the Order. In the government statement following the publication of the Cleveland Report, the Minister for Health, Mr Tony Newton, stated that an opportunity to challenge *ex parte* orders would be available after seventy-two hours (*Hansard*, HoC, 6 July 1988, Col. 1062). This time-limit corresponded with that proposed in the Beckford Report and represented a *volte-face* in official thinking. In the Review (DHSS, 1985), a seventy-two hour period was expressly rejected as giving insufficient time for the local authority to prepare its case and eight days was chosen as a realistic compromise. While not recommended in the report, it was a clear and practical outcome of the concerns at the centre of Cleveland related to the need to protect the rights of parents and the privacy of the family from unwarrantable intrusions.

The view that emerged from the report was that a highly interventionist and indiscriminate use of POSOs was wrong and that social workers should negotiate with parents where possible and that the coercive aspects of the law should be clearly accountable to the court and be held in reserve for 'real' emergencies. Child sexual abuse, in particular, was defined as rarely life-threatening and that to take precipitate legal action was unnecessary and positively unhelpful.

Misunderstanding of the nature of POSOs was also identified as a key to the extent of control assumed by doctors and social workers in Cleveland. In clarifying the respective rights and responsibilities of parents and local authorities, the Cleveland Report stood with the earlier Review (DHSS, 1985) in declaring that detention and removal was *not* admission to care. A POSO simply authorised the detention of the child and did not transfer parental rights to the local authority. Parents retained the majority of their rights and the professionals' power was highly limited. This meant, for example, that an initial medical examination to ascertain the health of a child would be within the scope of a POSO, but not repeat examinations for forensic purposes without the informed consent of the parents or an older child (following the *Gillick* case).[8] The report noted that the question of control over medical examinations needed consideration.

Likewise, the Cleveland Report doubted whether as a general proposition a POSO conferred on a local authority power to restrict the parents' access to the child. The report supported the White Paper that there should be a presumption that access should be allowed, recommending that whenever and however children come into care, social workers should seek agreement with parents on access. Should a local authority wish to suspend access during the eight-day period, the onus rested with it to return to court to obtain the requisite legal authority.

The net effect of this clarification of 'grey areas' of the law would be to strengthen the rights of parents and children *vis-à-vis* the local authority, and to subject the latter's actions to greater judicial review.

The Carlile Report had recommended that social workers should be given added legal rights of entry into homes with access to children believed to be at risk, based on the model of powers under the mental health legislation. This specific proposal was not taken further by the Cleveland Report, which instead advocated a 'disclosure order' to ascertain the child's whereabouts. Such an Order would carry the full weight of judicial authority, and the sanction of committal to prison for refusal to comply (p. 228). Nor did the Cleveland Report support the introduction of a Child Assessment Order.

Within the reports there was then a divergence of views on the need for additional powers. Whereas the Carlile Report envisaged a hierarchy of orders of ascending levels of control, Cleveland preferred to use the procedure for Emergency Protection Orders as an umbrella. This reflected different approaches to the common goal of simplification and clarification of the law: should it be achieved by multiplication and differentiation of statutory powers, or under a single unitary procedure? It is significant, too, that the Cleveland Report was reluctant to endorse non-judicial procedures which would permit independent action by social workers.

The report was clear that in relation to Care Orders, the White Paper proposals should be implemented. Thus the grounds and duration for interim care orders should be tightened up, while the grounds for care proceedings should be simplified and harmonised with 'family proceedings'. The recommendations of the Cleveland Report were limited to technical refinements.

Secondly, the report had numerous observations and re-commendations concerning possible procedural reforms. Since many of the procedural distortions and anomalies in care proceedings resulted from the initial focus of the Children and Young Persons Act, 1969 on the child *offender* rather than the child *victim*, the trend had been to move away from a quasi-criminal to a civil model of proceedings. Under Section 3 of the Children and Young Persons (Amendment) Act, 1986 (which came into force on 1 August 1988), parents were recognised as true contestants and given full party status. Beyond endorsing the White Paper recommendations, the Cleveland Report merely commented on the problems in relation to guardians *ad litems* exposed by the crisis. The report viewed the guardian system as problematic because of a perceived lack of independence from the local authority and as counter-productive because of delays associated with appointments.

Prefacing its summary of the wardship jurisdiction, the Cleveland Report commented: 'Wardship is not clearly understood by many who in case conferences or otherwise may have important decisions to make over future legal proceedings in respect of children in their care' (p. 230). Wardship was an ancient jurisdiction, based on the concept that the Crown as *parens patriae* had a duty to protect those subjects, such as infants, unable to help themselves. As an inherent jurisdiction, its flexibility had proved useful in recent years to local authorities wishing to supplement, or even by-pass, the statutory restrictions on care proceedings. Thus, in Cleveland, wardship 'came to the rescue of an otherwise over-burdened juvenile court' (p. 231). Heaping praises upon this 'invaluable procedure', which enabled 'difficult, complex and emotive issues to be fully considered and adjudicated upon', the report countred the possible implication in the White Paper that, in future, local authorities would not need to invoke wardship. It expressly doubted whether the proposed changes to care proceedings would of themselves substantially reduce reliance on the jurisdiction.

The report also considered that there was injustice in the ability of a local authority to issue wardship proceedings when parents do not have that right. This followed from the decision of the House of Lords in *A v. Liverpool City Council* (*Family Law Reports*, 1981, No. 2, p. 222) which rejected attempts by parents to use wardship to challenge local authority decisions about access and other matters in relation to children in care. Accordingly, the report recommended that the *Liverpool* case be considered.

Righting this particular injustice to parents carried with it the potential over-burdening of the High Court, and it recommended that the allocation of individual cases to the appropriate forum should be controlled by Registrars, in accordance with directions issued by the President of the Family Division. This would represent a significant step in bringing the two jurisdictions together, and it was in this context that the report recognised the procedural advantages flowing from the creation of a unified family court. However, this was not as ambitious as some of its supporters might have wished, since it assumed that magistrates would still hear the majority of care cases, with wardship remaining the 'Rolls Royce' procedure. The thrust behind the establishment of such a court was clarification and rationalisation. The lesson drawn from Cleveland was that the children suffer when the professionals were confused or misconceived the legal position (Secretary of State, 1988, p. 236).

With the wider consideration of setting up a family court in mind, the Cleveland Report suggested creating a new Office of Child Protection. The possible duties of the new office were outlined in the very last paragraph of the report, viz., to scrutinise local authority applications for a care order, commission additional investigations and administer the guardians *ad litem* panel (p. 254). The Lord Chancellor's Office promptly issued a consultation paper (Lord Chancellor's Department 1988). However, the responses to the paper were generally negative, primarily on the grounds of cost and duplication of effort, and the plan was shelved.

Conclusions

As with previous child abuse reports, a lack of resources was not seen as a significant factor in causing the crisis in Cleveland. While it felt that social workers, and to some extent medical staff, did have inadequate resources to cope with the number of cases at its height, this was seen as an effect rather than a cause of the crisis. The central causes were, in terms of professional response, the failure to prioritise and, particularly, manage. The reasons for the crisis were identified as: (*a*) a lack of proper understanding by the main agencies of each other's functions in relation to child sexual abuse; (*b*) a lack of communication between the agencies; and (*c*) the differences of views at middle management level which were not recognised by senior staff (p. 243).

While the response of some of the media, particularly the

serious newspapers, did attempt to communicate some of the complexity of the report, this was not the case across the board. Franklin has commented that:

> Most newspapers simply quoted the Report selectively to endorse their previous editorial line. The crude and simplistic reviews typically published in the press conveyed little of the complexities which Butler-Sloss had so thoroughly detailed. (Franklin, 1989, p. 7)

In part, this could be accounted for by the fact that the shortened version of the report (Cmnd 413), which was used by most journalists, had almost no critical comments of the police, police surgeons, magistrates or Stuart Bell. The comments on Dr Higgs, Dr Wyatt and Mrs Richardson were much fuller.

Thus, while the accusations originally levelled by Stuart Bell had been found by the report to be unfounded, they continued to frame and dominate the agenda. In his statement in the House of Commons, the Minister of State, Tony Newton, identified the central issue in the following way:

> The whole House will be united in its condemnation of sexual or other abuse of children, and in its support for proper action to protect children from it, but it will be no less united in insisting that this must be achieved in a way that does not trample on the rights of parents and inflict unnecessary distress on the very children we wish to be helped.
>
> It is clear from the Report that this *balance* was not achieved in Cleveland during the period in question. (*Hansard*, HoC, 6 July 1988, Col. 1061, my emphasis)

He confirmed that the Government were firmly committed to implement the White Paper proposals, modified in the light of the report and that a Bill would be brought before Parliament at the earliest practicable opportunity (*Hansard*, HoC, 6 July 1988, Col. 1062).

What emerged via the Cleveland Report was support for the legal framework outlined in the White Paper but modified to strengthen the rights of parents and making more explicit the move toward identifying the law itself as the crucial mechanism for both informing decision-making and resolving disputes.

This is not to say that social work was not given a significant space in these attempts to modernise and rationalise. For all the criticisms made of social work practice and the relatively undeveloped professionalism and professional power of social workers, the Cleveland Report underlined the crucial need to legitimate and enhance the role and practices of social workers. Nowhere was this more evident than in the focal function of the social assessment when attempting to identify sexual abuse and weigh the significance of certain signs and indices in relation to deciding whether a case was high risk or not and for determining the form that intervention should take. Similarly it was not sufficient for social work intervention to overly rely on coercive interventions as symbolised by the Place of Safety Order. In doing so social work was in danger of overlooking its distinctive rationale. What was crucial was that social workers interpret, construct and mediate the 'subjective' realities of the children and adults with whom they work. Social assessment could not be reduced to simply applying the apparently objective criteria derived from the physical sciences and traditional clinical medicine. While these were of importance they also needed to be interpreted so that their true significance could be weighed and judged.

Throughout, however, all needed to recognise, professionals and family members alike, that the auspices, and hence ultimate accountability for such social practices and interventions, lay with the law and its representatives. It was not simply a question of getting the right balance between family autonomy and state intervention but also getting the right balance between the power, discretion and responsibilities of the juridicial, the social and the medical and their respective agencies and professional representatives.

5

Co-ordination, Management and Social Assessment

The Butler-Sloss Report saw the central reasons for the crisis in Cleveland as residing with failures in inter-agency co-operation and poor inter-professional understanding. As a consequence, the cases were not managed sensitively and the respective expertise of the different professionals was not applied appropriately. The solution did not lie simply in changing the law for this was unlikely to provide the more detailed checks and balances that would be required to modify day-to-day practice and influence professional attitudes. No-one was suggesting that any agency or professional group should be excluded from this area of work; what was crucial was that their respective roles, responsibilities and interrelationships, together with their areas of expertise, should be clarified, developed and formalised. In his statement to the House of Commons on the day of publication of the Cleveland Report, Tony Newton, the Minister, announced that guidance circulars were being issued by DHSS (1988d), the Home Office (1988), and the Department of Education (1988) to their respective agencies, enclosing a comprehensive guide on inter-agency co-operation (DHSS 1988a). This was backed up by the publication of a Social Services Inspectorate survey of current arrangements in the area of sexual abuse (SSI, 1988) and guidance for doctors on the diagnosis of child sexual abuse (DHSS, 1988b), plus guidance for senior nurses, health visitors and midwives (DHSS, 1988c). He also announced that 'detailed professional guidance on social work practice is now being tested in the field and will be issued shortly' (Col. 1062), and this was published in late 1988 (DoH, 1988). The Government also responded to the concerns expressed in the report on the strategic significance of training for social workers who were seen as *the* central professional group. The Minister announced a grant of 70 per cent in support of expenditure of ten million pounds for social work training in this field (DHSS, 1988e; 1989a).

However, we should not see this emphasis on trying to finely tune the management of the problem and improving inter-agency co-operation as either new or something particular to child abuse. Throughout the 1980s there had been an increasing emphasis across the health, welfare and penal fields on the need for improvements in inter-agency collaboration. It was particularly evident in the area of community care (see, in particular, the Griffiths Report, 1988) and various initiatives in crime prevention (see Moxon, 1985). However, the issues related to sexual abuse were seen as being of particular significance:

> More than any condition adversely affecting health of children, child sexual abuse requires close coordination and exchange between the services, agencies and different types of professionals who are concerned with the overall wellbeing of children. (DHSS, 1988c, p. 2)

In fact, the major efforts in response to child abuse, since the mid-1970s, had been to establish and develop inter-agency and inter-professional mechanisms. In some respects, we should simply see the recommended changes in the wake of the Cleveland Report as further refinements to existing structures and practices. However, while the earlier attempts aimed to increase professionals' awareness of the problem of child abuse and hence increase their willingness and ability to protect children, current concerns were different. In particular, sexual abuse was seen to present new and qualitatively different demands and there was now much greater emphasis on the rights of different family members – both children and parents. While a co-ordinated multi-disciplinary approach was even more significant, the way this was legitimated, the form it should take and the practices it should set in place, changed in an attempt to take account of these new demands and tensions.

The Management of Child Abuse

The system of child abuse management was effectively in-augurated with the issue of the DHSS circular (DHSS, 1974) in April 1974 in the wake of the Maria Colwell Inquiry and followed earlier guidance in relation to 'battered babies' (DHSS, 1970; DHSS, 1972) (see Parton, 1985b, pp. 102–14). While paragraph 2 of the circular attempted to sensitise professionals to the 'first signs' of possible 'Non-Accidental Injury', the remainder was taken up with how to manage individual cases and the local organisation of agencies, professionals and resources.

It emphasised the need for teamwork and 'strongly recommended' the establishment of case conferences, area review committees and registers. Area Review Committees were to provide a forum for consultation between representatives of all local agencies and should be responsible for the formulation of local practice procedures, training, enquiries and general advice. Case conferences were to provide an arena for professionals who had knowledge of a particular child or family to share information and co-ordinate their efforts. The police were not crucial to the workings of a case conference at this stage as they were listed as 'others who may be invited'. The problem to be addressed was essentially of a health and welfare nature, for which health and welfare experts were crucial. However, the establishment of a register of cases was 'essential' as 'the outcome of any case will depend on the communicating skills of the professionals involved as much as their expertise'. By the end of 1974, Area Review Committees had been established across England and Wales, together with registers, while the convening of case conferences was 'recognised in all areas as a vital process in the handling of cases of children injured or at risk' (DHSS, 1976, para. 10).

The circular stressed that children should always be admitted to hospital if 'non-accidental injury' (NAI) was suspected and that 'the paediatrician will normally be responsible for an assessment . . . a case conference should be called as soon as possible. A place of safety may have to be obtained through the social services department, police or NSPCC and if parents propose to remove the child before investigations are complete, the paediatrician in charge should see them to explain the possible consequences of their action' (para. 5). If a child had to be removed from home for a period, this should always be on a statutory care order rather than by a voluntary admission. Once in the care of the local authority, the child should then only be returned home on the advice of the case conference. However, whenever there was evidence of NAI, it argued that decisions should only be made on the basis of 'social, material and psychiatric assessments' of the family and whether they would respond to the support and advice offered. Where it was felt that the child needed a clear separation from the family, this should be based on a comprehensive knowledge of the family situation.

This circular provided the catalyst for change in a period of considerable social, professional and organisational anxiety. The roles of paediatricians, GPs, health visitors and social workers were seen as crucial and the social services department, as the statutory child care agency, central. However, some police forces felt that they were not informed when cases came to light and the DHSS released a circular in November 1976 (DHSS, 1976) which aimed to promote a better understanding between the police and other agencies. While it recognised the 'difference of approach' of the agencies, it stressed the importance of close co-operation. The circular stressed that a senior police officer should be included on all Area Review Committees and case conferences. It also recommended that the police should release to case conferences and other agencies any relevant information about a family when they were 'assessing the suitability of a person to have care of children', including any relevant previous convictions, regardless of whether they were spent or not. We can see that the issue of police relationships with social workers and paediatricians was not something specific to sexual abuse or to Cleveland in 1987. It had been a tension running through the management of child abuse since its modern inception.

However, potential problems had been kept within acceptable bounds and had not surfaced into the public domain in any serious way.

The DHSS circular of 1980 (DHSS, 1980) attempted to rationalise the management and role of registers. In particular, there was an explicit move to broaden the criteria for including cases. Whereas the problem in 1970 had been officially termed 'battered babies' (DHSS, 1970), 'non-accidental injury' in 1974 (DHSS, 1974), by 1980 it had become 'child abuse' (DHSS, 1980). Such a broadening reflected debates in the literature which increasingly argued that the physical trauma dimensions of abuse did not take into account the often more damaging effects that resulted from neglect, emotional abuse and that older as well as younger children were 'at risk' (see, for example, Helfer and Kempe, 1976). The circular did not include sexual abuse though this had been considered, nor did it include 'babies at risk of abuse' or 'other forms of abuse' as outlined in the original draft circular (DHSS, 1978). The categories were: physical injury; physical neglect; failure to thrive and emotional abuse; and children in the same household as a person previously involved in child abuse.

The circular was split into four sections: introduction, minimum requirements, optional recommendations, and general advice. All the recommendations on broadening criteria were in the 'minimum requirements' section. The optional recommendations were concerned with the management and monitoring of registers. It recommended that the 'custodian of the register' should be a senior officer with considerable experience in the field of child abuse, that they should have adequate administrative support and that there should be regular updating and reassessments of cases on the register every six months. The final section, general advice, included issues which had direct implications for civil liberties and the way the child abuse system was experienced by parents – how cases could be taken off a register, informing parents and confidentiality – issues which, in 1980, were seen as good practice but not of top priority. There was never any suggestion that parents might have any involvement in a case conference, for:

unless in an individual case there are exceptional reasons for not doing so, *parents should be informed that it has been decided to place their child's name* on the register and should be given the opportunity to discuss and question the decision. (para. 4.6, my emphasis)

A primary reason why the recommendations were prioritised in this way was cost. The criteria for including cases on registers could be broadened at little or no cost, while employing senior staff to administer them would. The section on good practice was simply advice. Ironically, the BASW Report (1978), on which the circular claimed it had drawn extensively, specifically argued that its recommendations should not be prioritised or introduced partially. This was particularly the case if the criteria for including cases were broadened without improvements in the professional, administrative and hence resource base. If they were not introduced as a package, unintended and unforeseen implications for civil liberties, rights and the way social work interventions were experienced might follow.

Working Together

The early 1980s was a period of relative calm. The emphasis at the DHSS was on drawing out the common lessons that could be drawn from inquiries (see DHSS 1982). While there continued to be a number of tragic cases of children dying at the hands of their parents which did receive some publicity, and child abuse cases continued to be a high priority for social services departments, rarely did debate seriously filter into the public domain. This quickly changed, however, in 1985 with the furore arising from the Beckford case. Following the publication of the report, the DHSS responded in April 1986 with 'a draft guide to arrangements for inter-agency co-operation for the protection of children' entitled *Child Abuse – Working Together* (DHSS, 1986). As Norman Fowler, the Secretary of State, underlined in his covering letter, it attempted to pick up on the major problems identified in the Beckford Report in relation to inter-agency and inter-professional co-ordination and that it was important to ensure 'that all staff are fully aware of the legal framework in this area and how it affects the responsibilities which they bear'. The draft guide very much reflected the overall tone and agenda for change outlined in the Beckford Report and the BASW document on the management of child abuse (BASW, 1985) which had been prepared and presented in outline to the Beckford Inquiry. Individuals and organisations were asked to respond to the guide by the autumn of 1986 so that there was an expectation that the final document would be available during 1987. Before it was published, however, the Cleveland affair exploded onto the scene and its publication postponed so that the Cleveland Inquiry could be taken into account. It was eventually published and circulated on the same day as the publication of the Inquiry. While both the draft and the final document follow a similar format, there were significant differences and subtle changes of emphasis so that their overall meaning, together with their recommendations for policy and practice, can be read as quite different in important respects. The draft can be seen very much as a response to the Beckford Report, while the final version is much more a re-sponse to the Cleveland Report. While the phrase 'Working Together' in the draft made explicit reference to the need for professionals and agencies to work together, the final version puts much more emphasis on the need for professionals and agencies to 'work together' *with* parents and in some respects children – though the ultimate responsibilities and lines of accountability still clearly remained with professionals. In the process of these changes, the notion of child protection was subtly reframed. For while both explicitly framed their recom-mendations for change in terms of *child protection* (see Parton and Parton, 1989a 1989b), the draft saw this as essentially in terms of protecting children *from* parents and guardians *per se*, while the final guide saw the need to protect children without unwarrantable interventions into the family and hence also protect the rights of parents. Thus, while I will concentrate my analysis on the final 1988 *Working Together* guide, I will also draw attention to where and how this differed from the draft. Perhaps the most glaring difference was their length. While both were considerably longer than previous guidance, this was most evident in the final version which was over seventy pages long and reflected the complex issues it had to address. It attempted to make the roles and responsibilities of the different agencies, together with their interrelationships, as explicit as possible so that most eventualities were subject to detailed, though not necessarily unambiguous, comment.

As the circular (DHSS, 1988d) accompanying the guide (1988a) stated, the guide attempted to consolidate and update the existing guidance on inter-agency work in the field of child abuse and '*in the context of the wide statutory duties* of authorities for the health and welfare of children' (my emphasis). In fact, the whole of the first substantive section (Part 2) of the guide on the role of social services departments set this out in terms of their statutory responsibilities. Social Services Departments were identified as *the* central agency and this arose from statute. A detailed summary of all the relevant elements of the law was included. This was much fuller than in the 1986 draft, where a particular emphasis had been put on the Place of Safety Order. In 1988, Place of Safety Orders were outlined as simply *one* of the statutory responsibilities, together with: investigation; prevention; reception into voluntary care; care proceedings; and finally emergency situations.[1] Thus, while social workers were constituted as essentially statutory agents in both, this took on a subtly different guise. In particular, in the 1988 guide the use of a Place of Safety Order was simply one possible response and should only be used in very prescribed circumstances.

The range of other agencies with a role to play included hospital staff, midwives, health visitors, school nurses, GPs, dentists, opticians, teachers, education welfare officers, voluntary organisations and the community itself, as well as hospital doctors, the police and NSPCC. They should all 'be aware of the need to recognise the *signs of abuse*' (para. 3.8, my emphasis) and contact one of the statutory agencies if they were concerned about an individual child and should take advantage of their particular role to provide strategic 'surveillance' of the child population. A variety of community and clinic health professionals were able to fulfil such a task (paras 3.2 and 3.3) and 'teachers and other school staff are particularly well placed to observe outward signs of abuse, changes in behaviour or failure to develop' (para. 4.1). This was the first time that teachers were officially identified as having a significant role. To formalise this, each school should designate a senior member of staff to liaise with the social services department – as recommended in the Beckford Report. Teachers also had an important role to play in prevention via changing behaviour and attitudes via the curriculum.

A number of voluntary organisations, along with the community as a whole, were expected to bring 'children who are thought to be in need of protection to the attention of the statutory agencies' (para. 4.10) who in turn needed to be responsive to such referrals. It was everyone's responsibility, both professional and lay, to increase surveillance and thereby extend the net of the child abuse system.

While social services were at the centre of this net, the police were also 'involved in cases of child abuse as a consequence of their general responsibility for the protection of life and limb, the prevention and investigation of *crime* and the submission of cases for *criminal proceedings*' (para. 4.5, my emphasis). However, potential difficulties in the relationship between police and social and services, particularly during an initial investigation, were recognised. The police 'work to a standard of proof *beyond reasonable doubt* which is not the same as the *balance of probabilities* on which a juvenile court must be satisfied in care proceedings' (para. 4.5; my emphasis) and which was the central criteria for social services departments. In order to negotiate these differences 'in the interests of children, methods of joint working need to be established' of which Bexley was perhaps the most celebrated example (Byrne and Bloxham, 1986; Metropolitan Police and Bexley London Borough, 1987).

Part 5 was taken up with 'working together in individual cases' and stressed that 'inter-disciplinary and inter-agency work is an essential process in the professional task of attempting to protect children from abuse' (para. 5.1). It stated that:

> Working arrangements need to involve all agencies and *include* the handling of cases of child sexual abuse. The *thrust* now must be to ensure that professionals in individual agencies work together on a multi-disciplinary basis. (para. 5.2, my emphasis)

This marked an important change of emphasis to the 1986 draft guide. First, it explicitly stated that cases of sexual abuse should be included in such arrangements, whereas this had been simply assumed in 1986. Secondly, it said that the *thrust* should be on agencies working together. The emphasis in 1986 had been different, for:

> The development in interagency practice has not been fully matched by the development of practice in individual professions. The *thrust* in the next decade must be to develop knowledge and skills in the individual professions. (1986, p. 10; my emphasis)

This shift reflected the move from the Beckford Report, which saw the problems being located primarily in professional knowledge and practices, to the Cleveland and Carlile Reports, which saw the central problems being located in the inter-agency systems themselves.

The discussion on the 'exchange of information' was much expanded from the 1986 version and quoted at length from the Annual Report 1987 of the General Medical Council to underline that while information should be treated in confidence, confidence – in the context of child protection work – was 'not intended to prevent the exchange of information between different professional staff who have a responsibility for ensuring the protection of children' (para. 5.4) for 'arrangements for the protection of children from abuse, and in particular case conferences, *can only be successful* if the professional staff concerned do all they can to share and exchange relevant information, in particular with social services departments (or the NSPCC) and the police' (para. 5.3, my emphasis). While this was designed to address the problems where children had died because crucial bits of the jigsaw had not been pieced together, as in the Beckford case, the argument had to be clearly specified so that it was not seen as an unnecessary attack upon civil liberties and parental rights:

> staff in different agencies and other practitioners will maintain their own records of the case and such records should be subject to the arrangements for maintaining confidentiality within that particular agency. All agencies must establish procedures to safeguard information provided to them. (para. 5.6)

The guide then outlined the 'stages of work in individual cases'. The words chosen reflected not just an emphasis on systematic management, but ones which tried to avoid the use of technical terms in common use in any of the respective professions. The process was seen to fall into three stages: recognition and investigation; assessment and planning; implementation and review. It was hoped that the construction of these new terms would help frame a common language whereby all professionals and agencies could identify a common ground to work together. For 'if co-operation between agencies in providing protection to children is to be effective, it must be underpinned by a shared understanding of the handling of individual cases' (para. 5.7).

Social services departments, the NSPCC and the police were identified as the 'investigating agencies' (para. 5.8). The initial steps must establish the relevant factual circumstances of the child and the possible sources of harm or danger. For this to be effective, 'close co-operation between these agencies from the outset is essential and local guidelines should be agreed between them on the investigation of individual cases. These should include *strategy discussions* with each other, relevant agencies and medical personnel, at an early stage in the investigation. The purpose of these discussions is to ensure an early exchange of information and to clarify what action needs to be taken' (para. 5.11; my emphasis). This signposted an important development. For whereas in 1974 social workers and doctors, particularly paediatricians, had been identified as the central figures, and the police were to be invited to the initial case conference 'when appropriate', by 1988 the police had become one of the central 'investigating agencies', while medical personnel were, in effect, relegated to the equivalence of a 'relevant agency'. A subtle but important shift in professional power and hence the responsibilties for decision-making. The impact of Cleveland seemed evident because in the 1986 draft guide, 'the extent of police involvement will depend in part on whether it appears that an offence has been committed' (p. 12). The other new element was the introduction of *the strategy discussion*. This was something separate from a case conference and reflected the changed timing, function and composition of case conferences as will become evident below.

While professionals would have had such discussions in the past, this was the first time they had been given an official label and formal function. The 1986 draft guide made no such reference to strategy discussions.

While 'the dominant issue must be to ensure the safety of the child', we were reminded that removal could be 'either on a voluntary basis or by obtaining a Place of Safety Order' and that 'a Place of Safety Order should only be sought for the minimum time necessary to ensure the protection of the child'. The voluntary basis for removal had been explicitly criticised in the 1974 circular, while the emphasis on using Place of Safety Orders for the minimum time necessary had not been in the 1986 draft guide. The inclusion of both was indicative of the new *balance* that the 1988 guide aimed to construct. To ensure that this balance was negotiated in practice, it was recommended that such decisions should be brought to a multi-disciplinary case conference whenever possible.

It emphasised that 'the investigation of child abuse or risk of abuse *always requires social as well as medical assessment*' (para. 5.13, original emphasis). It also pointed out that doctors needed to record their findings and opinions at the time in order to contribute to future planning, including possible court action, thus stressing that such an examination was essentially forensic.

Whereas in 1974 a case conference should meet as 'soon as possible', in 1988 'the timing of the first inter-agency case conference will vary' (para. 5.15) and 'in some cases the first case conference will be held after the investigating agencies have held a *strategy discussion*, completed initial investigations and have taken urgent action to protect the child' (my emphasis). But essentially 'the investigating agencies need to act with the speed appropriate to the circumstances of the case ... in accordance with locally agreed inter-agency procedures'. Thus, while there seems to be more leeway for professional discretion, such discretion should take place in the context of the locally-negotiated multi-agency approach.

The investigative stage was concluded when a case conference 'is able to reach a view on whether or not the child's name should be placed on the local child protection register' (para. 5.16) which signified that such cases 'will then be subject to co-ordinated inter-agency planning and review'. For those cases not registered, they should be 'assessed and responded to by the relevant agencies as in other cases not involving child abuse procedures' for they may still need a variety of services. In effect, the investigative process had as its prime purpose judging whether a child was in immediate danger and should be removed, together with judging whether the case should be placed on the register. Registration signified that a case should be subject to child protection procedures.

Once registered, the process of assessment and planning should begin and one of the statutory agencies, that is, social services department or NSPCC, should carry responsibility for the case and one of its workers take on the role of 'key workers' for the purposes of co-ordinating inter-agency activity. While others may have far more active contact with the child and family, the statutory lines of accountability and ultimate responsibility were thereby underlined. The central role that social services departments and the NSPCC played in investigation should be maintained in the assessment and planning stage. This emphasis on the statutory mandate for the key worker role was much more explicit in 1988 compared to the 1986 draft guide. What was also evident was the clear move to see key workers as having a role as case planners and multi-agency co-ordinators, almost in the guise of that suggested in the Griffiths Report on Community Care (1988). We can see a distinct move away from constituting social workers as individual counsellors and case-workers to one as case managers, for:

> the *primary* task of the key worker will be fulfil the statutory responsibilities of his or her agency which will include the development of a multi-agency, multi-disciplinary plan for the protection of the child. The key worker's *secondary* responsibility is to act as leading worker for the inter-agency work in the case. (para. 5.20, my emphasis)

While short-term plans could be based on the assessment carried out during the investigation, '*longer term plans require a comprehensive social, medical and developmental assessment*' (para. 5.21, my emphasis) and for this the key worker was responsible. The assessment took on a crucial function for:

any action to provide for protection, treatment and other services for the child and family must be based on an assessment of the child's and family's needs, including an assessment of the levels of risk to the child. (para. 5.21)

Finally the case, together with the plan, should be reviewed at least every six months at either a case conference or via written reports to the key workers. The case should also be reviewed at any other significant points, for example when rehabilitation was being considered. A child's name should be removed from the register and hence no longer constitute a child protection case 'when the *professionals* who are working with the child and family *decide that the risk* to the child has been eliminated or reduced to an *acceptable level*' (para. 5.28, my emphasis). It was the professionals who were to decide what constituted an acceptable level of risk and, for this, assessment was crucial.

The register itself should be renamed the child protection register as it was concerned with the 'future protection of the child rather than past abuse' and was therefore to be made up of 'all the children in the area who have been abused or who are considered to be at risk of abuse and who therefore are currently the subject of an inter-agency plan to protect them'. In effect, the recognition of a child as abused or as at risk and the existence of a child protection plan were interdependent and, by definition, constitutive of each other. We were not told what would happen if a child was identified but no such plan existed!

Child abuse, for the purpose of registration, was categorised into: neglect, physical abuse, sexual abuse, emotional abuse and grave concern, where grave concern covered:

children whose situations do not currently fit the above categories, but where social and medical assessments indicate that they are at *significant risk* of abuse. These could include situations where another child in the household has been harmed or the household contains a known abuser. (para. 5.31, my emphasis)

While similar to the 1986 draft which also included sexual abuse, the final category of grave concern was more restrictive than in 1986 where it had been 'potential abuse' which referred to 'a high degree of risk that they might be abused in the future'. It was the first time, however, that official guidance had included such a catch-all category.

In effect, registers were the material outcome of the child protection surveillance net. The notion of a net was not simply analogous in this context because for families who move frequently 'there is a real danger that ... children can drop through the *safety net* and only reappear when serious harm has occurred' (para. 5.36, my emphasis). The custodian of the register, therefore, should have a specific responsibility to trace families who go missing and inform other areas when a family moves.

Case conferences were seen as an 'essential feature' of inter-agency co-operation as they:

> provide a forum for the exchange of information between professionals involved with the child and family and allow for inter-agency, multi-disciplinary discussion of allegations or suspicions of abuse; the outcome of investigations; assessments for planning; an action plan for protecting the child and helping the family; and reviews of the plan. (para. 5.39)

They should 'only be chaired by a senior staff member of the social services department or the NSPCC' (para. 5.44) who 'must be able to call upon the attendance of a lawyer from the local authority's legal section to assist in the evaluation of evidence indicative of care proceedings' (para. 5.39) under-lining again the essentially statutory nature of the exercise. At this point, however, a particular tension was evident, for while case conferences were defined as 'inter-professional meetings', as they had been since their formalisation in 1974, for the first time it was recommended that parents should have a role. This was a direct spin-off from the findings of the European Court of Human Rights and the Cleveland Report which were supportive of involving parents, and children, in decisions as far as possible – including case conferences.

While the 1986 draft guide was keen to encourage 'openness and honesty' and felt 'the ability of professional staff to confront parents with reality are an essential basis on which to build a foundation of understanding' (p. 18), this did not include parental participation at the case conference, for:

It may be helpful for the key worker and one or more members of the core group to meet as a group with parents from time to time in the course of work with the family. *Such meetings, however, should be clearly distinguished from formal interagency case conferences. It is not appropriate for parents to attend the latter which are professional meetings* focused on the details of interagency co-operation to protect the child and plan for the future. (DHSS 1986, p. 19, my emphasis)

By the 1988 guide:

Parents should be informed or consulted at every stage of investigation. Their views should be sought on the issues to be raised prior to a case conference to afford them the opportunity to seek advice and prepare their representations. *They should be invited, where practicable, to attend part, or, if appropriate the whole, of case conferences unless in the view of the Chairman of the conference their presence will preclude a full and proper consideration of the child's interests.* (DHSS 1988, para. 5.45, my emphasis)

While still an essentially inter-professional meeting, and it was professionals – particularly the chairperson, who had the power to decide what 'where practicable' and 'full and proper consideration of the child's interests' meant – it was a significant shift. It goes some way to explaining the emergence of 'strategy discussions' which were clearly of an exclusively inter-professional nature. Throughout, however, it was stressed, as in previous guidance, that the case conference was a 'consultative, advisory body' rather than one with executive powers. Each agency was responsible for its own decisions. Trying to maintain this 'balance' between agency independence and the multi-agency co-operation was a major focus of case conferences and the guide as a whole.

Sexual abuse was, for the first time, included in guidelines and was allocated a section in its own right. While sexual abuse was brought under the auspices of the child abuse system, it was recognised that there were certain factors associated with it which posed particular problems, particularly at the investigative stage. The discussion of these was much fuller than in 1986.

The shift in various *balances* resulting from Cleveland was evident at a number of points: (1) It pointed out that a 'high level of co-operation' between the agencies 'is essential during the investigation because of the likely nature of the *evidence. It is essential that no agency relies on any one criterion in isolation*' (para. 6.3, my emphasis). This final sentence was inserted following the 1986 draft. (2) It pointed out that 'sexual abuse does not necessarily call for an immediate emergency response or removal of a child from home' and had a quite new section on 'support for parents' which, among other things, said that the '"Code of Practice – Access to Children in Care" should be applied in every case'. (3) Whereas in 1986 'a child's statement that he or she is *being abused should be accepted as true* until proved otherwise', this had become in 1988 'a child's statement *about an allegation* of abuse, whether in confirmation or denial, should always be *taken seriously*' (para. 6.4, my emphasis). Not only was *abused* relegated to *allegation* but *accepted* was relegated to *taken seriously* and statements regarding denial as well as confirmation were included in the equation. (4) Similarly, while the 1986 guide simply said 'the child's welfare must be the overriding concern of professional staff who become involved', by 1988 this had been modified to:

in cases of child abuse, including child sexual abuse, social services departments will give *first* and *highest* priority to protecting the child. However, they *also* have responsibilities in relation to the child's parents and other family members or carers. (para. 6.7, my emphasis)

The guide argued that there was a particular need for highly skilled multi-disciplinary assessment 'where there is a suspicion of sexual abuse because of minor behavioural manifestations or inconclusive physical findings but where there has been no allegation or complaint of abuse by the child or a third party' (para. 6.11). However, there was only lukewarm support for the suggestion in the Cleveland Report to set up specialist assessment teams, for agencies are simply 'commended to consider carefully' such an option. Even so, assessment was the crucial element in attempting to address this sensitive area.

Finally, the prevention of sexual abuse consisted of encouraging '*earlier recognition* and referral of families under cases of suspected abuse' together with enabling children 'to protect themselves' (para. 6.16, my emphasis). While the latter had the greatest potential, the 'primary responsibility for this lies with parents' and to a lesser extent schools. Not only did this suggest a real tension – encouraging actual/ potentially abusing parents to help their children protect themselves – but both elements of prevention were essentially narrow and individualistic. There was no suggestion of any more wide-ranging preventive strategies.

The recommendations for developing and formalising joint agency policies and procedures in the guide built on the previous aproach but, reflecting tbe emphasis on *child protection*, re-designates Area Review Committees as Area Child Protection Committees. This conceptualisation of the work as child protection had clearly sharpened via the Cleveland Inquiry as the designation in the 1986 draft guide was as Joint Child Abuse Committees. To be fully effective, a joint forum needed to be accountable to the agencies which made up its membership who are 'jointly responsible' for its actions. ACPC members should be senior officers from the constituent agencies and they 'should have sufficient authority to allow them to speak on their agency's behalf and to make decisions to an agreed level without referral to the appointee's agency' (para. 7.5). While we can see a real effort to formalise the 'co-operation' between agencies and make the ACPC's authority and responsibilities clear in an attempt to overcome some of the failures evident in Cleveland, the recommendation stopped well short of the proposals in the Carlile Report.

The main emphasis was on formalising co-operation without mandating agencies, and underlined the centrality of the social services department. For the first time it was spelt out that 'the responsibility for the provision of the chairman and secretariat and support services for the committee should rest with the social services department'. The chairperson should be at least an Assistant Director of Social Services. However, it was not clear from where the social services department was to gain any extra power to carry out this responsibility if co-operation was not forthcoming. While 'each agency should accept that it is responsible for monitoring not only the performance of its own representative, but also that of the

ACPC' (para. 7.8), it was the social services' officers who should 'take the lead in monitoring implementation of the local procedures and the efficacy of arrangements' (para. 7.6). Thus, while the ACPC had the responsiblity for overseeing the net of the child abuse system, there was a potential for the net to come apart or go in different directions – the links were to be based on goodwill. It had no resources of its own, except that 'agencies should allocate funds to the ACPC in accordance with agreed arrangements at the beginning of each financial year so that the ACPC has an annual budget' (para. 7.11).

The ACPC had particular responsibilities for inter-agency procedural guidelines, inter-agency training and mechanisms for handling particular cases for which an inquiry was deemed necessary. Two interrelated new elements were recommended: ensuring that the constituent agencies produced quarterly management information on the level of child abuse work, type and trends and producing an annual review on its work and plans for the forthcoming year. We can see, therefore, another move to formally categorise and quantify an element of the social and professional world as child protection work such that its form, size and dimensions could be constituted.

The section on training recommended that 'agencies should establish joint annual training programmes on child abuse issues for all professional groups in direct contact with children' and that this should be made up of two types. First, all newly-appointed staff should be made aware of the 'signs of harm to children' and the local policies and procedures. Second:

> Specialist in-service training should be directed *primarily* to those involved in the *investigation* of abuse and *provision of protective services*. It should reflect the need for knowledge and skill within the context of *child care law, the concept of child protection and the assessment of danger, and alternative forms of intervention*. The central role of *social services* in child abuse work emphasises the need for this training for *social workers*. (para. 8.5, my emphasis)

Thus, the training of social workers involved in investigation work was prioritised and this should be made up of law, the concept of child protection and the assessment of danger, and alternative forms of intervention. We were given here a neat summary of the focal concerns and hence crucial elements of what child protection work consisted of.

Finally, the guidance included a recommendation that management in each agency should instigate a *case review* 'in all cases that involve the death of, or serious harm to a child where child abuse is confirmed or suspected'.

> The timely production of a well conducted case review report with clear conclusions, and where necessary positive recommendations for action should in mosc cases enable agencies to ensure that all necessary lessons are learned and *public concern satisfied.* (para. 9.1, my emphasis)

Clearly, a part of the management of child abuse included the management of public concern. Increasingly it seemed that the impact of public inquiries had been counter-productive and had had deleterious effects on both professional morale and public confidence. They demonstrated the essential problems and contradictions of the work and thereby the liberal state. Not only should such case reviews be concerned with fact-finding and staff interests, therefore, but public and media interests, for 'the importance of keeping the media and public informed should be recognised and there should be close co-operation between agencies on the release of statements' (para. 9.11). The ACPC should provide the focus for co-operation and co-ordination between agencies but also had a crucial public relations aspect to its work.

The Role of Health Professionals and the Status of Medical Diagnosis

July 1988 also saw for the first time the publication by central government of detailed guidance directed at the practices of those involved in the multi-agency response. The guidance for doctors on the diagnosis of sexual abuse (DHSS 1988b) was prepared by the Standing Medical Advisory Committee.

It stressed that medical aspects were only one element in the diagnosis which required close co-operation between agencies and professionals 'who are concerned with the over-all wellbeing of children' (p. 2). In effect, medical knowledge was secondary to social knowledge and both were subservient to the legal discourse.

> Doctors should be aware that the probability of finding definite clinical evidence is low, but absence of signs does not mean that CSA has not taken place. *It cannot be over-emphasised that legal proof does not necessarily depend on medical evidence.* Even in the absence of any clinical findings there may be other and adequate evidence of CSA. Medical assessment should be part of a multi-disciplinary process which includes a full family and social history. (paras. 5.4 and 5.5, my emphasis)

The statutory responsibility for the removal of a child lay with social services and should only take place when it was thought a child was in physical danger. The role of the doctor was circumscribed and their responsibilty to participate in the multi-agency system made clear:

> The main responsibilties of a doctor involved in a suspected case include seeking further advice and information and keeping an accurate record of what is known, or has been found. In particular, the doctor should contribute to case conferences, and attend court if requested. (para. 5.8)

The chapter on medical presentation of sexual abuse opened with a statement that the use of a Place of Safety Order was rarely necessary and outlined three levels of suspicion – serious, moderate and mild. *Serious* suspicion should be aroused when 'the child makes a clear, unambiguous, verbal allegation of abuse' (para. 8.4), while *mild* suspicion should be aroused in a variety of behavioural or emotional disturbances for which no other obvious cause is present. Certain family settings also gave rise to moderate or mild suspicion. An attempt was made to categorise for the purposes of assessing the existence of sexual abuse.

The guide also outlined, following the Cleveland Report, the form that interviews and the physical examination of children should take, including the way in which physical signs, particularly reflex anal dilatation, should be inter-preted.

While the role of the psychiatrist was important in some

cases in order to diagnose and treat emotional and behavioural disorders, there were inherent problems in such approaches for the purpose of establishing the existence of sexual abuse, for: 'Psychiatric techniques do not lend themselves easily to purely investigatory procedures, that is, to determine whether abuse has occurred' (para. 13.2). Similarly, the use of anatomically correct dolls and leading questions were 'controversial'. Such techniques 'should be used by people who are highly experienced and trained in communicating with children and would be able to justify their use and findings in court' (para. 13.4). Only one interview should be used and colleagues from other disciplines should be given the opportunity to observe via either a one-way screen or a videotape.

The net effect of the guide was to formalise the role of doctors in the diagnosis of sexual abuse and thereby subject its power and expertise to a variety of checks and balances in the context of the multi-disciplinary approach where the statutory role of social services departments meant social work and social knowledge was focal.

The guidance for senior nurses, health visitors and midwives (DHSS, 1988c) explicitly extended the net of child protection responsibilities to nurses in hospital accident and emergency and paediatric departments, health visitors, school nurses, district nurses, clinic nurses, practice nurses, midwives and others, but in the context of the multi-agency approach. Unlike doctors, the role of line management supervision was stressed, reflecting the quite different traditions of occupational control and clinical freedom.

Protecting Children: The Social Assessment

However, it was not sufficient to modernise and formalise the mechanisms for inter-agency working and the framework of the law alone. A major theme of recent reports had also been the crucial role of social assessment and that this had invariably been inadequate. On 24 November 1988, David Mellor, the Minister of State, launched *Protecting Children: A Guide for Social Workers Undertaking a Comprehensive Assessment* (DoH, 1988) as part of the overall package on child care emanating from central government which included *Working Together*, the Training Support Programme, the Children Bill and the various other circulars and guidances. The immediate history of *Protecting Children* came out of a Social Services Inspectorate Report (1986) (on the assessment and monitoring of cases of child abuse, subject to a court order but where children had been returned home), announced in April 1985 in response to the public attention focused on the case of Jasmine Beckford. The SSI report concluded that 'comprehensive assessments for the purpose of long-term planning were conspicuous by their absence in seven out of the nine authorities' inspected (p. 12). Not only would an improvement in assessments prove beneficial for the children concerned, but would increase the efficient allocation of scarce resources – particularly professional social work time – for:

> The Inspectorate estimates that it takes on average thirty-five hours to complete a comprehensive assessment. Initially some supervisors and workers were adamant that they did not have time to undertake assessments requiring this amount of time. However, during the inspection it became evident that workers often spend more than thirty-five hours gathering information about individual children and families, and in discussion and meetings with other disciplines. (p. 13)

The inspectors argued that:

> it was evident that as a result a considerable amount of social work effort and resources are being misdirected, but more seriously, children are returned home without a thorough assessment of the risks involved, and this may mean that they are inadequately protected. (p. 41)

One of the main recommendations was that the DHSS should set up a 'small group of social work practitioners skilled in child abuse work, including one or more with training expertise, to prepare a practice guide for social workers on assessment and long-term case management in child abuse work' (p. 50).

However, it took the furore related to Cleveland before the Minister announced, in July 1987, that such a group had been established. By then, the focus on assessment had been fuelled by other concerns. Not only did poor assessments waste resources and fail to protect children, they also failed to protect the rights of parents, particularly where sexual abuse was involved. The guide was not about assessment under-taken as part of an initial investigation but 'is about compre-hensive assessment for long-term planning in child protection cases'. As David Pithers has highlighted:

> The guide addresses the key issue of whether a family is considered safe for a child, or whether it can be made safe, or whether it is so potentially dangerous that alternatives have to be found. (Pithers, 1989, p. 18)

It was an attempt to ensure that the rationalisation of the inter-agency *procedures* was matched by attempts to develop the required *practice skills*. In doing so, however, it recognised that many of the tensions that pervaded at the level of the agency were just as evident at the level of practice:

> significant tensions and pressures remain within our society about when and how the state should intervene between parents and children. Such tensions and pressures place a particularly heavy burden on social workers, who by virtue of their statutory responsibilities have a central role in child abuse intervention. (DoH 1988, p. 3)

It accepted that child protection work could never be risk free and that there could be no guarantee of success, but it was argued that:

> a more systematic approach, based on a comprehensive assessment of the child and family should not only provide a better basis for decision-making but also allow for more effective evaluation of the models of intervention used. In addition, it should provide opportunities for more effective supervision and management of the social work task. (p. 3)

The guide provided a map via which practitioners could negotiate the tensions and pressures and thereby provided a picture of what constituted assessment for the purposes of child protection. In doing so, however, it recognised the dilemmas that arose from the *professionalised* nature of the task and the type of *knowledge* which should inform it. The guide was not designed to replace what practitioners 'know' but was presented as a framework for organising in a system-atic way. 'It should not, therefore, be used in isolation but as part of knowledge gained from the literature, training and the practitioner's own experience' (p. 5). Similarly, the guide attempted to find a middle course between being too prescriptive and too general and hoped practitioners would use it in different ways of depending on their own training, experience and style. It also drew attention to the importance of observing and noting the *processes* operating within families (and between families and practitioners) as well as the gathering of *information* about the child and the family for 'the recognition and understanding of roles and patterns of behaviour governing such interactions will often provide the key to understanding how and why a family as come to abuse or fail to protect a child' (p. 5). The guide was not offered as a universal prescription for 'all human beings and families are unique and intervention must be specifically tailored to their particular needs and circumstances' (p. 5).

In effect, the guide attempted to provide a framework for objectifying the subjective realities of children and families but mediated through the subjective realities of the social worker. It was an attempt to organise and classify for the crucial purpose of assessing and thereby making decisons. The tensions at the heart of this were demonstrated at the outset, for while *'defining what is unacceptable in parental behaviour presupposes a common understanding of what is normal in terms of parent-child interaction'* (p. 7, my emphasis), it was also recognised that *'judgement as to what constitutes abuse is therefore in part a matter of degree, opinion and values'* (p. 7, original emphasis). Knowledge of the causes of abuse and the best forms of intervention, particularly in relation to sexual abuse, was extremely limited and contested. Such problems were perhaps illustrated at their sharpest in the brief discussion on cultural sensitivity for 'a balanced assessment must incorporate a cultural perspective but guard against being over-sensitive to cultural issues at the expense of promoting the safety and wellbeing of the child'. Beyond this, however, little was offered as to the special knowledge that may be required for such work (see Channer and Parton 1990 for a further discussion).

It was important, therefore, to codify the basic principles that should underpin assessment work.

Children were defined as having basic needs for food,

warmth, shelter, health and education and that, while these were independent of those of their parents, it was parents who had the primary responsibility to assert and protect these. 'It is accepted that the basic needs of children in our society are best met within the family structure' (p. 9).

The state should only become involved when children and young persons 'come to the notice of the helping professions because of difficulties they or their families are experiencing'. The guide, reflecting the emphsis of the Cleveland Report and *Working Together*, stressed that while the child's interest should be given first consideration and children 'have a right to be consulted and their views taken into account', parents have a right to an open and honest approach and should have an opportunity to challenge information held on them and decisions taken. However, the ultimate responsibilities resided with social workers, so that the primary right for parents and children was procedural in terms of the assessment process rather than outcomes:

> they have a right to expect careful assessment of any problems prior to long term decisions being taken. Their views should be sought and taken into account, although engaging them in assessment and planning *does not mean a total sharing of the agency's responsibility for decision-making.* (p. 9, my emphasis)

The guide reiterated the importance of the multi-agency context and the nature of confidentiality in child protection work and listed the skills required.[2] It also specified the nature of authority in such work bearing in mind the potential for being overly soft, as in Beckford, and overly harsh, as in Cleveland.

> Child protection work inevitably involves the use of authority ... *the positive use of power and authority* can be a helpful tool in the therapeutic process as well as a means of protecting a child ... using authority and control does not necessarily involve initiating legal action to obtain control through a court order, but it does involve explaining to parents what the social worker's statutory duties and powers are and their relevance to the particular child's and family's situation ... authority should not however be exercised without responsibility or to excess. *An authoritarian and punitive approach will ultimately be destructive.* (p. 11, my emphasis)

Finally the guide, following the work of Peter Dale *et al.* (1986), hung its approach on the umbrella of 'Dangerousness', quoting a definition from Hamilton (1982) that dangerousness referred to the *potential* to cause physical and psychological harm to others. While discussions about dangerousness had been part of the language of the law and psychiatry for many years (see Foucault, 1978), in recent years its centrality for policy and practice had taken on a 'renaissance' (Bottoms, 1977; see Parton and Parton, 1989a 1989b). As we have seen, it was the Beckford Report which first introduced the notion into the official discussions about the best way of responding to child abuse.

There are three essential elements for understanding the meaning of 'dangerousness'. First, it is assumed that there are some individuals in the population who are prone to cause serious and lasting violence. As the guide argued:

> Although the number of such high-risk families who come to the attention of the statutory authorities as a result of child abuse is small, they are usually the families that feature in child abuse deaths and subsequent inquiry reports. (p. 12)

Second, while these individuals and families may come to official notice for relatively minor infractions, their propensity to violence, 'dangerousness', must become the central focus in any decisions about disposal – whether it is safe for the child to remain at home and under what circumstances. Third, it follows, therefore, that it is vital that we improve our predictions of dangerousness so that such individuals and families can either be changed or the children be placed elsewhere on a permanent basis. Assessments of actual and potential dangerousness therefore become central so that we can differentiate between those families that require authoritative intervention and monitoring and those that can, in effect, be left well alone.

Following Dale *et al.* (1986), the guide asserted that:

> Incidents of fatal or serious child abuse have to be understood in terms of the *total family dynamics*. Although the perpetrators in these cases are usually men, and often not the father of the child, the other partner has often been aware of the danger of the situation and significantly failed to protect the child from abuse. (p. 12, my emphasis)

It was the dangerous family, in the context of the extreme manifestation of family dysfunctions and the dangerous personalty – whether 'seriously immature', 'habitually aggressive' or 'over-inhibited' – which was causative of child abuse and which social workers needed to identify via their improved assessment skills. In order to do so, it was also important to avoid the ramifications arising from both professional and inter-agency dangerousness (see Forbes and Thomas, 1990; Frost and Parton, 1990 for further discussion).

The guide outlined the legal, agency and inter-agency contexts of intervention, together with the stages of intervention outlined in *Working Together*. However, the assessment had a strategic significance. It was the focal activity in allocating cases to their correct category and thereby co-ordinating the appropriate resources and expertise. It was not concerned with whether abuse had occurred or not, but 'to understand the child's and the family's situation more fully in order to provide a sound basis for decisions about future actions' (p. 21). The strengths and problems of a family and whether, in effect, it was viable for the child(ren) in question. A major element for judging such viability was how far the parent(s) accepted responsibility for what had happened, acknowledged problems and were ready and willing to co-operate. While there was a preference for working *with* parents, this took place within the statutory context, for:

> parental denial of responsibility for abuse or other causes for concern does not necessarily indicate that there is no basis for future work, although a total failure to find *any* shared acknowledgement of problems presents serious difficulties and the outcome in these situations will very much depend on the sufficiency of evidence to take legal action. (p. 23, original emphasis)

One hundred and sixty-seven questions, plus sub-questions were itemised as requiring consideration in a comprehensive assessment, and grouped into: the nature of the cause(s) for concern about the child; the child's physical and emotional development, health and personality; the composition of the family and its stage in the family life cycle; the financial resources and physical environment available to the family;

each parent's (or partner's) background, personality, attitudes; family interactions, including the couple's relationship with each other and the child(ren), with particular attention being paid to their ability to meet the child(ren)'s needs; the nature of the child's and family's networks of relatives, friends, and links with professional or other organisations.

The questions provided a basis for making *judgements* about viability in the context of potential change and potential resources available to bring about such change. For each group of questions, the social worker should consider: the main positive and negative features that had emerged; the main changes that were *necessary* (not simply desirable) to secure the future safety and wellbeing of the child; the judgement and the basis of this judgement, together with the resources needed about the likelihood for bringing about and sustaining such changes; the areas of disagreement between family members, between family members and professionals, and between professionals about these areas. In effect, the social worker was asked to make recommendations on the basis of 'the professional judgements about the relative weightings of the various constellations of factors' (p. 69). However, there was no set formula as 'one positive may be judged to outweight several negatives and vice versa' (p. 69).

> There can be no prescribed formula for balancing the pros and cons of each available option to be considered. This task is, and should remain, a matter for *skilled professional judgement*. Key decisions should be taken in consultation with supervisors, managers and others *in the multi-disciplinary network* and *after consultation with the child and the family*. (p. 75, my emphasis)

Thus, while the social workers were subjected to a variety of views and checks and balances from their own and other agencies and family members, they had the ultimate responsibility for carrying out the assessment and coming to conclusions as to the best options available. Three such options were outlined: the child remaining at home; short-term separation leading to rehabilitation; and permanent separation from parents. Whichever option was pursued, this should be on the basis of a realistic and achievable plan which avoided 'a never-ending high-dependency relationship with families' (p. 77).

The guide outlined techniques to help construct the assessment, including genograms, ecomaps and flow charts, together with summaries of likely relevant theoretical knowledge on the developmental progress of infants and young children and family lifestyle, together with essential reading. The primary focus was to help social workers decide on what constituted good-enough parenting in the context of the multi-agency response to child abuse. Knowledge about human development and skills derived from the modern systems approach to family work were seen as crucial in constructing an 'objective evaluation'. Ultimately, however, the mandate and legitimacy for such work was provided by the statutory context and the gaze of the court – something which social workers should be conscious of and explicit with family members, for in some cases: 'in the final analysis, the matter will be decided by the courts and parents and children must be made fully aware of their legal rights' (p. 70).

Conclusions

If the tensions and problems identified in the inquiry reports were to be addressed, it was clearly not sufficient to see the solutions in terms of the law alone. All the reports pointed to issues related to the functioning of the multi-agency approach and the activities of the different agencies and professions themselves. While we can see the range of different guidance published in 1988 as in some ways building on the framework established previously, in other ways they were quite different. First, they were much fuller and more detailed and more prescriptive about the roles and responsibilities of the different agencies. Second, for the first time, they were centrally concerned with sexual abuse. Third, they were much more concerned with trying to construct a balance in everyday practice between protecting children and protecting the rights of parents. No longer was the focus simply raising awareness of and responses to child abuse. They were now concerned with rationalising and modernising the responses of various agencies to each other *and*, intimately, the nature of such responses to different family members. Fourth, the role of social services departments and social workers was prioritised in a much clearer way than previously. Not only did social workers have the statutory mandate, but it was social knowledge which was crucial in constituting the nature of child abuse and the form that intervention should take. The social assessment was focal for identifying the high-risk cases and thereby protecting children and the rights of parents. At the end of the day, such assessments depended on professional judgements.

While such judgements and interventions took place under the auspices of the law, it was important for the more traditional agencies of law and order to modify their responses to take account of the particular issues at play – particularly with sexual abuse. An increasing emphasis was placed on social workers and the police working together via joint investigations, joint interviews, sharing information and providing specialist facilities (Home Office Circular, 1988). While the social agencies needed to be aware of the statutory context of their work, the agencies of the law, the police and the courts, needed to be aware of the problems with more traditional forms of investigation and evidence. While the police and social services became the primary agencies, particularly at the point of investigation, the health experts took on a much more secondary role and level of responsibility. If child abuse had previously been constituted as a disease, and thus a socio-health problem, the focus now was child protection, which was constituted as a socio-legal issue.

6

The Children Act 1989: Reconstructing the Consensus

When the Lord Chancellor introduced the Children Bill into the Lords at its second reading on 6 December 1988 he said:

> The Bill, in my view, represents the most comprehensive and far reaching reform of child care law which has come before Parliament in living memory. It brings together the public and private law concerning the care, protection and upbringing of children and the provision of services to them and their families. (*Hansard*, HoL, 6 December 1988, 2nd Reading, Col. 488)

It was an attempt to modernise and rationalise the law in the light not only of the Short Report, the Review of Child Care Law, the various child abuse inquiries, particularly that into the events in Cleveland for which the Minister of State had previously said the Government had delayed finalising the Bill, but also the Law Commission's report on guardianship and custody (1988). Hoggett (1989) said it was remarkable because: first, it brought together for the first time almost all the law relating to court procedures and social services for children and their families; and second, all the statutory remedies available to determine the upbringing of children were available in all courts and all proceedings. Such a rationalisation was important in order to make the law more readily understood to all those who operated it or may come under its auspices.

Clearly, however, this was more than a technical exercise,

for it was also crucially concerned with attempting to make both the content and the operation of the law seem fairer for all concerned. More particularly, it was concerned with constructing a new consensus, or what was often referred to as a new set of balances related to the respective roles and responsibilities of the state and the family in the upbringing of children. Defining this balance or constructing this consensus, particularly in the area of child protection, lay at the heart of the Bill.

The purpose of this chapter is to analyse how these balances were struck, the form that this new legislative framework was to take and to show how this related to the previous rcommendations for change that I have looked at in previous chapters. What were the essential problems and solutions? How did these differ from previous statements? And how did these problems and solutions shift in the process of the Bill becoming law? I will focus on the White Paper *The Law on Child Care and Family Services* (DHSS 1987), which was the forerunner of the Bill, only when it is apparent that the Bill had moved significantly away from it. Similarly, my central concern throughout will be on how the legislation attempted to reconstruct the boundary between state and family in the *area of public child care* and the way the relationship between different elements of the state child care apparatus was itself reconstructed.

The awareness of this need to create a new consensus in this sensitive area was apparent throughout the passage of the Bill. While there were wide political differences in the way state welfare provision should be framed in this area, together with numerous explanations of the recent malaise, the way this legislation was debated was far more amicable than with other legislation. There was a willingness on all sides to negotiate, wherever possible, cross-party support. For example, Mr Tom Clarke, the main front-bench Labour Party spokesperson in his opening speech in the Commons, having listed the main areas where the Labour party was critical, reduced such criticisms to mere context. For he concluded: 'the Bill is nevertheless a good Bill. The balance, in our view, is about right between parental responsibilities and children's rights' (*Hansard*, HoC, 27 April, 2nd Reading, Col. 1124).

Similarly, in the Commons the House only divided on nine occasions – five in committee and four during the third reading. While the Bill was subjected to detailed, and often wide-ranging criticism and debate, no one wanted to be seen as being unnecessarily obstructive. For the Conservative Government, in a period when the economy was proving difficult to control with increasing inflation and interest rates and highly-contested social policy change in the areas of education, health and local government, this was one of the few opportunities to pass legislation which was likely to receive wide political, professional and public support. In the words of Dame Jill Knight: 'It is nice, just for once, to discuss a Bill where surely sweetness, calm and light can obtain. Surely we must be at one in our desire to improve the lot of unfortunate children' (*Hansard*, HoC, 2nd Reading, 27 April 1989, Col. 1124). Such sentiments, however, were not only felt by Conservatives, for everyone was keen to demonstrate they were caring and concerned adults who could come together in the interests of children and the family.

While important political differences did emerge as to the best way to help and support the family, no-one disputed that the family was the building block of society and was by far the best place to bring up children, though there were rare occasions where children did suffer and where the parents were incapable. Again, differences emerged as to how this could be explained and the best way of solving such problems in the longer term. However, there was no major dispute that coercive state interventions to protect children should be kept to a minimum. All realised the framework and basis for such interventions needed careful thought and that, in the light of recent experiences, required the full support of as many as possible. As Keith Vaz (Labour) said: 'We all start with the presumption that the best place for a child is with his or her family and that the state should intervene only if that relationship goes wrong' (*Hansard*, HoC, Standing Com. B., 25 May, Col. 284), while Tim Devlin (Conservative) expressed it as follows:

> Family life is the foundation stone of society and we tinker with it at our peril. In exceptional cases, children are battered, beaten and sexually

abused by their parents, and an outsider should be empowered to intervene. But the powers given to an outside agency operating on behalf of the state must be drafted carefully in order that gratuitous and free-ranging interference by an over-powerful agency cannot take place. (*Hansard*, HoC, Standing Com. B., 25 May 1989)

The spectre of child abuse inquiries, and Cleveland in particular, never seemed far away. While many said that the Bill was much wider than simply concerned with avoiding such situations in the future and owed much to the work of the Short Report and the subsequent Review of Child Care Law, as clearly it did, there can be little doubt that for most MPs and Peers the child abuse inquiries were the primary backcloth for the debates. As a consequence, the need to reconstruct a consensus in the area of child protection was the priority – particularly for David Mellor, the Minister of State, who was guiding the legislation through the Commons. As we will see, the Government shifted its position quite considerably over the issues of emergency protection and child assessment orders. It was not prepared to shift its position in other areas, however. The further one moved away from child protection issues in the Bill, the more dissension was evident to the Government's proposals but the less did the Government seem willing to negotiate and compromise. Similarly, the further one moved away from ostensibly child protection issues, the less priority and significance to current concerns an issue seemed to have for the Government. As a consequence, it was not unusual for issues to be presented in terms of child protection in order that, at a minimum, they should be taken seriously. For example, the debates on day care and child minders had as a central theme how far such services were of use in preventing and monitoring possible child abuse, rather than simply being a positive contribution in their own right to parents, particularly women, caring for children in difficult circumstances.

Cleveland was present throughout in the guise of Stuart Bell and Tim Devlin, the MPs at the centre of the affair. Both were on the Commons Standing Committee and Stuart Bell made a point of sitting in front of the press bench throughout the Commons proceedings. Not only did they invariably make reference to Cleveland in their contributions but Stuart Bell,

likened by a Conservative MP, Richard Holt, to Barnardo
and Shaftesbury (*Hansard*, HoC, 27 April, Col. 1149), clearly
saw the Children Bill as a direct consequence of his interventions in Cleveland. As we will see, the final legislation was
different in many ways from the recommendations of the
Cleveland Report. What is important is that Cleveland and
the other child abuse inquiries, including that into the death
of Doreen Mason, which was awaited during the early stages
of the Bill (Area Review Committee for Lambeth, Southwark
and Lewisham 1989), provided the central concerns and
thereby constructed the agenda whereby the legislation was
debated.

Certainly for the press the Bill was concerned with meeting
the problems thrown up in Cleveland. For example, *The Times*
headline announcing the publication of the Bill read, 'Proposed new law on children sets up unified code to prevent
abuse in wake of Cleveland' (see *The Times*, 25 November
1988). For the press the Bill was framed as dealing with abuse
– but not of children so much as parental rights. *The
Independent* announced the Bill's publication with 'Parents
will get right to contest child care law' (see *Independent*, 25
November 1988). However, from then on, the most notable
fact about press coverage of the Bill was that it was virtually
non-existent. Apart from the split that later emerged about
emergency protection orders and child assessment orders, and
then only in the serious papers, the Bill received no coverage
except in some of the parliamentary reports. It was as if the
issues became too complex for the press to handle. This was
true of other areas of the media as well.

It was not surprising, therefore, that it was child protection
that David Mellor underlined when introducing the Bill to the
Commons at Second Reading, as I pointed out at the outset in
Chapter 1:

> As I hope I made clear, we have high ambitions for this Bill. We hope
> and believe that it will bring order, integration, relevance and a better
> balance to the law – a better balance not just between the rights and
> responsibilities of individuals and agencies, but most vitally, between the
> need to protect children and the need to enable parents to challenge
> intervention in the upbringing of their children. Recent well-publicised
> cases, including the tragic case of Kimberley Carlile, Doreen Mason and

the events in Cleveland in 1987, have graphically shown the consequences of getting that *balance* wrong. Of course, of itself, legislation
cannot stop such tragedies, but we hope *a clear legal framework will help
to make more likely clear-eyed judgements by key people involved in child
welfare*, whether they are in Social Services Departments, Health
Authorities, the police, education or the courts. (*Hansard*, HoC, 2nd
Reading, 27 April, Col. 1107–1108, my emphasis)

It was the construction of such a balance and thereby a new
consensus in the area of child protection that was the priority
and to which everyone needed to demonstrate their prime
commitment. The influence of the Short Report and the
Review of Child Care Law were very evident but they need to
be understood essentially in terms of a framework which took
as its starting point getting the balance in child protection
right.

Underlying Principles and Structure of the Bill

Public child care law, since its inception with the Prevention
of Cruelty to Children Act of 1889, has been made up of two
elements. First, the responsibility which Parliament gives the
executive, essentially the local authority, and thereby its social
workers, to intervene in private family life in order to protect
and help children; and second, the court processes for adjudication in respect of such intervention. Recent events had
apparently demonstrated that the former element, the activities of social workers, had ben given too much discretionary
power and their interventions were unsufficiently accountable
to and adjudicated by the latter – the courts. A major purpose
of the legislation was to modify this relationship so that social
workers became more accountable and courts the explicit
focus for adjudication where parental powers and responsibilities may be transferred.

Certain guiding principles informed the Bill throughout
and these closely followed the White Paper. (1) The upbringing of children was primarily a *parental responsibility*, but in
cases of *need* the state should be ready to help, especially
where doing so would lessen the risk of family breakdown. (2)
Such *services* to *families in need* should be arranged in volun-

tary partnership with parents and in a way that promoted family relationships as fully as possible, including where the child had to be *looked after* away from home, maintaining close contact with their family and reuniting them as soon as possible wherever appropriate. (3) Parents' legal powers and responsibilities for a child should only be transferred to a local authority *via a full court hearing* following due legal processes and the court should be satisfied that there was evidence of *significant harm* or the *likelihood* of such harm and that it was in the interests of the child. (4) In such proceedings, while the interests of the child were to be the primary concern, parents should be properly represented and, therefore, full parties to the proceedings in addition to the child. (5) *Emergency powers* to remove a child should be of *short duration* and subject to court review by the parent or child if *challenged*. (6) The legal responsibilities of local authorities caring for a child away from home, together with the powers and responsibilities of the parents in such circumstances, should be clear.

From the outset, the Government stressed that the Bill should be read as a whole, as the underlying principles and the essential structure of the legislation had an inherent logic and balance which could be seriously disturbed if any part was taken in isolation. In this respect, a crucial element of this logic and balance centred around the proposals for the new emergency protection order which was to replace the discredited Place of Safety Order. As David Mellor said at the outset:

> A vital part of striking the right balance is the introduction of a new emergency protection order to replace the present Place of Safety Order. This will give those with parental responsibility a right to challenge the order and power for the court to give directions on access and medical examinations. (*Hansard*, HoC, 2nd Reading, 27 april 1989, Col. 1108)

Part One of the Bill restated the keynote proposition of the existing law that the child's welfare should be the paramount consideration when the courts reach decisions about a child's upbringing. That principle was to govern not only the making of orders in private cases, such as divorce, but also the court's decision on whether to place a child in local authority care or under its supervision. In order to ensure that such a broad principle was not applied inconsistently, a checklist[1] was provided to guide the court. Similarly, because there was a danger that a child may be put into care because of inadequate home circumstances, but without evidence that the order would improve the situation, the court was always to be convinced that making the order would be better than making no order at all. Part One also underlined the notion of parental responsibility which drew attention to the view that the overwhelming purpose of parenthood was the responsibility for caring for and raising the child to be a properly developed adult both physically and morally.

Part Two introduced four new orders which underlined the notion of parties continuing to have parental responsibility. A 'residence order' focused on settling the arrangements about the person with whom the child was to live; 'contact orders' would allow the child to visit or have contact with a named person; a 'specific issue order' aimed to settle disputes about a particular matter, for example about where a child should go to school or whether they should have a serious operation; while a 'prohibited steps order' would prohibit any particular step being taken in respect of a child without the court's permission.

Part Three set out the principle responsibilities of local authorities to children in their area who were in need and their families, and to the children who they looked after. It brought together the main local authority responsibilities to families with children, including those previously set out separately for disabled children. The aim was to focus attention on the role of the local authority in supporting the family. Local authorities would have a new duty to promote the upbringing of *children in need* by their families so far as this was consistent with their welfare duty to the child. Further requirements designed to help children in need to continue to live with their families and generally to prevent the breakdown of families were itemised in Schedule 2. *Partnership with parents* based on *agreement* so far as possible was to be the guiding principle.

Such an approach also applied where children were provided with *accommodation* under voluntary arrangements because, for example, the parents were unable to care themselves. Provision of accommodation was to be seen as a *service* to the family without stigma. The Bill attempted to make clear the rights of the parents and the responsibilities of the local authority when this particular service was provided. Parents would no longer have to give notice before removing their children from voluntary arrangements and authorities would not be able to assume parental rights over children via an administrative resolution. The authority would have to promote contact between the child and family, consult both child and family on decisions and establish a procedure with an independent element for considering complaints.

While the family was constructed as an essentially private institution and the primary institution for rearing children, parents were seen as having responsibilities towards their children rather than holding, in effect, parental property rights as in the past. The role of parents was in far more active terms, and terms consistent with the Government emphasis on individuals and families taking responsibility for both their own behaviour and the quality of life of their dependents. While the state was seen to have an important role to play, this was to ensure that parents fulfilled such responsibilities. The role of the state was confirmed as residual and supportive rather than primary. However, it should work in partnership with parents on behalf of children in need. Such an approach clearly reflected the general approach of the Short Report, the Review of Child Care Law and the various research which informed it, but modified in certain ways.

In effect, voluntary care was to be replaced by accommodation in which children would be *looked after* by the local authority on behalf of their parents. The Government was determined not simply to get rid of parental rights resolutions but also to remove any ambiguity between the compulsory, perhaps coercive, aspects of the care system and the supportive voluntary services. Voluntary care was seen as stigmatising and as a last resort by both families and the social workers that used it. So that it could be seen as, and used as, a service by parents, in the way that many respite care services for handicapped children had developed in previous years, it was important that it be removed from the care system altogether.

If the local authority wanted to impose any controls over such situations, these would have to be taken to court in the same way as any other care proceedings.

Part Four was seen as constituting a major feature of the Bill, as it set out the new grounds on which the court would have to be satisfied before making a care or supervision order. The grounds were to be rationalised to (1) evidence of *significant harm* or the *likelihood* of such harm *in the future* and (2) that the harm was attributable to the care given to the child falling short of what a 'reasonable' parent would provide. In introducing the ground of *significant harm* as opposed to simply *harm*, as in the White Paper, the Bill was attempting to signify the gravity of harm deemed necessary to warrant state intervention.

Even when the grounds were proved, it needed to be demonstrated that it was in the child's interest so that the court was to be convinced that making an order was better for the child than making no order at all. We can see here an attempt to construct a new balance for legitimating state intervention. For while on the one hand, by including a fear for the future, there was a broadening of potential cases, by also saying these cases should show *significant* harm and that such intervention should be in the child's interests, there was an attempt to restrict such interventions to the exceptional. Whenever such cases were subject to state intervention, explicit due process should prevail thus making the accountability of local authority social workers explicit and giving the parents every opportunity to put their case and defend themselves.

Part Five was taken up with the reforms in relation to emergency protection. There was to be a new Emergency Protection Order limited to a maximum of eight days and extendable only once by up to seven days. As promised, and unlike the White Paper, there was to be a new opportunity for parents to apply to the court for the order to be discharged after seventy-two hours if they were not present at the initial hearing. According to the Lord Chancellor when introducing the proposals in the Lords:

> Here we seek to strike a balance between the need to protect children from harm in emergencies and the need to allow aggrieved parents to

challenge action taken in respect of their children – the need for which was graphically illustrated by what happened in Cleveland. (*Hansard*, HoL, 6 December 1988, Col. 492)

The holder of the Emergency Protection Order would be under a duty to take such action as was necessary, which included leaving the child where s/he was if thought safe, and a duty to return him/her if continued removal was to prove unnecessary. In addition, the court was to have powers to give directions on contact and medical examinations at any time an emergency protection order or interim care order was in force. These duties for the holder of the order and additional powers to the court to give direction were all added to the recommendations of the White Paper and reflected the added concerns arising from Cleveland. It would be granted on the grounds that the *Justices* and *not the applicants* were satisfied that 'there is reasonable cause to believe that the child is likely to suffer significant harm'. The applicant would be responsible for the child during the period of the order and, if the local authority was not the applicant, it would have to be informed and satisfy itself as to the child's welfare and apply for a transfer.

Part Five also allowed an emergency order to be enforced by a constable acting under a warrant, as previously, and would allow the holder of the order to locate other children on the premises who were thought to be at risk. Such police powers to take a child into police protection were to be limited to seventy-two hours and aligned with the other emergency protection powers as proposed in the White Paper.

Finally, in Part Five, as recommended in the Beckford Report, local authorities and other agencies would be required to co-operate in support of a more active investigative responsibility placed on social services departments.

The Government did not seek in the Bill to reform wardship as such, though it intended that the reforms both in private and public law would substantially reduce the need to invoke it. The conditions in the Bill which must be satisfied before the state could intervene in families (by seeking emergency protection, care or supervision orders) were designed as the minimum circumstances which could justify such action.

Accordingly, the Bill prevented the High Court's inherent jurisdiction, which would not be limited by such conditions, being used to confer compulsory powers on local authorities. It was recognised that, in practice, the High Court would not be likely to exercise its power in circumstances where a care order would not be justified under the Bill. As the Lord Chancellor argued:

> as a matter of principle it is important for the law in a free society expressly to protect the integrity and independence of families, save where there is at least likelihood of significant harm to the child from within the family. (*Hansard*, HoL, 2nd Reading, 6 December, Col. 493)

Parts Six and Seven were designed to replace, with amendments, the provisions of the Child Care Act 1980 on local authority community homes, the regulation of voluntary homes and the responsibilities to children accommodated in those homes. Parts Eight and Nine re-enacted, also with amendments, similar provisions for private children's homes in the Children's Homes Act 1982, which had never been implemented and those governing private arrangements for fostering children. The Government also announced its intention to revise, by amendment, the Nurseries and Child Minders' Regulation Act 1948, to regulate day-care facilities provided privately for children under five years of age. The Secretary of State's inspection and other supervisory functions and responsibilities were set out in Part Ten.

Part Eleven, which was concerned with a variety of outstanding miscellaneous and general matters, provided for the redesign of court arrangements and the procedures for child care cases. However, it stopped short of introducing a family court. From the outset, the Government argued it was first necessary to get the substantive law right before fundamentally restructuring the court structure and practices. In introducing concurrent jurisdictions, however, proceedings under the Bill could be allocated to different courts according to certain criteria including the level of difficulty of each case and the need to avoid delay. Under the Bill, most care cases would go in the first instance to the Magistrates' domestic court referred to in the Commons committee by the Solicitor-General as 'family proceedings courts'. When introducing the Bill in the Lords, the Lord Chancellor argued that the changes would create a flexible system under which cases could both be heard at the appropriate level in the court and enable all proceedings affecting a child to be heard in the same court and at the same time by magistrates and judges who were experienced and specialised in family work. It was anticipated that these powers would be exercised initially in relation to local authority care cases and adoption but would eventually cover all child care cases included in the Bill if that seemed appropriate. Such changes were presented as the beginning of a rolling programme towards the establishment of a family court (see Smith and Riches 1989, and Smith 1988).

While the Government did not proceed with the Cleveland Report recommendation to establish an Office of Child Protection following the lukewarm reception to the proposals from the Lord Chancellor's Office on the subject in 1988, the Bill considerably increased the role and responsibilities of guardians *ad litem*. This reflected the shift in the balance of power in the Bill from the local authority to the court. The guardian *ad litem* was constructed as the independent representative of the child's wishes and interests and their views and information were seen as crucial in helping the court come to its decisions. Not only would the range of cases to which guardians could be appointed increase, but the requirements to appoint would be strengthened. No longer would it be necessary to establish a possible conflict of interest between parent and child before a guardian could be appointed. Instead, the court should appoint one 'unless satisfied that it is not necessary to do so'. They were to be appointed in all but exceptional circumstances (see Munro 1989 and Smith 1989).

The Government was clearly pleased with the package it had produced in the Bill and was confident it would receive the wide support that was seen as so crucial. The Lord Chancellor made his hopes quite clear:

> I hope that the Bill will be seen on all sides of the House as a landmark in Children's legislation. It deals with important and difficult issues which require great care and sensitivity. The Bill will, in particular, establish a framework of rights and responsibilities with which to see that children in

need receive the care, upbringing and protection they require, and that parents and others with an interest in the child can play a full part in those crucially important decisions. I accordingly commend the Bill to the House. (*Hansard*, HoL, 2nd Reading, 6 December 1988, Col. 496)

In doing so, an attempt had been made to clearly demarcate the powers available to local authority social workers and the courts. While the courts were to be primarily responsible for adjudicating and deciding matters where the transfer of parental powers and interference in the family was at stake, it was the local authority which was to have prime responsibility for decisions once a child was in its care. In the process, the accountability of local authority social workers would be increased to courts on the one hand and families, primarily parents, on the other (Robertson 1989).

Alternative Interpretations: The Personal and the Political

While there was wide agreement that it was crucial to develop a new legal framework, it would be incorrect to say that this did not have to be carefully negotiated and in certain important respects modified in the process of the Bill becoming law. Not only were there different interpretations of the underlying causes of the recent malaise and the best ways of resolving it, but also a range of different pressure groups and professional bodies put forward their own views and amendments related to their particular priorities and interests. Thus, while there was general support for the overall tone and structure of the Bill, there were also numerous disagreements concerning certain of its details and, in some quarters, the way it related to other elements of the Government's social programme. Many argued that the Bill could not be seen in isolation so that its impact was crucially dependent on other much more significant changes in economic and social policy and society more generally.

What was evident in the debates in both Houses, but particularly in the House of Commons, was that while many contributions reflected a particular political perspective on the most appropriate relationship between state and family, they could not easily be reduced to party politics alone. There were other factors. First, those who brought forward amendments often did so because of a sympathy for, or formal links with, an outside organisation. The NSPCC, for example, had a noted Member in both Houses who spoke on its behalf and supported amendments drafted by the Society. Second, others were concerned because of a particular interest related to previous experiences or professional involvement. The legal profession was particularly well represented in this respect, as many either were or had been practising lawyers or barristers. Far fewer MPs had also been practising social workers. In reality just two former social workers, both on the Labour benches, Hilary Armstrong and David Hinchliffe, were actively involved throughout. The validity and utility of the changes, therefore, was often debated on the basis of previous professional situations or cases known personally to the contributors. Finally, individuals' often very personal experiences also played a part, and these reflected a whole range of social, familial and age-related factors. This was perhaps at its most explicit in the attempts to increase the influence of grandparents over court decision-making when the child's future was at stake. Many MPs were categorical that their interest arose primarily because they were grandparents, thus reflecting the age makeup of the House of Commons.

The issues at hand were thus sensitive to a range of perspectives and interests which Peers and MPs brought to bear covering the political, the professional and the intimately personal. As a consequence, the contributions were not necessarily consistent and the potential for conflicts deriving from these different elements was never very far away. This can be illustrated from an example in the Lords. The Conservative Peer, Lord Mittistone, made it known early on that he was speaking on behalf of the NSPCC and that he received most of his briefings from that quarter. This did not stop his personal views and experiences coming to the fore on occasions however. Speaking during the Lords' Committee he opposed an amendment which would have prevented anyone becoming a foster parent unless they had signed an undertaking not to subject the child to corporal punishment. For

> When I was brought up in the 1930s there was not the same complaints about bad behaviour as there are today. It may be that there is more publicity today. I was last *beaten* at the age of 19 as a midshipman for misbehaving. It did not create in me a feeling of antagonism and make me want to behave badly. I think that I have been reasonably well controlled, except perhaps in this Chamber. It seems to me that one can become obsessed with the thought that corporal punishment – *beating* – of a child by a parent is wicked. (*Hansard*, HoL, 7 February 1989, Col. 1446. My emphasis)

However, the issues could not be divorced completely from explicit political analyses. These were most in evidence in the earlier stages of debate in the Second Reading of the House of Commons. Invariably these were presented in terms of the way child abuse, in its various forms, could be explained and what would constitute the most appropriate medium and longer term solutions.

Dame Jill Knight expressed a not uncommon perspective on the Conservative benches when she argued that child abuse arose primarily from the failure to recognise 'the crucial importance to society of stable family life' and the consequences of the 'pressure for permissiveness' heralded by Roy Jenkins in the 1960s and the ease with which parents could now get divorced. She therefore welcomed both the emphasis on keeping families together and the fact that it would no longer 'be possible for children to be torn from the family home and kept away for weeks as happened under the truly disgraceful regime of Dr Marietta Higgs' (*Hansard*, HoC, 27 April, 2nd Reading, Col. 1124–25). Similar sentiments were expressed by Teresa Gorman who was particularly concerned that 'the Bill tends to perpetuate the ideas that powers given to professional workers to protect children are necessarily a good thing'. She did not think so and wanted to see a greater emphasis placed on what she called 'the natural neighbourhood network of protection for children' in the guise of the teacher, neighbours and the police rather than the 'so-called professionals'. Most particularly, however, she wanted to see much greater attention given 'to children as independent citizens with the right to speak up in their own defence' – an issue she argued for throughout the passage of the Bill (ibid., Col. 1173). Such perspectives were generally in tune with recent Conservative philosophy which wished to free the market and the family, reduce but strengthen the state and which was very suspicious of the expansion of modern welfare professionals in the postwar period, of whom social workers were perhaps the most evident example. Rather than strengthen the family, they only acted to undermine its internal and natural morality, responsibility and authority. Such views were subsequently expressed in their most explicit and articulate form in a pamphlet, in which Teresa Gorman played a part, published by the Centre for Policy Studies – a body which has been seen as reflecting ideas held dear by Margaret Thatcher (Gledhill, 1989; see also Jervis, 1990).

Such views held important similarities with some expressed on the Labour benches where Stuart Bell was a significant participant throughout. Initially, we can interpret his interventions as essentially continuing the priorities and concerns he expressed throughout the Cleveland affair. For him, as we have seen, the Bill constituted the natural conclusion of those interventions. He was keen to defend the traditional authority and responsibility of parents and, perhaps more accurately, those of fathers (see Bell 1988 and Frost 1990 for a critique). In the process, however, he was more concerned to clarify the roles of social workers rather than sideline them altogether.

> Family life has come under a fundamental and serious attack over the years. For a variety of sociological reasons, as well as others, we have seen a steady erosion of the family base. The Bill should seek to restore the balance in the family and should also clearly state the role of the local authority. We need training for social workers. They find themselves in sensitive and difficult situations. We need to share the burden among those who are involved in child care work. It should not be right for one individual to take full responsibility for a particular incident. (ibid., Col. 1138)

However, he also seemed to share, along with David Mellor and the Lord Chancellor, the belief that it was changes in the law which would prove crucial in overcoming the recent problems. David Mellor and Stuart Bell were both barristers and it was this belief in the law which was to prove crucial for their respective support for the changes in the emergency protection provisions at the report stage. Throughout the whole period Stuart Bell seemed committed to a mission and saw himself as behaving as a great statesman who on occasions had to go out on a limb to show others the light and to stay true to his own conscience.

> I am reminded of the words of Winston Churchill in the 1930s, who said that the only shield of a Member of Parliament is his conscience. I refer, too, to the words of John Fitzgerald Kennedy, who said that a man must do what he must in spite of all opposition, and that was the basis of all human morality. (ibid., Col. 1138)

What he had in common with many, including Jill Knight and Teresa Gorman, was a belief that the Cleveland parents were 'innocent' and while some children did suffer abuse, it was a very small minority and needed keeping in proportion so that other children did not suffer as a result of unwarrantable state interventions. Many believed that child abuse occurred in a small number of situations and was caused by exceptional circumstances. While Richard Holt (Conservative) saw this as because of 'human nature' (ibid., Col. 1149), Rosie Barnes (SDP) argued that 'we are beginning to recognise that there is an unfortunate group of people in society who gravitate towards children for the wrong reasons' (ibid., Col. 1156).

On the Labour benches, however, there was a much greater willingness to argue that not only was the problem of child abuse perhaps larger than such explanations would suggest, but that a crucial factor in its genesis was related to social deprivation and what were seen as the socially divisive Government policies of recent years.

Max Madden reminded the House that the debate was taking place against the background of child benefit having been frozen and other cuts in welfare expenditure and that over two million children were living at, or near, the poverty level.

> The Government's response is to threaten to punish still further the parents of those children rather than dealing with the cause of the problem which, as has been said so often today, is the problem of

poverty, deprivation and disadvantage. It is all very well to build a framework which we hope will protect children more effectively than has been the case in the past, but the Bill will be no more than words on paper unless we ensure that Britain's children and families receive a fair share of the wealth that they have been creating over the years. (*Hansard*, HoC, 2nd Reading, 27 April 1989, Col. 1175–6)

Hilary Armstrong went further, for not only did she argue that the living standards for the poorest had dropped in the previous ten years but that, drawing on a study by Becker and MacPherson (1988), there was both quantitative and qualitative evidence to suggest there was a causal link between poverty and abuse, particularly neglect. Many Labour MPs argued that unless the Bill made attempts to reduce the inequalities arising from social class, its impact on abuse and deprivation would be minimal. It was similarly argued that because it was women who carried the main responsibility for children, it was women who suffered the most stress and hardship. Improving the lot of women would improve the lot of children. This was a major factor behind Hilary Armstrong's attempts to broaden the local authorities' statutory responsibilities for day care. However, this was a difficult issue for those on the left, for while there was a recognition that those in care were, following the Short Report, almost exclusively from the poor and that prevention should be on a wide-ranging basis, there was also a reluctance to suggest that there was a direct link between abuse and poverty as this might suggest that child abuse was exclusively a problem amongst the poor.

This problem perhaps arose because a feminist perspective emphasising the significance of gender inequalities, male power and masculinity in relation to the family and sexuality in particular, was virtually absent from the proceedings. Clare Short and David Hinchliffe were perhaps the only MPs who made any such reference. David Hinchliffe rejected the 'disease model' of child abuse as this 'largely ignores the very important economic and social context in which parenting takes place'. Drawing on the work of Christine Parton (1990), he continued:

> I would argue in particular that nowhere is the individual pathology model more questionable than with regard to sexual abuse . . . the roots

> of child sexual abuse are not so much in deviant family and sexual values, but in normal ones ... we need to address in particular male socialisation, sexual attitudes and expectation of women and the portrayal of women in society. (*Hansard*, HoC, 27 April 1989, Col. 1162)

There were clearly, then, a range of political, professional and personal experiences to be drawn upon – there were few, however, who had the detailed knowledge of the area or the existing law to criticise the content of the Bill and put forward detailed amendments. For this, the extra parliamentary professional, interest and pressure groups were important.

The Process of Lobbying

Not only was the Bill generally recognised as the most important in the field of child care this century, but also that it was likely to provide the framework for policy and practice for many years to come. Not surprisingly, therefore, the voluntary, professional and local authority groups involved were keen to influence its passage through Parliament and ensure that their particular interests or concerns were catered for. They had made efforts to lobby in relation to the children's legislation of 1975 and 1980, but had done so, on the whole, quite independently so that on numerous occasions they had lobbied against each other, thus cancelling out their efforts. In effect, the Governments of the day had been allowed to do what they wanted. A number, therefore, felt it sensible to try and co-ordinate their efforts so that at a minimum each knew what the others were proposing. David Mellor, the Minister of State, also made it known informally that he would welcome the opportunity to meet with such bodies in an attempt to ensure the Government got it 'right'. He seemed to feel that it was important that the response of those organisations whose responsiblity it would be to operate the legislation should be listened to in an attempt to increase its chances of success. For such a dialogue to develop, however, it was important that it take place under neutral auspices and thereby gain the respect and trust of all those organisations which might wish to contribute.

Shortly after the Bill was published in November 1988, representatives from the Association of Metropolitan Authorities (AMA), the Association of County Councils (ACC), the Association of Directors of Social Services (ADSS) and the British Association of Social Workers (BASW) had met to begin to formulate their own responses. Peter Westland, the Permanent Under-secretary for Social Services at the AMA, took the initiative to broaden the group in order to improve their co-ordinating efforts and raise the profile of the lobbyists on all sides of the House.

Following a meeting between Peter Westland and Peter Riches, the then Assistant Director (Development) at the National Children's Bureau, it was decided to centre the co-ordinating efforts at the National Children's Bureau.

Peter Smith, Senior Development Officer at the NCB, was seconded to the co-ordinating task on a part-time basis until the passage of the Bill was completed; originally planned for July 1989. The main constituents, including the AMA, ACC, BASW and the larger voluntary organisations, all put a few hundred pounds together to cover Peter Smith's salary, while the smaller organisations were asked to contribute a nominal sum to register their commitment. About forty organisations were involved, though the reality was that only between fifteen and twenty did so in any sustained way. However, the momentum for producing amendments, particularly in the latter stages, seemed to come from a group of highly-motivated women, most of whom combined part-time work with domestic child care responsibilties. Mary Ryan (Family Rights Group), Rachael Hodgkin and Nicola Wyld (Children's Legal Centre), Avril Wilson (NSPCC) and Deborah Cullen (BAAF) were very much at the centre of things. Peter Smith took on the task just after the Second Reading in the Lords in December 1988.

Thereafter, before each stage of the Bill in both the Lords and the Commons, there would be a meeting to which each organisation would bring drafts or finalised amendments that it wanted considering. Where there were a number of organisations with similar issues in mind, an amendment would be worded so that they could all put their names to it. Where there were disagreements, everyone would know where the differences were and what their nature was. While it seems there was much common ground, different organisations focused on issues of special interest to them. For example, the National Children's Home and Barnardo's were concerned that the balance had shifted too far away from the best interests of the child, BASW was determined to ensure full party status for children in proceedings and the independence of guardians *ad litem* from local authority management and control, the Family Rights Group promoted parental rights and the Children's Legal Centre complaints procedures and post-Gillick rights for older children (see Osmond 1989c). Similarly, while initially the ADSS argued for a single Emergency Protection Order, almost all the others favoured an additional Child Assessment Order.

Not only did the group help the constituent organisations to rationalise and co-ordinate their efforts, it provided the Government, the Lords and MPs with a ready reference point. The co-ordinating group issued one set of amendments but indicated the main supporters and drafters of each one. It was a new way of organising lobbying efforts, and one which was well received by most MPs. Andrew Rowe, the Chair of the All-Party Social Services Panel in Parliament and a member of the committee in the Commons, for example, recommended this 'highly sophisticated lobby' to the Social Care Association in his keynote address to the Association in November 1989, as one that should be emulated in the future in order to influence the progress of legislation (see Murray 1989).

At the same time, Baroness Lady Faithfull, who had previously been Children's Officer in Oxford, organised all-party meetings when the Bill was in the Lords, where the representatives could put forward their views and discuss with Peers who were interested in presenting and speaking to an amendment. It provided a vehicle whereby initial contact and subsequent briefings could take place. Similar meetings took place with the Labour Group in the Commons who were going to sit on the committee so that again individual amendments could be picked up and briefings take place. Contacts were developed with Conservative Members, but these tended to be a little more *ad hoc*. Certainly, however, Tim Devlin and other Conservative members were more than prepared to table and speak on behalf of amendments supporting the introduction of Family Courts. Peter Smith would prepare a regular paper in the form of a parliamentary briefing which would be circularised to the various organisations, but also to others including the professional press. This provided a summary of the progress of the Bill and an outline of the issues where it seemed the main concerns were developing.

Throughout, the lobbyists had meetings with Peers and MPs, and officials at the Department of Health who drafted the Bill and the subsequent Government amendments. During the summer of 1989, when stringent efforts were being made to resolve the outstanding contentious issues, there were a number of meetings which involved not just representatives of the lobbying groups and civil servants, but also meetings containing Members of the Commons Committee from all parties. Such dialogue was very unusual during the progress of legislation – particularly when a Government had a large majority and much of its previous legislation has been pushed through in the context of stiff parliamentary and extra-parliamentary opposition. It would be misguided to read this dialogue, however, in terms of the lobbyists getting what they wanted, that the Government was willing to give way on its original plans, or that Government resistance to change did not lead to the outbreak of strong criticisms. There were important differences but there was a keenness on all sides to maintain a mutual respect so that the new balances and consensus that people were searching for did not collapse. There is little doubt that senior civil servants played a crucial role in this. In particular, Rupert Hughes, the Assistant Secretary at the Department of Health who had been the main drafter, was central. He had been in post since 1983 and had been involved throughout the whole period of policy discussion from the Short Report through to the Butler-Sloss Report. He chaired the group which produced the Review of Child Care Law and was the one constant figure throughout, the one most on top of issues and the technicalities and as committed as anyone to seeing the legislation onto the statute book. The *Times Diary* of the 14 March 1989, described his significance as follows:

At the centre of a web of connections is an Assistant Secretary in the Department of Health, Rupert Hughes. A genuine policy expert and an accomplished fixer, Hughes has greased the machine so well that what might otherwise have been a highly contentious rewriting of the law affecting child care is slipping easily through. Even David Mellor, not a Minister to miss a chance of playing to the gallery, is onside. When Lord Mackay and Baroness Faithfull have completed their double act in the Upper House, Hughes will take up his position in the official's box in the Commons and continue shepherding. (p. 16)

Main Areas of Political Dispute and Professional Concern

By the time the Bill was about to start its passage through the Commons in April 1989, it was clear that while there was general agreement that it provided a considerable improvement on the previous inadequate and muddled state of child care law, there were also significant areas of concern evident amongst the lobby groups and expressed by MPs from all parties. It had become clear by this stage, however, that while the Government might consider minor changes, it had little intention of modifying the structure, underlying principles or major clauses of the Bill. Thus, while it was presented as consensual legislation, major limits were placed on the room for manoeuvre. These limits were most in evidence whenever changes appeared to have resource implications or they seemed to compromise changes in other policy areas – particularly social security or housing.

For example, children being at risk via the parents' homelessness was seen as a housing problem; the increasing stress in families following the introduction of the social fund was seen as a social security issue; and, perhaps most dramatically, the increased problems facing older children leaving care as a result of the reduction of income support levels for young adults was similarly seen as a social security issue. The latter led to considerable criticism, but little movement on behalf of the Government. The Social Security legislation offered no relief to 16–18 year olds, and little to 18–25 year olds, but the Children Bill offered only a discretionary power for Local Authorities to help in exceptional circumstances once a young person left care. The Social Services Select Committee stated that the Bill fell 'substantially short' in this area and took the unprecedented step of putting forward amendments to oblige local authorities to offer advice and to provide assistance, including cash help, to care leavers (Social Services Select Committee, 1989).

The Social Services Select Committee, along with most others in the children's lobby, also felt that the section on prevention was much more restricted than the recommendations in its original report (Short Report). Not only was the focus on children 'in need' but the use of cash assistance by local authorities was possible only in 'exceptional circumstances' and was a power rather than a duty. Many were concerned that while the *concept* of prevention had been broadened, this might prove meaningless in a context of resource restraint and would receive a low priority. Numerous attempts to remove children 'in need' and 'exceptional circumstances', increase the power to a duty and place the local authorities preventative duties in the main body of the Act, as opposed to Schedule 2 at the end, all failed.

Similar criticisms were made of the day-care provisions. During the Committee stage in the Commons, the Government moved its long-awaited new clauses to replace the Nurseries and Child Minders' Regulation Act 1948. Many pressure groups and the Labour group led by Hilary Armstrong, felt the new regulations were weak and failed to ensure comprehensive provision for all who may require it. There was concern at the lack of breadth and quality of reviews; at the failure to define the criteria for defining quality in childminding; that the requirement to levy charges for the registration of child minders could act as a disincentive to register and therefore increase the number of unregistered child minders; to ensure regular and authoritative inspections; at the deregulation of facilities for older children. More generally, there was a concern that day-care had not been given the central role that was vital in any strategy that was serious about prevention. It was an area where it was not possible to find a cross-party consensus. The Government resisted attempts by the opposition to lay a duty on the Secretary of State to publish a response within three months to the local authorities' regular reviews of day-care in their areas. The Government was accused of seeing the state as providing day-care only 'when a mother's life has collapsed' (Hilary Armstrong, *Hansard*, HoC, 3rd Reading, 24 October 1989, Col. 776). What is of note is that the opposition ultimately justified their wishes for a much more broad-based universal day-care provision on essentially child protection grounds. For, Hilary Armstrong asserted:

> If we want to protect children, what is the point of developing a structure to protect them from abuse, or to help us to identify abuse and protect them? We want children to be in a protected and supported environment from the beginning. (ibid., Col. 779)

The centrality of concerns about child protection – but different ways of approaching it – in the context of day-care was made most explicit by David Hinchliffe (Labour):

> Day-care has a particular preventive and rehabilitation role in providing social needs. I fail to understand how social workers in authorities that provide minimal, if not non-existent, day-care can operate effectively in their monitoring and child protection roles. I have always thought that day-care provision was a central part of this work. (*Hansard*, HoC, Committee, 16 May 1989, Col. 112)

The other main area of dispute in relation to prevention related to the new concept of accommodation. What this debate illustrated was the Government's determination to underline the essential independence and privacy of the family, in effect parents, unless the state had taken over parental powers under care proceedings. The Government was determined to construct the provision of *accommodation* for children being *looked after* as a *service*, thus reducing the suspicion and stigma associated with it by parents, and thereby 'avoid a hybrid arrangement between voluntary and compulsory' (*Hansard*, David Mellor, HoC Committee, 18 May 1989, Col. 152). Not only did it wish to get rid of parental rights resolutions, it was determined that there would be no powers vested in a local authority whereby it could take over or vary parental powers without going to court. As a result, the recommendations relating to 'shared care' and 'respite care' in the Review of Child Care Law were not taken up because they seemed to cloud and confuse where parental powers and responsibilities lay. The Government similarly resisted the universal clamour from the professional lobbyists to include a brief period of notice of removal of a child by parents from accommodation, even of twenty-four hours, to allow a degree of planning to take place for such children. It was argued that if an authority was so concerned, it should apply to the court for emergency protection or care orders.

This clear division between care and accommodation was perhaps at its most stark in the debates about written agreements. In an attempt to increase the principles of partnership and co-operation between parents and local authority when a child was away from home, the White Paper had argued that:

> matters such as initial placement, schooling and access, and subsequent changes to these arrangements should be settled by mutual agreement. An arrangement under which parents will give notice that they wish to take the child back should also normally be settled by mutual agreement between the parents and the local authority in order to prepare a child for returning home. (para. 23)

However, numerous attempts by the Family Rights Group, supported by the National Foster Care Association, ADSS, Barnardo's and National Children's Homes, to require local authorities and parents to enter into written agreements when children came into local authority accommodation and following the wording of the White Paper, were resisted on the basis that the Government wanted to underline that voluntary really was voluntary. What became apparent was that the Government had reframed the notions of 'partnership' and 'participation' which had been central to the Short Report and the Review of Child Care Law, according to much more consumerist criteria, where the consumer was seen as the parents. In the process, voluntary care was redesignated as 'accommodation' and the powers of the supplier, the local authority, to influence the terms of the exchange were curtailed. The concern of the lobbyists was that the Government had gone much too far so that local authorities would be reluctant to use such a response except with the short-term admission. Whenever a child was likely to come into care for any longer period, the local authority was more likely to resist the admission altogether, fall back on pursuing a care order through the courts or offer 'accommodation' with conditions on a take it or leave it basis. The result would be the opposite for policy and practice to what was intended in the Short Report.

Thus, while the Government agreed that written agreements would be an important means of clarifying the respective responsibilities and actions of all parties when children were looked after in local authority accommodation, it did not agree that such agreements should be defined in the Act, nor that such agreements should contain a clause defining a period of notice for removal of the child. It seemed particularly mindful of the recent developments for handicapped children where their parents were much more instrumental in deciding when, where and how they wished to use residential and foster care services. The net result was that, rather than an essentially social democratic notion of partnership and negotiated contract informing the relationship between local authority and parents, as in the Short Report, the more obviously consumerist notion of freedom of choice came to the fore. In the process, the room for independent manoeuvre on behalf of the executive, local authority social workers, was potentially much more contained.

Other criticisms related to the role and funding of guardians *ad litem* and the failure to introduce a family court. While it was clear that guardians would play an important role, there was concern that the proposals would not ensure their independence. The Government supported the establishment of local authority consortiums rather than taking the service outside the local authority altogether, something which was again likely to cost more. Many felt the establishment of the family courts, administering guardians, was the best way forward.

For all the apparent success of the Family Court's Campaign (see Smith, 1988), the Government insisted that while the establishment of family courts was part of its 'rolling programme' of change, it wished to get the substantive law right first before making such fundamental changes in court philosophy, procedure and processes of decision-making. All-party amendments to introduce family courts in the

Commons Committee led to a debate in which all members who spoke, thirteen in number, were in favour of such a change as was the case at the Commons Report Stage before it went to a division.

However, perhaps the issues which divided both Houses on party political lines the most, and which gave considerable concern to the various professional and interest groups, related to resources and, to a lesser extent, training. The Labour group in particular stressed that many of the good intentions of the Bill would be lost and a range of unintended consequences come about if the resources made available were inadequate.

It was argued that if the key professionals were not fully trained to implement the Act, the quality of service to both children and families would not improve. Following all-party concern in the Lords, there was a small amendment requiring the Secretary of State to review training. While the Government subsequently said that £2.5 million would be devoted to training staff prior to implementation, a consortium of national and London-based organisations said that double that amount would be required (*Community Care*, 1989).

There were other areas besides training, however, where it was argued that expenditure would be required. A report to the AMA stated that the cost of implementation would be more than £13 million in excess of the Government's estimates, while Joan Lestor, Labour spokeswoman on children and a member of the Commons Committee, claimed it would cost £65 million for the whole country (reported in *Social Work Today*, 10 August 1989, p. 4). The shorter time limits attached to emergency protection responsibilities, together with the increased information that courts would require so as to decide on directions regarding parental contact and medical examinations, would all require a concentration of effort and skills. Similarly, the wider preventive powers and responsibilities, if they were to be provided in any comprehensive and integrated way, would require increased resources.[2]

The position of the Government, however, was very different and reflected its general scepticism towards local government's ability to use resources effectively and efficiently. This was most evident in its statements on large Labour-controlled inner-city authorities. Writing in *The Times* in December 1988, in relation to the Doreen Mason Case, David Mellor (1988) said:

> A Southwark MP, Simon Hughes, has spoken of 'a tragically incompetent department'. We shall see if that description is justified. But Southwark's reputation in social services was depressingly low even before this case, and illustrates another problem. A big spending authority, constantly propagandising about 'services', can nevertheless, despite spending money like water, appear to run a pretty poor show. What we do not want are predictable excuses about 'lack of resources', if the real problems are, as many suspect ones of organisation, management and individual judgement. (p. 12)

While such attitudes were rarely expressed during debates about the Bill in the Commons, they were never far below the surface. Certainly, Margaret Thatcher, Vice-President of the NSPCC, had never hidden her admiration for voluntary organisations as opposed to local authorities in this area of work.

For all the criticisms, however, there were very few either inside or outside Parliament who were prepared to go as far as to say that their concerns were so gross as to invalidate the whole package. Only the Association of London Authorities argued it was 'worthless as the blueprint for the next decade' (ALA, 1989). Most were concerned to get the legislation onto the statute book, trying to improve any inadequacies where these were seen to exist but recognising they were restricted by the Government's financial restrictions and underlying philosophy.

The Emergency Protection of Children

The issue which provided for the most conflict and dissent was that related to the legal mechanism(s) to protect children in emergency situations. What the arguments and subsequent resolutions demonstrated was that not only were these issues central to the legislation, but that also how important it was for the Government to construct a set of balances which would receive wide support.

As originally drafted, the Bill closely followed the recommendations of the Short Report, the Review of Child Care Law and the White Paper but, following the Butler-Sloss Report, further strengthening the rights of parents, who could make a challenge after just seventy-two hours if they had not been present at the original application. Similarly, the primary ground was to be *significant* harm, rather than simply *harm* as in the White Paper, and if, upon investigation, the child was found not to be at risk, the child was not to be removed. It was the *court* which had to be satisfied that the grounds for such an order existed, rather than the *social worker*, under the Place of Safety Order, believing them to exist. The Bill also gave the court the power to make directions on contact with the child and medical examinations at the time the Order was made. There was a clear effort to ensure that state intervention into the family should be reserved for real emergencies and that the gravity of such interventions required the full authority of the court behind it. The influence of Cleveland was evident. When he launched the Bill in November 1988, David Mellor said that the events of Cleveland and 'the devastating effect' of the removal of children from their families had shown all too clearly the problems that could blow up as a result of over-zealous action. He said, 'I hope the Bill proves the Government takes parental rights very seriously indeed' (see Gibb, 1988).

The Government initially took the view that the EPO provided sufficient powers for social workers to protect children. The Bill did not include a Child Assessment Order (CAO) as originally recommended in the Carlile Report. However, David Mellor did say at the outset that he was well aware of the case for such an Order and would listen to all sides of the House before deciding whether to introduce such an amendment. Ironically, it was the running debate on this issue which caused the greatest dissension and eventual opposition from numerous quarters. The issue accounted for much time, energy and debate. By the end, many felt the reforms which had received much support at the outset had so significantly been changed that it was no longer appropriate to see the Bill as having the same heart. Many felt it underwent a fundamental transplant such that it was much more difficult to hold on to the notion of a consensus on the issue. The irony is that this transformation seemed to come about in an attempt to find just such a consensus.

The CAO was not new to MPs, for following the Carlile Report, Virginia Bottomley (Conservative MP and former social worker who subsequently succeeded David Mellor at the Department of Health in November 1989) introduced a Ten Minute Bill on 13 January 1988 called the Medical Examination of Children at Risk Bill. While it was accepted that such Bills rarely become law, it was hoped to raise the profile of the issue so that it would be included in any subsequent overhaul of Child Care Law. The purpose of the Bill was to ensure that there was a power to require parents to produce a child for *medical examination* within three days. The child would be neither removed from home, nor would parental rights be transferred. The Bill would have introduced a new lower order to ensure that a child for whom there were not grounds for a POSO, but where the child had not been seen could be medically examined: 'Under the Bill, parents have a right of appeal; it is rather like paying a parking ticket. They must either produce the child for a medical within the required time of three days or appear in the juvenile court, or before a Magistrate to explain their objections' (Virginia Bottomley, *Hansard*, HoC, 29 April 1988, Col. 691). The Bill received wide cross-party support together with that of the NCB, NCH, the Children's Society, ADSS, BASW and NSPCC. There was no-one in obvious opposition. While the Bill did run out of parliamentary time at its second reading, in replying for the Government, Tony Newton, Minister of State, said that all could be assured that the issue would be re-examined in the light of the Cleveland report when the new Bill was being drafted.

However, the Cleveland Report had felt that the inclusion of a CAO would confuse the issue for social workers and put its weight behind the EPO alone. As a consequence, some of the major recommendations of the Carlile Report were not included in the Bill. According to Margaret Jervis (1989):

Once the Cleveland Report had arrived, the majestical force of Lord Butler-Sloss won through. Department of Health Officials, guided by the

ADSS, drafted one emergency protection order and police order and scrapped the Section 40 police warrant. The right of entry without an order for social workers didn't get a look in and nor, it seemed, had the Child Assessment Order. (p. 18)

Clearly, however, the issue of a CAO was a live one which could be seen as Cleveland *vs.* Carlile or, as it was to develop in the initial stages, ADSS *vs.* NSPCC. John Chant, then Director of Somerset Social Services, had been a member of the Butler-Sloss Inquiry Team while Jim Harding, Head of Child Care at the NSPCC, had been a member of the Carlile Inquiry.

It also seems that when the Bill was published, there were differences of opinion in the Government, for while David Mellor had made it known he was willing to listen to arguments regarding a CAO, the Lord Chancellor gave the impression that he would have nothing of it. In the first full debate in the Lords, at Second Reading in response to Lord Moston's question regarding the 'deliberate omission of provision for medical assessment orders' (*Hansard*, HoL, 6 December 1988, Col. 500), the Lord Chancellor replied that he felt such concerns were covered by an EPO as long as the court was asked to give its direction on a medical examination. He could see little point for a CAO (ibid., Col. 540).

Early in the life of the co-ordinating group based at the NCB, it became clear that there was interest in the proposal to include a CAO, following that originally suggested by Virginia Bottomley. The NSPCC was particularly keen and took the lead. It was quickly apparent, however, that the ADSS was against this, but that it was out on a limb. For while most thought the EPO a massive improvement over the Place of Safety Order, many of the original supporters of Virginia Bottomley's Bill thought it still worth pursuing. During the winter of 1988–9, a wide division opened up between the ADSS and the NSPCC. Not only did this quickly move into the House of Lords, but into the public domain. A number of articles were published in the professional press by representatives of ADSS and NSPCC, putting their respective cases.

The NSPCC argued that the benefits of a CAO order were essentially fourfold (see Harding, 1989; Wilson, 1989). First, that parental responsibility would be retained by the parents throughout and would, therefore, create the least possible stress within the family. Second, the child would be seen by the family doctor in a familiar environment, thus protecting the child from distress and worry. Third, the parents would be likely to co-operate so that the social work relationship with the family would not be damaged. And, finally, but most importantly, the child could be protected in serious, but not emergency, situations. The Child Assessment Order was not seen as an alternative to an EPO but as an alternative to being unable to do anything. In this respect, the EPO and CAO were seen as complementary and providing child care professionals with real options for investigating alleged abuse depending on the circumstances.

In contrast, the ADSS argued that the reasons pertaining when Virginia Bottomley introduced her Ten Minute Bill no longer existed. The CAO was not trying to overcome the problems with the Place of Safety Order, which was to be abolished, but had to be located in the overall rationale of the Children Bill. In this context, social workers needed to draw upon their negotiating skills in an honest and open way with parents so that children, where there was concern, could be seen and medically examined with the full agreement of the parents. If this was not possible, an EPO should be sought but if, when the child was examined, the concerns were not confirmed, the child should not be removed. The ADSS considered that an additional order, the CAO, would confuse staff and there would be a tendency to apply for the 'lesser order' putting the child 'at risk'. For if upon examination under a CAO the concerns were substantiated, an EPO would still have to be applied for necessitating delay, leaving the child exposed to further harm.

The two positions seemed irreconcilable throughout the Bill's progress through the Lords. Both sides felt that their proposals provided the best legal mechanism for protecting children. The Lord Chancellor took the ADSS position but bolstered this further with his primary concern for protecting the rights of parents and the overall structure and logic of the Bill. Lord Mottistone tabled an amendment drafted by the NSPCC, following that of Virginia Bottomley's Bill, and presented it as filling the gap in the 'otherwise excellent child protection provision' but designed for those 'borderline cases where there is serious but not urgent concern for the child'. However, not only did the Lord Chancellor feel the EPO would cover the circumstances which Lord Mottistone had outlined but also argued that:

> The Child Assessment Order would necessarily be a major interference in family life. One can make it as little as one likes but it is a compulsory intervention that is in question, and it would raise the unsettling prospect of further intervention. (*Hansard*, HoL, 16 February 1989, Col. 316)

Earlier the Lord Chancellor had been at pains to distinguish between a medical examination and a developmental assessment where the latter was likely to involve numerous meetings over a period of time and thus could not rationally be included within the auspices of an order, the EPO, which only covered eight days:

> We must be careful to distinguish between examination and assessment. While an examination may take place on a single occasion for a particular purpose, an assessment, or a developmental assessment is likely to involve a series of examinations, meetings or interviews over an unspecified or even indefinite period of time, and it may involve various professional persons. However it is defined, it will inevitably be a relatively lengthy consideration of a child's circumstances. As such, I do not think that it would be appropriate for a court to be able to give directions concerning such an assessment when making an emergency protection order which at that stage can last for no more than eight days and will often be of shorter duration. (*Hansard*, HoC Committee, 19 January 1989, Col. 433–4)

This was to prove a most salutory argument in the light of the way the CAO was to be modified for final inclusion in the Act over the coming months.

However, during the debate in Committee in the Lords, Lord Mottistone used a case in illustration where, while there was no direct evidence of serious harm, the social worker could not gain access on four occasions. In response, the Lord Chancellor argued that:

> if access is refused therefore we would say where there is a *prima facie* indication that something's going wrong, that the proper step is to try

and investigate. If you cannot, if you are frustrated in your investigation by action taken by the parents or on their behalf, the next step should be an application for an Emergency Protection Order. The serious concern that led to the approach to see the child in the first place, combined with the refusal to allow him to be seen, makes action urgent and should, together with the relevant surrounding circumstances, be adequate to meet the grounds for an Emergency Protection Order. (*Hansard*, HoL, 16 February 1989, Col. 315)

Lord Mottistone was not convinced, however.

I should have thought that some people might say – ordinary people like magistrates, and I am not sure that clerks to the justices might not say this – 'it is all very well; you have come to me and told me this story about this child who you have not been able to see four times and the parents did not take it to see the doctor when you said they should, but I do not think that this is evidence of significant harm'. They might say that, and I do not see why they should think it was significant harm. It depends on how the story is told and the circumstances if we create this particular situation. If we are to drop this idea of a Child Assessment Order, we have to tackle more seriously what is really required to issue an emergency protection order. (*Hansard*, HoL, 16 February 1989, Col. 317)

During the Report Stage in the Lords, Lord Mottistone moved his Child Assessment Order Amendment[3] which he subsequently withdrew. It transpired, however, that since the Committee, Lord Mottistone and the Lord Chancellor had exchanged letters and met, for the Lord Chancellor recognised that the grounds for an EPO may need to be clarified to cover the problems with access outlined by Lord Mottistone and which the magistrates may not feel sufficient for an EPO. The Lord Chancellor admitted that he was considering:

whether there is a case for putting something into the Bill that might help in that connection. The difficulty is that one also has to take into account of the right not to be interferred with improperly; not to be interfered with for too little reason. (*Hansard*, HoL, 3rd Reading, 16 March 1989, Col. 401)

The issue regarding the CAO Order and the disagreement between the ADSS and NSPCC left the Lords for the Commons quite unresolved. By this stage, however, the debates about the CAO had also raised doubts about whether magistrates would accept continual denial of access together with the original concerns as constituting grounds for an EPO.

By the time the Bill was debated at Second Reading in the Commons, it was clear that this was the major outstanding issue which the Government saw as needing resolution, even though nearly all the lobbyists saw other things as more important. However, whereas the Lord Chancellor continued to hold as a priority, the need to keep interference in the family to a minimum, for David Mellor it seems the prime concern was 'to be satisfied that mechanisms proposed are sufficient to ensure proper protection for the child' (HoC, 2nd Reading, *Hansard*, 27 April 1989, Col. 114). It seems likely that his concerns over the way the case of Doreen Mason had been handled made a particular impact upon him and provided for a different perspective to those of the Lord Chancellor.

During April and early May there was a considerable number of meetings and much activity. Not only were officials from the Department of Health trying to find a resolution to the dispute between the NSPCC and ADSS, but the Government was working on an amendment to the EPO to overcome the problem pointed up by Lord Mottistone. In early May, the Government issued an amendment it intended bringing to the committee stage in the Commons. The amendment, in effect, included new grounds that spelt out that, in the context of a social worker investigating an emergency, the court could make an EPO if access to the child was being *unreasonably refused*. The EPO would act as a directive to any person who was in a position to do so to produce the child to the social worker holding the Order. Such a development quickly raised the heat of the debate as many felt that not only had the value of the CAO been overlooked, but the grounds for the EPO had been fundamentally broadened. Mary Ryan, the Family Rights Group solicitor, took the initiative on behalf of the children's lobbying groups to brief those MPs on the committee about the concerns.

The briefing strongly opposed the proposed amendment which was seen to radically alter the grounds on which an EPO could be granted. The briefing summarised the criticisms of the research in the early 1980s of the fundamental problems with the Place of Safety Order and that the Review of Child Care Law, the White Paper and the Cleveland Report all stressed that the abrupt removal of children from home should occur only *in a genuine emergency*. It argued that 'if these amendments are passed there is a real danger that children will continue to be inappropriately removed from home' and that it was quite unrealistic to expect that a social worker, having been granted an EPO on the grounds of frustration of access, would feel able to leave the child at home. If the social worker's level of anxiety about the safety of the child had been such that they had applied for an EPO, it was likely that they would also remove the child even if, when seen, the child was safe. It was argued that 'it is unsatisfactory to attempt to incorporate some form of child assessment order into a clause relating to emergency protection' which should be about the need to take immediate action to protect the safety of the child. The Family Rights Group, British Agencies for Adoption and Fostering, BASW, the Children's Legal Centre, the NCB and the AMA all came out strongly against the EPO amendment.

As an alternative to the broadened EPO they – including the Family Rights Group who had previously sat on the fence – redoubled their efforts in support of a separate CAO. While not involved in putting down the amendment, it was also clear that PAIN (Parent Against INjustice) was also in support of a CAO (Marshall 1989). Roger Sims, briefed by the NSPCC, tabled the CAO amendment (similar to that of Lord Mottistone's in the Lords) for the Commons Committee. It was argued that the major advantage of such a CAO over the EPO amendment was that the application was on notice and was for the *parents* to take the child for a medical or psychiatric examination, something which would be quite normal for parents to do with their children. The EPO should be restricted to where there was evidence of an *emergency*. If there was no evidence, but concern about what might be happening, then a CAO should be applied for. Such an Order would give protection in cases similar to that of Kimberley Carlile, where there may be insufficient information to provide grounds to apply for an EPO, and would also prevent the unnecessary and traumatic removal of children in circumstances where there was no immediate threat to the child.

There were a number of meetings with the DoH officials, including Rupert Hughes, who essentially reiterated the ADSS argument that such a CAO was not needed, that it would confuse social workers and that they might use a CAO as a 'soft option'. The newly-amended EPO was seen as much more preferable.

Then in mid-May, once the Commons Committee had started work, there were rumours circulating amongst the lobbying groups and the corridors at Westminster that the NSPCC and ADSS had resolved their differences and that a likely outcome was the inclusion of a new clause introducing a CAO as well as the amendment to the EPO.

At a meeting with officials of the DoH on 22 May, the NSPCC and ADSS both agreed to support not only the Government amendment to the EPO, but also the inclusion of a new clause on a CAO. The NSPCC and ADSS published a joint press release announcing the 'glorious peace'. The Government was clearly pleased.

NSPCC and ADSS said they were both happy with the EPO amendments and were delighted that the Government was to introduce a separate CAO designed to deal with situations where the child may be in need of help, but where the case was not an emergency. It was thought to be of particular use where parents were unwilling to co-operate in cases of longer-term neglect and chronic emotional abuse. While not an emergency, such situations were seen to require a thorough assessment of the nature and degree of risk to the child. The CAO would be granted if the *social worker suspects* that a child was likely to suffer significant harm. The child could then be assessed to establish if this was the case, and what harm, if any, the child was suffering. The order would be made on notice so that parents and the child could seek legal advice and a guardian *ad litem* would also be appointed. There was to be no question of the child being removed from home or parental responsibility being transferred to a local authority. Under the original amendment presented to the Commons Committee, the Order would have been for up to twenty-eight days to allow full family and psycho-social assessment as well as medical examination and developmental tests to take place.

Initially it seemed that the NSPCC had got what it wanted and that the ADSS had backed down. However, Robin Osmond, the main ADSS representatives during negotiations with the NSPCC, explained that 'what is now proposed is an amendment to the EPO, so that if access to a child by a social worker is frustrated that could be a ground for an EPO. This leaves the Child Assessment Order free to be used in non-emergency cases. In those circumstances, we have no objection to the lesser Order' (see Edwards, 1989, p. 11). It seemed that in the process of trying to satisfy both ADSS and NSPCC, what had been negotiated was a fundamentally different set of legal mechanisms for intervening in child protection situations. Not only had the grounds for the EPO been broadened, to take account of the concerns for which the original CAO had been designed, but a completely new non-emergency Order had been inserted. What was very clear was that the new CAO Order bore little similarity to that recommended in the Carlile Report, Virginia Bottomley's Ten Minute Bill or Lord Mottistone's and Roger Sims' amendment to the Bill. Even so, the NSPCC Child Care Director, Jim Harding, stated, 'I'm very heartened by the news of these amendments and by the fact that the NSPCC and the ADSS – the two main providers of child protection services – are able to stand together in welcoming this package' (see McMillan 1989, p. 1).

It quickly became apparent, however, that while the new amendments might have the support of the NSPCC and ADSS, they were opposed by virtually everyone else. If the amendment to the EPO had not been bad enough, the addition of this quite new CAO was seen to make things much worse. Not only had the battle lines been redrawn with ADSS, NSPCC and the Government facing the rest, but the nature of the concerns had fundamentally shifted.

The two sets of amendments were discussed for the first time in the Commons Committee of the 25 May, just three days after the NSPCC–ADSS meeting. The lack of time gave the opposition little opportunity to consider an overall strategy.

In presenting the proposed amendment to the EPO, David

Mellor argued that it did not seek any 'major extension of its scope' – it was simply making explicit what had always been intended. He stressed that it was 'not a snoopers' charter' and that 'had such specific provisions been in place when Kimberley Carlile's case was being considered, earlier and decisive action by the Social Services Department involved could not have been avoided' (*Hansard*, HoC Committee, 25 May 1989, Col. 282). What then ensued, however, was not a debate about the EPO amendment at all but the new CAO. In fact, the introduction of the CAO had caught people so off guard and touched such a range of anxieties that it was this that received the attention. In effect, the frustrated access ground for the EPO was never debated. This was clearly noted by David Mellor who said that he would retable it in its present form at Report Stage.

Stuart Bell was in attendance throughout and gave the amendment, subject to a minor observation, his blessing. Such a lack of debate was not the case with the CAO. While David Mellor was clearly convinced by now about the need for such an Order, he was undecided about the exact way in which it should be drafted. He particularly noted that the twenty-eight-day-period that was being suggested might be too long and in particular, following a contribution again from Stuart Bell, saw that twenty-eight days resurrected the spectre of the Place of Safety Order. Clearly, however, he had something in mind much broader than a simple medical examination and much more in line with the full social assessment outlined in the DoH Guidance on Protecting Children (DoH, 1988 – see Chapter 5 in this volume):

> The guidance from the Department of Health suggests that a full and proper assessment of a child's developmental progress goes much wider than a medical examination and could take up to three months, but when I originally envisaged a Child Assessment Order I did not imagine a period as long as twenty-eight days. I wish to take away with me the clear steer from the Committee that it is too long a period. (ibid., Col. 317)

Both amendments were withdrawn from the Committee though it was clear that the frustrated access clause to the EPO would be represented at the Report Stage in the autumn with very little change. Clearly, however, further work needed to be done on the CAO. David Mellor promised that he would keep both MPs and the interested groups informed and involved. Even tough clear dissension had broken out, he was determined to carry as many with him as possible. The summer recess consisted of many exchanges, meetings and behind the scenes manoeuvres – many of these quite unusual. It included all-party members of the Committee in meetings with civil servants and the Minister, as well as meetings involving the Minister and the lobby groups.

At this point, the focus of concern for the lobby groups shifted to try and influence the new CAO and virtually all efforts were given up at trying to avert or modify the Government's intentions regarding the EPO. All the lobbying groups, with the exception of the NSPCC, made it clear they wanted the new CAO dropped altogether – but recognised that this was unlikely. A letter to all concerned from David Mellor at the end of July indicated that the maximum length would now be fourteen days. He also stressed that a child could only be kept away from home for assessment in accordance with the direction of the court, and that it would be made clear in guidance that this should be required in only exceptional circumstances.

BAAF, the Children's Legal Centre and the Family Rights Group came together to front the criticism of the new CAO, pointing out that nearly all those who had been in favour of the original CAO at the start of the year were now set against it. They also drafted a new Order, subsequently tabled at Report Stage by Keith Vaz (Labour), called a Child Production Notice.[4] This would be a statutory notice served by a local authority on parents, requiring them to produce the child within twenty-four hours at a specified time and place to the social worker, but also perhaps a doctor, nurse or health visitor as specified. It was much closer to the original CAO than that currently being supported by the Government.

What emerged during the discussion over the summer was that the Government and the DoH officials saw the main purpose of the new CAO as bringing home to *unco-operative parents* their child's needs without the necessary expectation of any further Order. As a consequence, it was argued that it should not be used as a backdoor way of removing the child for fourteen days. The opposition, however, was concerned that: (*a*) the grounds were drawn so wide that it would be difficult for parents to challenge the professionals' claims in court without producing their own expert evidence; (*b*) there may be a further clash of expert opinion as to what constituted a 'satisfactory' assessment; and most importantly (*c*) it would undermine the good practice in working on a voluntary basis with children and families which was the whole philosophical basis of the Bill – it would prove too easy for social workers to issue threats of court action early on.

As late as the 17 October 1989, it was evident from David Mellor's communications that not only was he keeping to the essential principles of the CAO, but that fourteen days was seen as the appropriate length of time because 'it was clear from the response of the professional medical bodies we consulted that up to fourteen days may be required in complex cases'. By this stage, the opposition had even given up on having any success with the Child Production Notice and simply concentrated its efforts on trying to tighten the CAO.

When the final clause outlining the CAO was presented to the Report Stage in the Commons, however, the length of time had been further reduced to seven days. It had become clear during the meetings that there was, in legalistic terms, an anomaly whereby the lesser Order, the CAO, could lead to a child being away from home for fourteen days, while a stiffer order, the EPO, would only lead to an eight-day removal. It was important, therefore, that the CAO should be a lesser 'penalty' than an EPO. David Mellor commented: 'I do not believe that the Child Assessment Order, as we have it, is an unnecessary intrusion. By reducing the period from twenty-eight days to seven days, we have shown a marked concern that the order should not be excessive' (*Hansard*, HoC, Report Stage, 23 October 1989, Col. 593).

In effect, the Government having decided on a CAO, had to compromise between the contradictory criteria that such an assessment should fulfil. While the criteria for the social assessment suggested three months, the criteria of the judicial tariff system suggested less than eight days. It was the latter which eventually took precedent. The validity of such an exercise in more strictly social assessment terms, however, was clearly compromised. In the end David Mellor was reduced to arguing that:

> There is genuine anxiety lest Child Assessment Orders be used as an oppressive instrument. After careful consideration, I reached the conclusion that a sensible assessment could be made within seven days in almost every case. (ibid., Col. 594)

While clearly determined to introduce the CAO, he also wanted to re-establish a consensus across the range of interest and professional groups so that it would receive as wide a support as possible. In this respect, it was clearly politically important and symbolically very powerful when Stuart Bell said, during the debate on the CAO at the Report Stage, that: 'If the assessment order leads to a multi-disciplinary assessment in non-emergency situations, *I support and favour it*' (ibid., Col. 597, my emphasis). The net result, however, according to David Hinchliffe (Labour) was that

> in doing his best to be reasonable and conciliatory the Minister has made assessment orders effectively inoperable. He has disappeared into his own reasonableness, which is most unfortunate because he has tried, as members of the committee have tried. (ibid., Col. 605)

What concerned some of the lobbyists was that not only was the distinction between an EPO and a CAO very unclear, but that in reducing the order to seven days, it increased the likelihood that social workers, if the new Order was going to be used, would need to remove the child and engage the family in a concentrated and intrusive way during the seven-day period.

Conclusion

The Children Bill was not, as many have argued, a direct consequence of Cleveland, nor was it a direct consequence of all the other major child abuse inquiries throughout the decade. It does seem, however, that it was concerns about child abuse or, as it became known, child protection, that proved the major focus throughout its passage through both the Lords and Commons. While it is very clear that it did take much of its inspiration from the Short Report, the Review of Child Care Law and the various research that informed them, it would be inappropriate to say that they provided the main driving forces for change. For while the Short Report recognised the problems associated with child protection, including the potential abuses of the Place of Safety Order, these were located in its central concerns about recreating a well-resourced, preventative *child care* service that worked in partnership with families. While similar concerns informed both the structure and underlying principles of both the Children Bill and final Act, this may not be so clear-cut. The level of priority and the amount of time allocated to the discussions about the more obviously child protection clauses of the Bill was considerable.

Similarly, it was in these areas that the Government, together with the opposition, was most committed to negotiating a new set of balances which respected the privacy of the family while protecting children and which would provide a new professional, public and political consensus. In the process, however, not only were the grounds for the EPO broadened, but a new non-emergency CAO was introduced, which many felt had gone a long way from the original intentions of the Bill. Rather than reducing the likelihood of increasing state intervention in the family, it may have increased.

While there is little doubt that the Act aimed to remove much of the previous discretionary paternalistic power of social workers and make them much more accountable to the courts, it did not necessarily follow that the new principles of minimal intervention in, and voluntary support for, children in their own families would come to fruition. The potentially low priority given to resourcing prevention, together with the emphasis on parental responsibility was as likely to provide the opportunity for a clear demarcation between consumer-(parent) led child care or child welfare *services* and child protection *systems*. In a context where the time and energy allocated to making the right decisions regarding child protection is dominant, and where they are hedged around with numerous guidelines and tight court oversight, opportunities for imaginative preventive strategies which cost money may well be poorly supported and become the province of the non-statutory sectors.

The impact of the various lobby/pressure groups upon the passage of the Bill is difficult to assess. While the Government was clearly not keen to change the structure and philosophy of the legislation, the lobby groups were particularly active in helping to refine it in certain respects. It is clear that they were well organised and well received on all sides and in both Houses. Equally it was important, if the Government was to create a new consensual framework for child care, that it had the support of as many groups as possible. The net result was that on occasions the impact of diverse lobbying efforts gave rise to compromises which many found difficult to support. This seems particularly to be the case with the introduction of the CAO and the broadened grounds for the EPO.

7

A Contemporary Political Economy of Child Protection

The central purpose of this final chapter is to draw some overall conclusions from what has been an essentially detailed and perhaps overly descriptive analysis of recent policy statements and legislative developments in child care. All the time I have had in mind the likely significance such changes might have – for the experiences of practitioners and family members; for our understanding of changes in social policy more generally; and for debates about the nature of contemporary social regulation.

To begin, I will return to the questions that were posed at the outset. How have these changes come about and what were the central problems they were attempting to address? What forms of social regulation have emerged – in particular what major classificatory systems have been put in place, who should operate these and based on what types of knowledge? More specifically, how far can we see these changes as being an instance of the law being colonised by the 'psy' complex or 'social' practices?

Legalism in Child Care

For the moment, it is important to differentiate between the law *per se* and legalism which refers to a particular set of assumptions regarding the best way that society should be organised. It is a particular discourse which, according to Judith Shklar (1964), refers to 'the ethical attitude that holds moral conduct to be a matter of rule following and moral relationships to consist of duties and rights determined by rules' (p. 1).

In the child care field, this morality is focused upon the relationships between professionals, particularly local authority social workers, and their clients, parents and children. It involves the superimposition of legal duties and rights upon the therapeutic and preventative responsibilities, essentially for the protection of clients. Within an emphasis on legalism, the rule of law as judged by the court takes priority at the expense of other considerations, including that which may be deemed, by the professionals concerned, as optimally therapeutic or 'in the best interests of the child'.

It is perceived as necessary to provide a check upon social work as a system of state intervention which is powerfully legitimated by therapeutic discourses. Thus apparently soft forms of control, because they function more by a particular set of values, moral persuasion, helping, images of benevolence, and paternalism, can be seen to require legal scrutiny so that any threats they may pose to civil liberties and individual rights can be kept to a minimum, or deflected altogether. It would certainly seem that a major focus of recent changes, particularly in the Children Act 1989, has been to make social workers more accountable and in particular to transfer to courts the responsibility to make the ultimate decisions when the transfer of parental rights to the local authority is at stake. This proved a major theme throughout the 1980s from the Short Reports onwards.

Changes around the axis of legalism, in areas where the role of the law is controversial, can provide an important indicator of wider social and political changes. In the way in which Durkheim drew upon the changing form of legal sanctions as a *visible symbol* of underlying shifts in the type of social solidarity or moral integration in a society (see Durkheim 1964, p. 64), so the degree of legalism in the regulation of certain social practices can provide an index of important changes in the relationship between the state and civil society and in this case, particularly, the state and the family.

As I argued in Chapter 2, the establishment of the child care service in England and Wales in the postwar period coincided with the growth of social intervention, culminating in the establishment of the welfare state. In many respects, the legitimisation and growth of state social work in Britain was interrelated with, and dependent upon, the postwar consensus and the nationalisation of the welfare state during the 1950s, 1960s, and early 1970s. The recent emergence of legalism may, therefore, be interpreted as evidence of the collapse of the political consensus upon which the institutional fabric of the welfare state was so dependent and the development of an influential liberal individualist critique of the professionalised paternalism and bureaucratic decision-making which seemed to characterise local authority social work.

The optimism and confidence evident in social work at the time of the Seebohm reforms was dealt a series of severe blows during the 1970s, and these increased further during the 1980s. Some of the anxieties emanated from within social work itself and concerned the apparent poor and even deteriorating quality of child care practice in the newly created social services departments. The poor quality of skills in this area, and the failure to capitalise on the emphasis on prevention in the 1960s, were the central concerns of the National Children's Bureau working party (see Parker, 1980). They were similarly to prove central to the various DHSS and ESRC research studies and the Parliamentary Select Committee (Social Services Report, 1984). However, it was child abuse inquiries that provided the major catalyst for venting, in a very public way, major criticisms of social work in the area of child care. While these were clearly evident from 1973 onwards following the Maria Colwell inquiry (see Parton, 1985b), they gained a new level of intensity from the mid-1980s, particularly via the Beckford, Henry, Carlile and Cleveland inquiries. The major criticisms of social work expressed in the inquiries, however, need to be understood in the changing political climate within which they were located. In many respects, they connected with and gave expression to a whole range of different critiques which were developing in the polity. While the source, force and nature of these criticisms were quite different, their net effect was to dent the confidence of social workers and to undermine the political and public support for social work in the area of child care. We can interpret the changes emanating from central government in the guise of different guidances, and the Children Act as an attempt to construct a new set of political and professional balances whereby public confidence could be re-established.

The criticisms focused around four sets of prime concerns, each of which represented very different, though overlapping, constituencies. Firstly, from the 1960s onwards, with the growth of the women's movement and the recognition of violence in the family, there was a feeling that not only may the family not be the haven it was assumed to be, but that its more powerless members, women and children, were suffering a range of abuses at the hands of men. Much of the early critical analysis and action was directed at improving the position of women and it was only in more recent years, with the growing concerns about sexual abuse, that much of the energy was directed to the position of children (Parton, C., 1990; Parton, N., 1990). What such critiques helped to effect was a severe questioning of the family 'blood-tie' and disaggregate the interests of individual family members and hence they helped support the sometimes contradictory growth during the period of the Children's Rights Movement (see Freeman, 1983; Franklin, 1986; Freeman, 1987–8). During the 1980s, this was to find a common ground with the more traditional child rescue sentiments and received their most explicit expression with the Childwatch programme and the subsequent establishment of ChildLine (see Chapter 4).

Secondly, and running in parallel, was the establishment in the late 1960s of a more obviously civil liberties critique which concentrated upon the apparent extent and nature of intervention in people's lives that was allowed, unchallenged, in the name of welfare. Initially, this was directed at the issues of mental illness and delinquency. In both, the theme proved central for developments in both critical theory and supposed progressive practice in terms of patients' rights and the justice model (see Taylor *et al.*, 1980; Ingleby, 1982; Unsworth, 1987). In the child care field, such arguments were initially associated with critiques specifically related to parental rights resolutions and the reform of the juvenile courts, but were increasingly focused around criticisms of the Place of Safety Order. More generally, they were concerned with protecting the inherent rights of 'parents' over the 'natural' sphere of the private family from state interference.

Thirdly, and very much related, we have articulated the critiques of liberal, due process lawyers who drew attention to the way the administration of justice was unfairly and often unjustly applied in various areas of child care. It was argued that the priorities of practitioners, together with the processes of decision-making failed to give due weight and consideration to the different and perhaps competing interests of family members as opposed to the concerns of the professionals themselves and their agencies which may be overly influenced by, amongst other things, protecting themselves from outside criticism.

The latter two elements made their most explicit appearance with the establishment of a number of pressure groups which put particular emphasis on the need to protect and enhance individual clients' rights. The National Association for One Parent Families, Justice for Children, the Children's Legal Centre and the Family Rights Group were perhaps the best known. They helped construct a new set of priorities and debates around child care rarely articulated in the postwar period. The Children's Legal Centre and the Family Rights Group were particularly active in trying to influence the passage of the Children Bill. They, together with the more traditional and longer-established child care voluntary organisations, provided a continuous input and dialogue with civil servants, MPs, Peers and Ministers.

During the mid-1980s, however, the parents' lobby gained its most coherent voice with the establishment of Parents Against INjustice (PAIN) (see Chapter 4). While its direct influence and lobbying upon the Children Bill was marginal, there is little doubt that its existence, even though it was a small group with few resources, was important in helping to frame some of the central issues at play during the Cleveland affair, particularly in the way it was presented in the media. As a consequence, the right for children to be left at home, free of state welfare intervention and removal, as well as the right of children to be protected from parental violence, was placed on the political and professional agenda.

Finally, however, there were a whole series of criticisms levelled at social workers for being overly soft and permissive and, as a consequence, failing to stand up to cruel parents and protect children in 'obviously' dangerous situations. Most of the child abuse inquiries produced a catalogue of events and conclusions that suggested the tragedies had been 'predictable and preventable' if only social workers had intervened authoritatively, using the full statutory powers vested in them. It was their attitudes, knowledge and use of the law which was usually found wanting.

While all quite different in terms of their social location and their focus of criticism, we can see a growing set of constituencies developing during the 1980s which emphasised the need for a greater reliance on individual rights firmly located in a reformed statutory framework where there was a greater emphasis on legalism.

The Prioritisation of Dangerousness and Likely 'Significant Harm'

The other crucial element to emerge was in terms of the criteria that were to be used for making decisions. As I demonstrated in Chapters 3 and 5, the criteria of 'dangerousness' or 'high risk' has become central. In theory, the identification of the dangerous individual or family would provide the mechanism for both ensuring that children are protected while also avoiding unwarrantable interventions. It could provide the social and professional rationale for satisfying the demands of both the child rescue lobby and the family rights lobby. Not only does it offer the promise of identifying, isolating and removing children permanently who are in high-risk situations, but also ensures that the innocent and low risk are left alone. Such an approach is fundamental to the Children Act 1989, where there is to be a clear division between the voluntary services available to children in need and the care system, the criteria for which is 'that the child concerned is *suffering, or is likely to suffer significant harm*' (31(2)(a)).

It seems that the same conditions of possibility which emphasised the need for greater legalism also provided the opportunity for the 'renaissance of dangerousness' (Bottoms, 1977; 1980) and the decline in the belief in the rehabilitative ideal (Allen, 1981). During the mid- to late 1970s, the idea of dangerousness became a major topic of discussion for a number of prestigious groups and reports on penal policy, including the Working Party on Dangerous Offenders, set up by NACRO and the Howard League for Penal Reform, of which Louis Blom-Cooper, chair of two subsequent child abuse inquiries, was a member (Floud and Young, 1981). The increased official interest in the idea of dangerousness coincided with the growing tendency in penal policy to advocate or impose more severe penalties for offenders regarded as 'really serious', while advocating a reduction in penalties for the ordinary or run-of-the-mill offender. The use of long sentences *increased* in a period when there was a general *decrease* in severity – what Bottoms called '*bifurcation*'. For bifurcation to become a reality, one has to believe in the possibility of separating the dangerous from the rest and have the expertise to carry that through. Assessments of actual and potential dangerousness, therefore, become *the* central concern and activity. As Walker commented, 'what has made the concept of dangerousness a really live issue is the shortening of the periods of detention which legislators, sentencers, and psychiatrists regard as justified on other grounds' (1978, p. 38). Similarly, beliefs about the prognosis of dangerousness are significant in the operation of the Mental Health Act 1983, and the judgements of Mental Health Review Tribunals when making decisions about compulsory confinement. In both the penal and mental health fields, where the increased emphasis is upon keeping people in the community, the dangerousness criterion seemed to offer an objective yardstick for deciding who is not safe to be let out. It has become the crucial focus in modern classificatory systems for the purposes of allocating people to different forms of social regulation. As Cohen (1985, p. 195) has argued, while 'it used to be "moral character", sometimes it was "treatability" or "security risk", now it tends to be "dangerousness" '.

Shifting Political Foundations

Such developments should not, however, be seen in isolation from the more wide-ranging changes that were taking place in the political environment. During the 1970s, an increasing disillusion was evident about the ability of the social democratic state to both effectively manage the economy and to overcome a range of social problems via the use of wide-ranging state welfare programmes. The growth of what has been termed the Radical or New Right (Levitas, 1986), during this period, led to the election of Margaret Thatcher to the leadership of the Conservative Party in 1975 and Prime Minister in 1979. For the New Right, which was to dominate political discourse throughout the 1980s, the problems in the economic and social spheres were closely interrelated. They were seen to emanate from the establishment and increasing pervasiveness of the social democratic state. For the New Right, therefore, the prime focus for change was to be the nature, priorities and boundaries of the state itself.

Two factors were seen to lie at the core of Britain's problems and local authority social workers were to be implicated in both. First the state was seen as a burden on the wealth-creating and productive sections of society. Social services, as with any state activity, generated higher taxes, increased budget deficits, acted as a disincentive to work and encouraged an overloaded class of unproductive workers. Local authorities were particularly guilty in this respect, for while central government had expanded its activity by 14 per cent in the decade up to 1972, local authorities had done so by 53 per cent. The cycle of increased state action, higher taxes, rising unemployment, growing inflation and falling investment and profitability had to be broken (Bacon and Eltis, 1978).

Secondly, it was argued that state welfare, in the hands of the new professions of which social work was perhaps *the* prime example, encouraged soft, permissive attitudes to deviance, feckleness and the actual and potentially violent. Both Margaret Thatcher (1990) and Kenneth Baker (1990) have recently argued that the erosion of the family unit and the growth in single parenthood over the last twenty years can be traced to the period of 'permissiveness' in the 1960s and early 1970s. Permissiveness did not simply drain resources, but undermined national and traditional responsibility and morality. The family was at particular risk as a consequence. The decline in the central economic and social institutions was seen to require stern measures.

The failure of, and unintended consequences of, state benevolence were not only criticised by the New Right, but was also found wanting in a number of research studies, not only in relation to crime and delinquency (Croft, 1978; Gaylin, *et al.*, 1978) but also, as we saw in Chapter 2, in relation to child abuse and child care more generally. In the context of a deteriorating economy, the research seemed to suggest that rather than concentrate efforts on time-consuming casework and wide-ranging preventative programmes, it was better to retrench and emphasise 'less harm rather than more good'. It seemed that the confident belief that even the most recalcitrant individuals could be made to improve via state interventions should be replaced by a far more pessimistic or at least 'realistic' approach.

According to Andrew Gamble (1988), recent government policies have been premised on the twin pillars of the 'free economy and strong state', which has attempted to integrate the main philosophies from both the liberal and traditional conservative tendencies within the Conservative Party.

> To preserve a free society and a free economy the authority of the state has to be preserved. Apart from its libertarian wing all strands of New Right opinion see this as essential ... what sets it apart is the combination of a traditional liberal defence of the free economy with a traditional conservative defence of state authority. (Gamble, 1988, p. 28).

Such an approach stresses the importance of individual responsibility, choice and freedom; supports the disciplines of the market against the inference of the state urging reductions in taxation and public expenditure; and, while stressing the need for a reduced state, requires a strong state to establish certain modes of family life and social discipline. The strategy has consisted of a coherent fusion of the economic and the social. It has at its root an individualised conception of social relations whereby the market is the key institution for the economic sphere, while the family is the key institution for the social sphere. The family is seen as an essentially private domain from which the state should be excluded but which should also be encouraged to take on its natural caring responsibilities for its members – including children. The role of the state should be reduced to *(a)* ensuring that the family fulfils these responsibilities and *(b)* ensuring that no-one suffers at the hands of the violent and strong. Freedom, while central, is constructed in negative terms as freedom from unnecessary interferences. Clearly, however, a fine balance has to be struck between protecting the innocent and weak and protection from unwarrantable interference – particularly from the state. In such circumstances, the law becomes crucial in defining and operationalising both 'natural' rights and 'natural' responsibilities.

For in trying to redistribute resources away from more generalised welfare provision towards law and order, and in trying to free the market and the family as the best ways of allocating resources and ensuring individual freedoms, the role of the law becomes primary. Not only must it provide the framework to underwrite contracts between individuals and between individuals and the state, it also aims to make the rationale for intervention by state officials into the natural spheres of the market and the family more explicit and their actions more accountable. While a move towards legalism may minimise state interventions, this does not necessarily follow. Individual freedoms are to be defended under the purview of the law, but when the state does intervene, it does so with the full weight and legitimacy of the law, in the guise of the court, behind it. Clearly, the number of such interventions may increase or decrease. The primary significance of a move to legalism in child care is that the form of interventions will change and, perhaps more crucially, the boundaries between the private family and the state and between different state agencies should, in theory, become much clearer. As Nik Rose (1986) has argued in a different context: 'Rights-based strategies do not transform the relations of domination between professionals and those subject to them, but redistribute status, competence and resources, amongst the professionals of unhappiness' (p. 209).

Similarly, the centrality of a binary classification based on dangerousness has become even more explicit in the political economy of the 1980s, for while the state is rolled back in some areas, it is strengthened in others. The role of the state is not so much reduced but redirected. It is the notion of dangerousness which provides the criteria whereby such a sifting process is to be articulated and legitimised. It provides the yardstick for allocating cases for the purpose of allocating scarce resources and expertise. In the context of contemporary policies, few grey areas are allowed, in theory, to be justified. For while the hard end becomes harder and subject to the full plethora of the more coercive aspects of the law, the soft end contracts.

The Emergence of Child Protection

It is this context, of the increased emphasis on legalism and dangerousness, that gives the clue as to why the issue of *child protection* came to such prominence during the 1980s. However, while it is concerns related to child protection which lie at the heart of the Children Act, it is not the case that all formalised child protection policies and practices are directly accountable to the courts. The 1988 *Working Together* guidance formally set in place child protection strategy meetings, child protection case conferences, area child protection committees and child protection registers, all of which operate under the auspices of the respective professionals and agencies and outside the explicit gaze of the court. Most social services departments have child protection officers and teams, as do the NSPCC, while many area health authorities and police forces have personnel specifically designated as specialists in child protection. The 1980s witnessed the growth of a new language and set of practices around the notion of child protection. At its simplest, we could say that the policies and professional practices previously designated as child care, which formed the basis of the Children's Departments and formed a central plank of the Seebohm reform of local authority social work in the early 1970s, have not just been redesignated, but have been reconstructed around the axis of child protection.

It is perhaps ironic that one of the net outcomes of all the criticisms directed at social workers and others to fulfil their responsibilities to protect children appropriately was to confirm and construct child protection as *the* central responsibility for social work. Thus, rather than being simply one of the range of child care services and skills that social services departments offered, it became the main priority and the one that dominated thinking and priorities (see Corby 1987).

As I have argued elsewhere (Parton, 1985b, Ch. 5), this process started in the mid-1970s following the Maria Colwell Inquiry when departments were trying to respond to the 'newly discovered' problems of battered babies, non-accidental injury and subsequently child abuse. What happened during the 1980s was that these activities were reframed in terms of child protection. A number of factors fed into this. First, the nature of the problem of child abuse was officially broadened to include neglect, physical abuse, sexual abuse, emotional abuse and grave concern. Second, and in parallel with this, public, professional and political awareness of child abuse grew considerably. This was perhaps signified most explicitly with the media launch of ChildLine in 1986. The net result was that the number of cases coming to official notice escalated tremendously. ADSS figures showed that the number of children on registers increased by 22 per cent in 1985–6 alone (*The Guardian*, 31 August 1987, p. 4), while the number of children registered on NSPCC child protection registers increased from just over one per 1000 children aged 0–16 in 1984, to 2.66 per 1000 in 1988 (NSPCC 1989; Creighton and Noyes 1989).

Third, in the fall-out from the Cleveland affair, it became clear that social workers not only had a responsibility to ensure that children did not suffer in the family, which had been the central message from previous inquiries, but that parental rights and the privacy of the family were not undermined. Child protection involved a fine balancing act. The Cleveland affair also demonstrated the need for social workers to stand back from and authoritively judge the nature and quality of information provided by other experts, particularly medics, who traditionally had been allotted considerably more status and power in decision-making. Social workers were the central profession and the social services department the lead agency in the inter-agency and inter-professional systems that were set up to respond.

Such developments were taking place in a changing economic and social environment which had a direct impact on social services departments. First, the number of potential clients grew as increasing sections of the population became marginalised from the mainstream of the economy. The numbers at or below the supplementary benefit level increased from 5 140 000 in 1974, to 9 380 000 in 1985 (17 per cent of the population). By 1985, there were 15 420 00 (29 per cent of the population) with incomes at or below, 140 per cent of the supplementary benefit levels (CPAG, 1988). This expansion largely reflected the growth in unemployment and consequently a greater proportion of the total were children and families. By 1987, there were estimated to be about two million children at or below the supplementary benefit level (Piachaud, 1987). The potential clientele for social services departments arising directly from the deteriorating material circumstances and increased social stress on children and families increased considerably.

There were also severe limits on the resources available to other state welfare agencies during the same period. Their sphere of operations changed to fit in with current political and economic imperatives. The changes in social security and the introduction of the social fund were perhaps the most evident, but also the reductions in council housing and the increases in homelessness and overcrowding. The net result was again an increase in demand upon social services departments and upon the time and expertise of social workers.

At the same time, however, it was clear that social services departments did not have the resources available to meet this vastly increased potential need. Spending on the personal social services, starting from a very low initial base, grew by 63.4 per cent between 1970–71 and 1974–5. As Ferlie and Judge (1981, pp. 313–14) commented: 'The golden age for spending on the personal social services was quite clearly the first half of the 1970s'. Growth subsequently slowed following the establishment of a 2 per cent annual growth target intended to take account of demographic changes. While the growth in departments was quite diverse, Webb and Wistow, having surveyed the patterns of spending between 1978–9 and 1983–4, concluded that '2 per cent appears to have been an insufficiently accurate estimate by even the most modest of standards of growth and resources required annually to prevent a decline in the level of service provision' (1987, pp. 169–73).

The increased actual and potential demand in the context of reduced, or, at best maintained, resources, meant that social workers and social services departments had difficulty in developing the more wide-ranging preventative strategies with children and families and clearly there was scepticism as to whether this was appropriate and feasible anyway. Priorities and choices had to be made, choices not just between the more traditional child care responsibilities and responding to child abuse, but also choices and priorities in relation to child abuse itself. It is in this respect that the assessment of dangerousness took on its particular purchase. The crucial focus becomes differentiating the 'high-risk' or dangerous cases from the others. In doing so, children can be protected, parental rights and responsibilities respected and scarce resources directed to where they will, in theory, be most effective. The comments of the Beckford Report seem particularly pertinent in this respect:

> society should sanction, in 'high-risk' cases, the removal of such children for an appreciable time. Such a policy, we calculate, might save many of the lives of the forty to fifty children who die at the hands of their parents every year, and at the same time would concentrate scarce and costly resources of Social Services Departments to the 'grey areas' of cases where something more than supervision, and something less than long-term removal, is indicated. (London Borough of Brent, 1985, p. 289)

It is in these 'grey areas' that we can see the recently constituted systems of child protection operating and where resources and skills are directed ostensibly to sift out the high risk, particularly when high risk cannot be clearly demarcated. Where there is insufficient knowledge to demonstrate that the family is safe, systems of monitoring, observation and surveillance take on a major significance. It is in these grey areas outside of the gaze of the court and the principles of legalism that the disciplinary mechanisms seem to have become so central and it is these which are crucial for understanding what child protection means in day-to-day practice. It is here that Stan Cohen's images of social control in terms of dispersal, blurred boundaries, increased invisibility and penetration between the public and the private are most suggestive. It is in these grey areas where the more voluntaristic, indirect and universal child care services have been remodelled and refashioned to meet the needs of the child protection system which emphasises much more the targeting of provisions and concentrates on the direct observation and regulation of behaviour. Nowhere is this more evident than in the replacement of day nursery provision with family centres.

However, to go further and suggest that this simply reflects the increasing pervasiveness of the modern state, and that such systems essentially emanate from the top and that they mesh neatly together, is simplistic. It is clear from all the official statements, guidances and reports that have been published in recent years, that the problems of different agencies and professions working together for different elements of the state apparatus are immense. Far from being characterised by co-operation and rationality, they are characterised by conflict, different interests and mistrust. It is just as naive for social theorists of social regulation to assume that such systems do and can work functionally together as it is for central government guidance (see Stevenson, 1989).

In fact, to assume that policy and practice for children and families can be so neatly demarcated between a care system and a voluntary system for children in need, where the demarcation is 'significant harm' or dangerousness, seems naive. Considerable research and literature is available demonstrating the problems of predicting dangerousness not only in mental health and crime, but increasingly in child abuse (see in particular Parton, 1985b, Ch. 6; Parton and Parton, 1989a; Parton, 1989; Dingwall, 1989). The knowledge base for carrying out the task is limited. It is not perhaps surprising, therefore, that by far the biggest category designated on the newly-constituted child protection registers is that of 'grave concern'. The first national statitics for England on child

protection registers for 31 March 1988 showed a total figure of
39 200 children registered, of which 37 per cent were made up
of 'grave concern' (DoH, 1989). By 31 March 1989, the total
figure had increased to just 40 700, of which 41.1 per cent was
'grave concern' (DoH, 1990). Whether and how this picture
might change when departments try to include parents and
perhaps children more seriously in the case conferences and
the broader implications of the Children Act, it is difficult to
assess.

Alternative Futures

According to Stan Cohen (1985), in a political climate dominated by the New Right and where the criteria of dangerousness becomes dominant:

> Health, education and welfare budgets are cut, certain social services
> shifted to the private sector; ideals such as treatment or rehabilitation
> become irrelevant and expensive ... what remains of the soft edge is
> understood either as just benign watchfulness or as symbolic exercises of
> legitimation, serving to 'cover' and deflect attention from the repressive
> moves happening elsewhere. (pp. 108–9)

How appropriate is this judgement for the child care services
and how far will policy and practice continue to be dominated
by child protection issues?

Cohen's scenario seems particularly pessimistic, as it fails to
take into account the variety of influences that have fed into
recent changes and the perhaps unusual pervasiveness of
more obviously social democratic influences and ideas which
were not only central to the recommendations of the Short
Report, Review of Child Care Law and the White Paper, but
continued to influence the final legislation. There are elements
of the Children Act which do seem out of step with recent
social policy initiatives. Particularly, the emphasis on partnership, participation, prevention and the positive rethink on the
purpose and uses of care. Clearly, the approach was subsequently subject to a more consumerist set of criteria but the
central philosophy was not lost. The local authority is seen as
having the major role in providing support for children in

need and some role for all children, and it is social workers and parents and, to a degree, children, who should negotiate the nature and terms of what such support might be. In many respects, the concept of prevention in the act is much broader than anything officially conceptualised previously.

There seems little doubt that the role of certain civil servants was crucial in keeping such ideas to the fore and that Rupert Hughes was crucial in this. He was the senior civil servant who drafted and guided the Bill and had been the central architect of the Review of Child Care Law and the White Paper which followed the Short Report. All were supported by the availability of a range of interrelated and consistent research reports on the problems and the way they should be overcome. Such a momentum received wide support from the various professional and voluntary agencies which campaigned for change. There is little doubt that the Act does provide the opportunity for helping parents and children in the community in a supportive and participatory way which emphasises prevention and would keep coercive interventions to a minimum. To do so, however, may require a change of attitude on the part of some practitioners and a change of organisational culture on the part of some agencies. Even so, there are sufficient of the original recommendations for change from those earlier reports in the Act to suggest it may be possible to develop a form of policy and practice which is sympathetic towards a more obviously social democratic conception of the relationship between state and family and which would provide the space for social work to develop an approach to *child care* which aims to build on the good practices evident in the 1960s.

However, it is important not to exaggerate either the significance or potential of these social democratic elements because, as we have seen, in other respects, particularly the emphasis on legalism and dangerousness, the changes are quite consistent with recent policy. Perhaps most crucially the Government made clear through the passage of the Bill that extra resources would not be available and other policy changes, particularly in the social security and housing fields, could not be compromised. In this respect, developments in this field are of minor significance in the context of the overall changes taking place in social policy which have an impact on children and families and, more importantly for our purposes, for the way social work is organised.

While it is difficult to assess at this stage how the changes and priorities articulated via the Children Act and the various guidances will redirect day-to-day practice with children and families, to get a more realistic appraisal it is also important to look at changes in related areas. Apart from changes in social security, housing, NHS and education, the impact of the community charge on local authority services is only just beginning to be grappled with. However most crucially for social services departments are the implications of the White Paper on Community Care (1989) which is incorporated in the NHS Bill 1990. Both the changes arising from the Children Act and those from the White Paper were due to be introduced in 1991.[1] Certainly, the Government sees the two as being compatible, for in the White Paper it is stated that 'The Government is pursuing separately in the Children Bill ... a major reform of children's services ... the two programmes are consistent and complementary, and taken together, set a fresh agenda and new challenges for social services authorities for the next decade' (para. 1.3). It similarly states that 'there is no intention of creating a division between child care and community care services; the full range of social services authority functions should continue to form a coherent whole' (para. 1.3). While nothing further is stated, it is evident that many of the central principles of New Right political economy and philosophy have been brought to bear on this reorganisation of services for elderly and handicapped people in a far more thoroughgoing way. In terms of expenditure, rather than children, it has been the growth in the numbers of elderly people assumed to be dependent upon the state for care that has been the major challenge confronting the social services departments both over the past decade and into the 1990s.

The proposals take further the main thrust of policy over recent years in terms of reducing the role of local authorities as service providers, while encouraging the growth of informal, voluntary and private welfare. Alan Walker (1989) has argued that it provides a specific illustration of four of the main manifestations of the New Right philosophy that has dominated the Thatcher Government since 1979, 'antagonism to-wards public expenditure on the welfare state, increasing emphasis on self-help and family support, extension of the market and commodification of social relations, and the general breakdown of the social democratic consensus' (p. 204).

The direction of change for social services had been indi-cated by Patrick Jenkin, the Secretary of State for Social Services, in a speech to the ADSS in 1980. He described social services departments as 'a long stop for the very special needs going beyond the range of voluntary services' (Jenkin, 1980). The scenario was developed further by Norman Fowler, Jenkin's successor as Secretary of State, in a speech to the 1984 Joint Social Services Conference. He argued that there are three paramount responsibilities of social services depart-ments: to take a comprehensive strategic view of all the sources of care available in the area; to recognise that the direct provision of services is only part of the local pattern; and that a major part of their function is in promoting and supporting the fullest possible participation of other different sources of care. The fundamental role of the state is 'to back up and develop the assistance which is given by the private and voluntary support' (Fowler, 1984, p. 13). The role for social services departments was clearly seen as residual. But not as previously – residual in the context of the other universal statutory services, but residual to the family, com-munity and the market. The orthodox role of the social services departments in services for elderly and handicapped people should increasingly be moving away from providing and funding to one of enabling, subsidising and regulating.

> The Conservative blueprint for social policy in the 1990s does not so much resemble a wholesale abdication of state responsibility for either funding or provision of services, as, rather, a reformulation of what those responsibilities really mean. Service boundaries, resource allocation and assessment and the means to 'police' and review each are key deter-minants of the new welfare. (McCarthy, 1989, p. 46)

For all the hopes and aspirations evident in the Children Act, it is difficult to avoid the conclusion that it will be these criteria which dominate local authority services to children and families as well as other client groups.

Conclusions

What is perhaps ironic in the light of all the criticisms made of social work, particularly via the child abuse inquiries, is not just that social work is still seen to have a role in the reconstructed set of balances in child protection work, but has *the* central role. Even though the practices and knowledge base of social work had been seen by many as untrustworthy, far from being marginalised it now, more than ever, moves centre stage. While the various guidances all stress the crucial need for inter-agency and inter-professional co-operation, and the police are seen as having a much more crucial role than previously, it is the social services department which is the lead agency and the local authority social worker who is the focal professional, particularly in the crucial activity of assessment for the purposes of identifying dangerous individuals and families.

What the Cleveland Report argued in relation to sexual abuse, and what the parents' lobby had stressed throughout was that 'medical' assessment alone was quite inadequate. What was required was a thorough 'social' assessment of families in terms of their history, relationships and the views and experiences of individual family members – both parents and children. In order to judge whether a family could be deemed safe for a child, a thorough insight was required into the subjective reality of family life, but mediated via a framework which could be presented to the court as 'evidence' if required. While medical expertise should make an important contribution to such assessments and any subsequent judgements, it could only be partial in this respect. Nor were there any readily available checklists or scientifically proven criteria which could be learned for making such decisions. While these might be helpful in framing questions and coming to conclusions, as the DoH guidelines (1988) on undertaking a comprehensive assessment for the purposes of protecting children and the Children Act stress, they could be no substitute for *professional judgements* which rely on a much more fluid, interpretive, knowledge base.

This is not to say that social workers are to be allowed free-rein and wide-scale discretion. Such professional judgements are to take place in the context of the different health and welfare agencies, including the police, working together. Similarly, they are not to be given the ultimate responsibility for transferring parental powers – these are to rest clearly with the court. However, the type of 'evidence' and the form of expertise which is most vital in helping courts make such sensitive decisions is to be derived more than any other from social work. Not only will it be local authority social workers who will apply for Emergency Protection Orders, Child Assessment Orders and Care Orders, but the independent experts who the courts will draw upon for their advice in the guise of guardians *ad litem* will also be social workers. This reliance upon social workers for the purpose of making such crucial decisions continues to give some political commentators, like Teresa Gorman MP, as we saw in the previous chapter, cause for particular concern. Similarly, while the lack of resources for training, guardians and social services departments, may put the whole system at risk, what cannot be denied is that social work and the social work discourse is central. Thus, while the reconstituted system of child care is indeed subject to an increased emphasis on legalism and accountability to the court, there can be no doubt that the forms of knowledge and the types of expertise which are seen as crucial in helping to make decisions are crucially dependent upon social work. It is social workers who are constituted as experts in the social.

It is the tension between, and the ongoing search to find the appropriate balance between, this more explicit legalism while giving social workers sufficient room to carry out these social assessments for the purposes of identifying dangerousness which was the central issue throughout the debates at the heart of the Children Act 1989. It is not adequate to simply argue that either legalism or the disciplinary techniques of the 'psy' complex won the day – it was the balance and relationship between the two that was crucial and in this respect we can see some important developments.

If the emergence of child abuse as a problem requiring a response was conceptualised during the 1970s as a disease or 'medico-social' problem requiring the expertise of doctors, particularly paediatricians, and social workers, the increasing concern with child protection indicates something rather different. The discourse of child protection sees it as a socio-legal issue where social workers continue to be central, but where the agencies of the law (courts, police and lawyers) play a crucial role in helping to constitute what the problem is and what should be done about it. In the process, the nature of social work is itself refashioned.

What is also suggested is that social work takes on a crucial constitutive role in relation to how we experience family life which is the most private and intimate sphere in modern society. According to David Held (1987, p. 293), the sphere of the intimate refers to those circumstances of everyday life where 'people live out their personal lives without systematically harmful consequences for those around them'. But who is to decide what is harmful, how harmful consequences can be avoided and who is to guarantee the absence of harm? What I have argued in this book is that it is primarily social work that has this role and that it is professional judgements that constitute particular instances of harm. In the process, we are reminded that the 'freedoms' of family life, far from being 'natural', are constantly governed by a host of assumptions embedded in the practices of public life about what constitutes proper behaviour, and these crucially influence what we regard as private (Rose, 1990). What the recent, very public, debates about sexual abuse and parental rights have provided is not simply a vehicle for reconstructing and rethinking the nature of child protection practices and social work, but the form and nature of the family itself. If governing the family is to be successful, it means that most of us must know what good child care and good parenthood 'is' and what constitutes normal family relationships without ever having contact with a social worker. In attempting to delineate the boundaries between the public and the private, the state and the family, social work is confirmed in a crucial mediating role. At the same time, social workers' 'professional judgements' become central in constituting the nature of 'normal' family relations.

Notes

Chapter 1

1. Hall, Land, Parker and Webb (1975) applied a systems model (see Easton 1965 and Jenkins 1978) of the political process to six case studies of change in social policy to try and advance 'propositions about what determines the priority that an issue attains' (Hall *et al.*, 1975, p. 475) and hence why some issues become of significance for social policy initiatives and others do not. Phoebe Hall has since used a similar approach in her study of the reorganisation of social service departments in the late 1960s early 1970s (Hall, 1976). From the comparative study of six diverse case studies in the field of social policy, they argued that what is crucial is how far the authorities believe an issue measures up against the three broad criteria of legitimacy, feasibility and support.

   In order to judge legitimacy, we should ask 'is this an issue with which government considers it should be concerned?' (p. 476). The answer will depend upon features internal to the system, for example, government ideologies; and external factors, for example, the state of opinion amongst the general public and important interest groups.

   Three elements are identified in terms of feasibility in order to assess whether it is considered feasible that something can be done (pp. 479–80). First, 'feasibility is, in its broadest sense, determined by the prevailing structure and distribution of theoretical and technical knowledge' (p. 479). Second, the concept 'is not entirely independent of who does the judging' and, third, feasibility 'is rarely immediately apparent'. Judgements have to be made which have as their particular concerns questions about resources, collaboration and administrative capacity.

   The third general criterion, support, is concerned broadly with who in the population is likely to be affected and with what consequences for the government standing. 'Because policy change alters, or is thought to alter, some features of an existing distribution of power, influence, status or values, inevitably it will create some satisfaction and some discontent. The notion of the political feasibility of an issue is closely connected with

215

its implications for this balance. Two considerations determine how it is estimated by authorities. The first is *whose* discontents and *whose* satisfactions are involved, and the second is the general state of the reservoir of support' (p. 483).

Hall *et al.* also argue that the degree of success of an issue in being seen to meet these three general criteria will be significantly affected by the 'image' attached to it. Six such elements are identified: (*a*) whether the issue is associated with other issues and hence may have wider implications and scope; (*b*) how far does the issue seem of crisis proportions requiring a swift response; (*c*) whether it is believed to be getting worse and may constitute the 'tip of the iceberg' thus requiring preventive measures; (*d*) which individuals or groups are seen to be associated with the issue – what is the prestige, expertise and power of those sponsoring it; (*e*) are the 'facts' and information available to substantiate the existence and urgency of the issue to be addressed; and (*f*) does the issue accord with the prevailing ideology of those in power and how far is it seen as non-ideological and thus a priority across a broad political spectrum which on other issues may be in sharp opposition.

Chapter 2

1. The membership of the working party was: Professor R. A. Parker, School of Applied Social Studies, University of Bristol; Professor H. K. Bevan, Faculty of Law, University of Hull; Mrs Mary Evans, previously Inspector of Special Education with ILEA, then Co-Director of the Schools Council Project, 'The Education of Disturbed Pupils'; Mr Michael Fitzgerald, Child Care Advisor; Dr Robert Holman, Community Social Worker, Church of England Children's Society; Dr Iris Knight, Senior Clinical Medical Officer, Essex Area Health Department; Mr Martin Manby, Assistant Director (Field Work), Islington Social Services Department; Dr Mia Kellmer-Pringle, Director of the National Children's Bureau; Miss Jane Rowe, previously Director of ABAA, then researcher on the 1975 Children Act and freelance worker; Mr George Thomas, Director of Social Services, London Borough of Harrow; The Baroness Young, former Chairman of Oxford City Children's Committee.
2. The reasons for the decline in practice standards were seen to reside firstly with the loss of specialised skills with the introduction of the generic worker who was expected to cover a range of expertise and client groups; secondly the high turnover of staff arising in particular from the promotion, secondment and movement of social workers at the time of, and subsequent to, the reorganisation of social service departments in 1971 and local government in 1974; thirdly the rising level of demand for

social services and hence the increasing pressure of work on social workers; and fourthly the growth in size and complexity of the new departments, together with insufficient resources to meet the higher level of service required.

3. The discussion papers covered: prevention and rehabilitation; voluntary reception into care; grounds for compulsory admission and parental rights resolutions; compulsory admissions to care and parental rights resolutions – legal effects; supervision orders; Place of Safety and interim care orders; court procedure and related issues; parental rights resolution procedure; discharge of care orders and ending parental rights resolution; leaving care; access to children in care; powers and duties of local authorities in respect of children in care and other children in need.

Chapter 3

1. Jasmine Beckford died on 5 July 1984 at the age of four and a half at the home of Morris Beckford, her step-father, and Beverley Lorrington, her mother, in North West London, of cerebral contusions and subdural haemorrhage, as a direct result of severe manual blows inflicted on the child's head. She was also emaciated as a result of chronic undernourishment. She and her sister, Louise, were made the subject of Care Orders to the London Borough of Brent in August 1981 after both children had been admitted to hospital with severe injuries, including a broken arm and broken femur. From September 1981 to April 1982 they had been living with foster parents but were returned 'home on trial' in April 1982, still being subject to the Care Order. When Jasmine was discharged from hospital after being taken into care, she weighed 18lbs 14oz. Seven months later when she was returned home after being fostered she weighed 25lbs 5oz. When she died she weighed 23lbs. Morris Beckford was convicted of manslaughter and was sentenced to ten years' imprisonment, while Beverley Lorrington pleaded guilty to child neglect and was sentenced to eighteen months' imprisonment. At the trial, Judge Pigot said that the social worker, Gun Wahlstrom, had shown a 'naivete almost beyond belief' and called the Assistant Director of Social Services to be examined on oath about the work of his department in relation to the case. The panel of inquiry was set up by Brent Borough Council and Brent Health Authority.

2 In the 1985–6 parliamentary session, Dennis Walters MP introduced a Private Member's Bill in response to the Beckford case which would have required social workers to obtain the consent of a magistrate before a child in care could be returned to its parents. This was subsequently watered down when the Government took it over, as the Government stressed it was currently working on its much more widespread child care

reforms which would take such issues into account and the original Bill as drafted would have led to unnecessary expense. In the event, the Children and Young Persons' (Amendment) Act 1986 for the first time made parents parties to the case and introduced tighter regulations for when children were returned home on trial. These came into effect on 1 June 1989 as the Accommodation of Children (Charge and Control) Regulations, S1 2183 of 1988. Before returning a child on a Care Order home, the local authority had to seek the written views of various parties including the district health authority, and the person receiving the child (usually the parent) was required sign a written agreement that the child could be removed if the authority was not satisfied the placement was furthering the child's welfare, and set out the arrangements for social worker visits. The authority was required to visit every six weeks in the first year and every three months thereafter. Also the person visiting must 'so far as practicable see the child alone on each visit' (see Rutherford, 1986; Drewry, 1987).

3. It seems that the original idea for a Child Assessment Order had been outlined by Cyril Greenland to the Beckford Inquiry and followed closely a clause in the Child and Family Services Act 1984 in Ontario. While such a legal mechanism was not appropriate for the recommendation to overcome the circumstances in that case, Louis Blom-Cooper, who chaired both inquiries, thought it would be very pertinent to the circumstances outlined in the Carlile case.

4. Interestingly two recent child abuse inquiries do not seem to have been so circumscribed. The report into the death of Liam Johnson (London Borough of Islington, 1989) could find no serious errors of judgement in the way in which the professionals, and particularly those in social services, handled the case. It explicitly took issue with a statement from the Minister of State, David Mellor, prior to the inquiry and demonstrated that there was no evidence that 'something went wrong'. The report went further and argued that the attitude that all violence to children is predictable and preventable was a dangerous attitude for 'the reality is very different' (p. 10). Similarly it stated that 'if we have reached a stage at which even limited contact with social services is sufficient to raise a hunt for scapegoats, the implications for these services is appalling' (p. 11).

The panel of inquiry report into the death of Stephanie Fox (London Borough of Wandsworth, 1990) concluded that while a lack of resources alone was not the only reason for the child's death it did affect the services delivered and materially had an impact on the quality and nature of both day-care and social work provided.

Neither report, after assessing the evidence, saw it as appropriate to allocate blame for the tragedy in an individualised way to the professionals involved.

Chapter 4

1. The Minister also informed the House that he was in the process of arranging with local authorities and the NSPCC 'for the collection of national statistics on child abuse' (*Hansard*, HC, 9 July 1987, Col. 526). The lack of such statistics had been raised on numerous occasions and was to surface as a significant issue in the Cleveland Report. While the NSPCC had published regular statistics on the registers for which it was responsible, these only covered 9 per cent of the child population and were not necessarily typical. While many recognised the problems in the variability of such figures and the fact that they represented an insight into social and professional response rather than the size and nature of the problem, it was generally agreed that there would be value in having such national material readily available. Such a development could be seen to represent a further twist in the computation and calculation of child abuse and thus the way it was to be constituted.

   The Minister also said that preparation of the final version of guidance to the agencies who should work together in this field was pressing ahead and would be issued 'as soon as possible, after taking account of any lessons from Cleveland and the current inquiries into the deaths of Tyra Henry and Kimberley Carlile' (*Hansard*, HoC, 9 July 1987, Col. 526). Also the standing medical advisory committee had been asked to prepare guidance for doctors on the clinical diagnosis of sexual abuse and practice guidelines were also to be prepared for social workers and nurses, including health visitors (see Chapter 5 where these guidelines are discussed at length).

2. The five cases established three separate breaches of the European Convention: a failure to consult parents before decisions to end access were taken; the inability of the parents to challenge such decisions in the courts; and the undue delay in the decision-making processes in one of the cases. The European Court also identified a fourth area where it felt the Government needed to act: the fact that local councils could use wardship proceedings to keep children in care, even though a juvenile court had discharged the order when such a procedure was unavailable to parents.

3. Mrs Justice Butler-Sloss, then aged fifty-three, had been a judge since 1979, and was the sister of the then Lord Chancellor, Lord Havers. She had been a Conservative parliamentary candidate in 1959 and was Registrar in the Family Division from 1970 to 1979. She was made a Dame in 1979 and was Vice-President of the Medico-Legal Society. For several years, she had been the Family Division Liaison Judge for the North-Eastern circuit, sitting in Newcastle, Leeds and Sheffield. She had also sat in Teeside (Cleveland).

4. The Report completely failed to address the question of how many of the

children had been abused and the issue returned with a vengeance early the following year when eleven paediatricians wrote to *the Guardian* claiming that 'more than 90 per cent' of the 121 Cleveland child sex abuse case diagnoses were correct (see *Guardian*, 18 February 1989, Letters, 'Cleveland childcare mythology must be exploded', p. 20) and led to a re-emergence of many of the previous allegations and counter-allegations in the media for the next three weeks. It was also announced that the medical findings which underlay this support for Dr Higgs and Dr Wyatt were to be published in *The Lancet* towards the end of 1989. The article has not yet been published. However, the issues became embroiled in attempts by the Northern Regional Health Authority to end Dr Higgs' temporary secondment to a Newcastle Hospital and prevent her working in Cleveland and from child sex abuse work anywhere in the region in the future. While the case went to the Court of Appeal, it was eventually settled out of court in April 1990 when Dr Higgs accepted a permanent post in Durham.

5. Members of the study group that met at the CIBA Foundation between September 1981 and March 1984 were:
Dr Arnon Bentovim,* Consultant Psychiatrist, the Hospital for Sick Children, Great Ormond Street, London; Det. Chief Sup. John Bisset, Devon and Cornwall Constabulary; Professor Sydney Brandon, Department of Social Psychiatry, University of Leicester; Mr James Christopherson,* Department of Social Administration and Social Work, University of Nottingham; Dr Christine Cooper, Children's Department, The Royal Victoria Infirmary, Newcastle-upon-Tyne; Dr Hugh de la Haye Davies, Police Surgeon, Northampton; Dr Tilman Furniss, Department of Psychological Medicine, The Hospital for Sick Children, Great Ormond Street, London; Mr Paul Griffiths, NSPCC, Birmingham; Professor Lionel A. Hersor, Children and Adolescents' Department, The Maudesley Hospital, London; Dr Anthony D. M. Jackson, Consultant Paediatrician, The London Hospital; Ms Helena A. Hennedy, Barrister-at-Law, London; Dr Margaret A. Lynch,* Department of Paediatrics, Guy's Hospital, London; Ms Carolyn Okell Jones,* Child Guidance Training Centre, London; Dr Ruth Porter, Deputy Director, CIBA Foundation; Mr Dennis Tunney, Assistant Chief Probation Officer, London; Mr Richard White,* Solicitor, London.

6. In its first year, ChildLine counselled more than 22 000 children and the largest category was sexual abuse (5865 cases) followed by physical

* All of these also served on the BASPCAN Sub-Committee on Child Sexual Abuse, chaired by Ms Carolyn Okell Jones, which produced the BASPCAN (1981) *Child Sexual Abuse* pamphlet. The only other two members on the BASPCAN sub-committee who were not members of the CIBA Foundation Study Group were Dr Brendan MacCarthy, a child psychiatrist and psychoanalyst, and Ms Jean Renvoize, an author.

abuse (3838 cases) with the overwhelming location being the home and main perpetrator the father. ChildLine answered about 700 of the 8000 calls that came in most days (ChildLine, 1987).

7. The full directions of the memorandum of 29 May 1987 were:
'In order to safeguard the welfare of children, pending guidelines from the Joint Child Abuse Committee, the following steps should be taken in case of alleged or suspected sexual abuse:

(1) Medical examinations should be carried out in hospital by a consultant paediatrician.

(2) Initial protective action should be via admission to hospital. Where the consultant paediatrician is of the opinion that there is medical evidence of sexual abuse, an immediate Place of Safety Order should be taken to protect the child's interests during investigation.

(3) The police should be informed in all cases. Every effort should be made to conduct a joint police/social worker investigation with the child.

(4) The obtaining of a disclosure from the child should be the key focus. The child should be interviewed as promptly as possible, preferably not in the presence of the parent, which may inhibit disclosure. Parental access may, therefore, need to be suspended or restricted during initial investigations.

(5) Any siblings should also be seen and medically examined.

(6) Repeat examinations should be avoided. Where a statement is available from a clinician, it is not necessary for the police surgeon to re-examine the child. Forensic tests should be arranged in consultation with the consultant paediatrician, who will be able to assist the police surgeon as necessary.' (Secretary of State, 1988, p. 65)

8. Under the Family Law Reform Act 1969, a young person of 16 years was allowed to consent to medical treatment as if of full age. The case of *Gillick* v. *West Norfolk & Wisbech AHA* (1985), 1 FLR224, established that a child under sixteen years had legal capacity to consent to such treatment if s/he possessed the requisite maturity and understanding of the nature of the treatment proposed and its consequences.

Chapter 5

1. In 1986, a Place of Safety Order was to be considered 'to prevent immediate harm and allow for proper consideration of how to ensure the continued safety and welfare of the child' (para. 1.1), while in 1988 it was to be considered 'when it *is* suspected that a child *is being ill-treated or is in some other grave danger* ... to secure the immediate removal of a child from home' (para. 2.8, my emphasis).

2. The guide said that agencies should ensure that 'social workers involved in child protection work are able to:

- observe, identify and describe those factors which suggest that harm or abuse has taken place or is likely to occur;
- investigate allegations or suspicions of abuse, and assess objectively, both initially and comprehensively, the needs of the child and the family, including the risks of abuse and the need for protection;
- understand and explain their role, and plan, monitor and evaluate their intervention;
- involve parents as fully as possible in the process;
- seek the child's wishes and take them into account, having regard to his or her age, understanding, cultural and religious background;
- undertake direct work with children with skill, using play and an activity-based approach where appropriate;
- record carefully and be able to prepare thorough and *objective* reports, to be used not only in the case conference and the courts but as the basis for longer term decision-making;
- inform, involve and work with other agencies and professionals in accordance with agreed procedures and the needs of the child and family;
- keep up to date with child care legislation, practice and research;
- ensure that their own values and prejudices do not detract from their professional *objectivity*;
- use supervision and consultation appropriately, including consultation on cultural and ethnic issues.' (DoH, 1988, p. 10, my emphasis)

Chapter 6

1. *Welfare checklist to which the Court should give particular regard when considering whether to make an Order*
   (*a*) the ascertainable wishes and feelings of the child concerned (considered in the light of his age and understanding);
   (*b*) his physical, emotional and educational needs;
   (*c*) the likely effect on him of any change in his circumstances;
   (*d*) his age, sex, background and any characteristics of his which the court considers relevant;
   (*e*) any harm which he has suffered or is at risk of suffering;
   (*f*) how capable each of his parents, and any other person in relation to whom the court considers the question to be relevant, is of meeting his needs;
   (*g*) the range of powers available to the court under the Act in the proceedings in question.
2. Subsequently, the AMA carried out a survey exercise of authorities to estimate the additional costs that would be necessary to properly implement the legislation. If the average figures were grossed up to

national levels, it estimated additional costs of the order of £168 million. It estimated an average increase of 67 per cent which local authorities might be expected to incur when the Act became fully operational (see Jones, 1990).

3. *Lord Mottistone's Amendment (No. 44) on a Child Assessment Order*

(1) Where any local authority, NSPCC officer or authorised person (the 'applicant') applies to the court for an order under this section with respect to a child, the court may make the order if it is satisfied that there is reasonable cause to believe that:

(*a*) the child concerned may be suffering harm; and

(*b*) any of the following have failed or refuse to produce the child for prompt medical or psychiatric examination on request –

(i) a parent;

(ii) any person who is not a parent but who has parental responsibility for him;

(iii) any person with whom the child is living.

(2) An Order obtained under this section (Child Assessment Order) means that the child shall be produced by any of the following:

(*a*) parent;

(*b*) any person who is not a parent but who has parental responsibility for him;

(*c*) any person with whom the child is living, for medical or psychiatric examination.

(3) In this Act 'medical or psychiatric examination' may include developmental assessment, and may be extended to further examination after the initial one.

(4) A Child Assessment Order shall specify the time and place of the assessment which shall take place within 24 hours.

(5) Where there is a failure to comply with a Child Assessment Order without reasonable cause, the applicant shall immediately apply for an Emergency Protection Order.

(6) In this section 'the applicant' means a local authority social worker or an NSPCC officer, or an authorised person.

4. *Child Production Notice – Drafted by BAAF, the Children's Legal Centre and Family Rights Group and tabled by Keith Vaz (Labour) at HoC Report Stage*

(1) Where a local authority is making enquiries with respect to the child under Section 39(1)(c) and any officer of the authority

(*a*) is refused access to the child concerned; or

(*b*) is denied information as to the child's whereabouts the authority may serve a notice on:-

(i) the child's parents

(ii) any person who is not a parent of his but who has parental responsibility for him

   (iii) any other person with whom the child is living requiring him to produce the child to the person named in the notice at the time and place specified in the notice which shall be within 24 hours.

 (2) The Secretary of State shall make regulations governing the form of the notice to be served under this section which may in particular make provision for:-

  (*a*) the requirements for service of the notice

  (*b*) the notice to include:-

   (i) a statement that an unreasonable failure to comply with the notice may constitute grounds for the granting of an emergency protection order;

   (ii) details of the time and place at which application will be made for an emergency protection order if the notice is not complied with;

   (iii) details of the person or persons to whom the child is to be produced which may include a registered medical practitioner, registered nurse or registered health visitor and must include an officer of the local authority.

Chapter 7

1. At the time of writing, however, in late June/early July 1990, it seemed increasingly likely that the introduction of the community care proposals were going to be postponed or, more probably, 'phased in'. It had become increasingly clear as 1990 progressed that the Government was facing major political problems over it's introduction of the community charge or poll tax. The Government feared the introduction of the new system of financing community care, where the local authority would be the lead agency, would make it even more likely that the level of community charge may be further increased thus making it even more of a political liability. Such timing, just one year before a general election, for a Government that was already lagging in the polls, was seen as too much of a political risk. Short term political imperatives therefore needed to take priority over longer-term policy development.

Bibliography

Adcock, M. White, R. and Rowlands, O. *The Administrative Parent – A Study of the Assumption of Parental Rights and Duties* (London: BAAF, 1983).

Aldridge, M. 'Social Work and the News Media – A Hopeless Case?', *British Jnl. Social Work*, 20(6) (1990).

Allen, F. A. *The Decline of the Rehabilitative Ideal: Penal Policy and Social Purpose* (London: Yale University Press, 1981).

Area Review Committee for Lambeth, Southwark and Lewisham, *Report of the Inquiry into the Death of Doreen Mason* (1989).

Armstrong, D. *Political Anatomy of the Body: Medical Knowledge in Britain in the Twentieth Century* (Cambridge: Cambridge University Press, 1983).

Armstrong, D. 'Foucault and the Problem of Human Anatomy', in G. Scrambler (ed.), *Sociological Theory and Medical Sociology* (London: Tavistock, 1987).

Association of London Authorities, *Children First* (London: ALA, 1989).

Bacon, R. and Eltis, W. *Britain's Economic Problem: Too Few Producers*, 2nd edn (London: Macmillan, 1978).

Baher, E. Hyman, C. Jones, C. Jones, R. Kerr, A. and Mitchell, R. *At Risk: An Account of the Work of the Battered Child Research Department* (London: RKP, 1976).

Baker, K. *The Disraeli Lecture* (1990).

BBC, 'Childwatch – National Survey on Child Abuse', BBC Press Briefing, 9 July (unpublished, 1987).

BBC, *Childwatch: A Briefing* (London: BBC, unpublished, 1986).

Becker, S. and MacPherson, S. *Public Issues and Private Pain: Poverty, Social Work and Social Policy* (London: Social Services Insight Books, 1988).

Bell, S. *When Salem came to the Boro: The True Story of the Cleveland Child Abuse Crisis* (London: Pan Books, 1988).

Bentovim, A. Elton, A. Hildebrand, J. Tranter, M. and Vizard, E. *Child Sexual Abuse within the Family* (London: Wright, 1988).

Berridge, D. *Children's Homes* (Oxford: Basil Blackwell, 1985).

225

Bishop, M. (with A. Fry), 'The Trial of Working through a Nightmare', *Social Work Today*, Vol. 19, No. 44. (7 July 1988) 12–13.

Blom-Cooper, L. 'Legal Lessons from Cleveland', *New Law Journal*, Vol. 138, No. 6365 (15 July 1988) 492.

Blom-Cooper L. (with T. Philpott), 'What Social Work Must Learn from Carlile', *Community Care*, No. 693, (7 January 1988) 12–15.

Bottoms, A. E. 'Reflections on the Renaissance of Dangerousness', *Howard Journal of Penology and Crime Prevention*, Vol. 16, No. 2 (1977) 70–96.

Bottoms, A. E. 'An Introduction to the Coming Crisis', in A. E. Bottoms and R. H. Preston (eds), *The Coming Penal Crisis* (Edinburgh: Scottish Academic Press, 1980).

Bottoms, A. E. 'Neglected Features of Contemporary Penal Systems', in D. Garland and P. Young (eds), *The Power to Punish: Contemporary Penality and Social Analysis* (London: Heinemann, 1983).

Bronfenbrenner, U. *The Ecology of Human Development* (Harvard: Harvard University Press, 1979).

British Association for the Study and Prevention of Child Abuse and Neglect, *Child Sexual Abuse* (BASPCAN, 1981).

British Association of Social Workers, *The Central Child Abuse Register* (Birmingham: BASW, 1978).

British Association of Social Workers, *The Management of Child Abuse* (Birmingham: BASW, 1985).

British Medical Journal Editorial, 'Sexual Assaults on Children', *British Medical Journal*, Vol. 2, (16 December 1961) 1623–4.

British Medical Journal Editorial, 'Incest and Family Disorder', *British Medical Journal*, Vol. 2, No. 5810 (13 May 1972).

Butler-Sloss, Lord Justice E. *The Brian Jackson Memorial Lecture*, (Huddersfield Polytechnic, 4 November 1988).

Byrne, K. and Bloxham, R. 'When Sensitivity is on Trial', *Social Services Insight* (20–27 April 1986) 20–1.

Campbell, B. *Unofficial Secrets: Child Sexual Abuse – The Cleveland Case* (London: Virago, 1988).

Channer, Y. and Parton, N. 'Racism, Cultural Relativism and Child Protection', in the Violence Against Children Study Group, *Taking Child Abuse Seriously: Contemporary Issues in Child Protection Theory and Practice* (London: Unwin Hyman, 1990).

Chant, J. (with A. Fry), 'Time to Dim the Blue Light of Dramatic Intervention', *Social Work Today*, Vol. 19, No. 44 (7 July 1989) 16–17.

ChildLine, 'ChildLine: The First Year', Press release (30 October 1987).

The CIBA Foundation (ed. by Ruth Porter), *Child Sexual Abuse within the Family* (London: Tavistock, 1984).

Clarke, J. 'Social Work in the Welfare State', *Block 3. Unit 14. Social Problems and Social Welfare*, D211 (Milton Keynes: Open University Press, 1988).

Clarke, J. Langan, M. and Lee, P. 'Social Work: The Conditions of Crisis', in P. Carlen and M. Collinson (eds), *Radical Issues in Criminology* (Oxford: Martin Robinson, 1980).

Clayden, G. 'Anal Appearances and Child Sex Abuse', *The Lancet* (14 March 1987) 620–621.

Cohen, S. *Visions of Social Control: Crime, Punishment and Classification* (Cambridge: Polity Press, 1985).

Cohen, S and Scull, A. (eds), *Social Control and the State: Historical and Comparative Essays* (Oxford: Basil Blackwell, 1983).

Comment, 'Social Work in Trust', *Community Care*, No. 590 (12 December 1985) 1.

Community Care, 'Lack of Funds May Blunt Act', No. 790 (23 November 1989) 6.

Conrad, P. and Schneider, J. W. *Deviance and Medicalisation: From Badness to Sickness* (London: C. V. Mosby, 1980).

Cooper, J. *The Creation of the British Personal Social Services 1962–74* (London: Heinemann, 1983).

Corby, B. *Working with Child Abuse: Social Work Practice and the Child Abuse System* (Milton Keynes. Open University Press 1987).

Court, J. 'The Battered Child: (1) Historical and Diagnostic Reflection (2) Reflection on Treatment', *Medical Social Work*, No. 22 (1969) 11–20.

CPAG, *Poverty: The Facts* (London: Child Poverty Action Group, 1988).

Creighton, S. J. and Noyes, P. *Child Abuse Trends in England and Wales 1983–1987* (London: NSPCC, 1989).

Crewdson, R. and Martin, C. 'The Great Ormond Street Policy on Video Recordings', *Family Law*, Vol. 19. (April 1989) 161–2.

Croft, J. *Research in Criminal Justice*, Home Office Research Study, No. 44 (London: HMSO, 1978).

Dale, P. Davies, M. Morrison, T. and Waters, J. *Dangerous Families: Assessment and Treatment of Child Abuse* (London: Tavistock, 1986).

Dartington Research Unit, *Place of Safety Orders: A Study for the DHSS Review of Child Care Law* (University of Bristol, 1985).

DES, *Working Together for the Protection of Children from Abuse: Procedures within the Education Service*, Circular No. 4/88 (1988).

DoH, *Protecting Children: A Guide for Social Workers Undertaking a Comprehensive Assessment* (London: HMSO, 1988).

DoH, *Working with Child Sexual Abuse: Guidelines for Training Social Services Staff* (London: DoH, 1989a).

DoH, *Survey of Children and Young Persons on Child Protection Registers Year Ending 31 March 1988 England* (London: HMSO, 1989b).

DoH, *Children and Young Persons on Child Protection Registers Year Ending 31 March 1989 England: Provisional Feedback* (1990).

DHSS, *The Battered Baby*, CMO2/70 (1970).

DHSS, *Battered Babies*, LASSL 26/72 (1972).

DHSS, *Non-Accidental Injury to Children*, LASSL (74)(13) (1974).

DHSS, *Non-Accidental Injury to Children: Area Review Committees*, LASSL (76)(2) (1976a).

DHSS, *Non-Accidental Injury to Children: The Police and Case Conferences*, LASSL (76)(26) (1976b).

DHSS, *Child Abuse: The Register System* LA/C396/23D (1978).

DHSS, *Child Abuse: Central Register Systems*, LASSL (80)4, HN(80), (20 August 1980).

DHSS, *Child Abuse: A Study of Inquiry Reports 1973–1981* (London: HMSO, 1982).

DHSS, *Review of Child Care Law: Report to Ministers of an Inter-departmental Working Party* (London: HMSO, 1985a).

DHSS, *Social Work Decisions in Child Care: Recent Research Findings and their Implications* (London: HMSO, 1985b).

DHSS, *Child Abuse: Working Together. A Draft Guide to Arrangements for Inter-Agency Co-operation for the Protection of Children* (London: DHSS, 1986).

DHSS, *Working Together: A Guide to Inter-Agency Co-operation for the Protection of Children from Abuse* (London: DHSS, HMSO, 1988a).

DHSS, *Diagnosis of Child Sexual Abuse: Guidance for Doctors* (London: DHSS, HMSO, 1988b).

DHSS, *Child Protection: Guidance for Senior Nurses, Health Visitors and Midwives* (London: DHSS, HMSO, 1988c).

DHSS. *Working Together for the Protection of Children from Abuse*, LAC (88)10 (1988d).

DHSS, *Social Services Training Support Programme (Child Care): Financial Year 1989–90*, LAC (88) Draft (1988e).

Dingwall, R. 'The Jasmine Beckford Affair', *Modern Law Review*, Vol. 49, No. 4 (1986) 488–518.

Dingwall, R. 'Some Problems about Predicting Child Abuse and Neglect', in O. Stevenson (ed.), *Child Abuse: Public Policy and Professional Practice* (Hemel Hempstead: Harvester-Wheatsheaf, 1989).

Dingwall, R. Eekelaar, J. and Murray, T. *The Protection of Children: State Intervention and Family Life* (Oxford: Basil Blackwell, 1983).

Dingwall, R. and Eekelaar, J. 'Families and the State: An Historical Perspective on the Public Regulation of Private Conduct', *Law & Policy*, Vol. 10, No. 4 (October 1988) 341–61.

Dominelli, L. 'Betrayal of Trust: A Feminist Analysis of Power Relationships in Incest Abuse and its Relevance for Social Work Practice', *British Journal of Social Work*, Vol. 19, No. 4 (August 1989) 291–307.

Donzelot, J. *The Policing of Families: Welfare Versus the State* (London: Hutchinson, 1980).

Donzelot, J. 'The Promotion of the Social', *Economy and Society*, Vol. 17, No. 3 (August 1988) 395–427.

Douglas G. and Willmore, C. 'Diagnostic Interviews as Evidence in Cases of Child Sexual Abuse', *Family Law*, Vol. 17 (May 1987) 151–4.

Drewry, G. 'The Parliamentary Response to Child Abuse', in *After Beckford? Essays on Themes Related to Child Abuse*, Department of Social Policy, Royal Holloway and Bedford New College, Social Policy Paper No. 1 (1987).

Durkheim, E. *The Division of Labour in Society* (New York: Free Press, 1964).

Edwards, K. 'Back to the Drawing Boards', *Social Services Insight* (7 June 1989) 11.

Eekelaar, J. 'Family Law and Social Control', in J. Eekelaar and J. Bell (eds), *Oxford Essays in Jurisprudence*, Third Series (Oxford: Clarendon Press, 1987).

Eekelaar, J. and Dingwall, R. *The Reform of Child Care Law: A Practical Guide to the Children Act 1989* (London: Routledge, 1990).

Easton, D. *A Systems Analysis of Political Life* (New York: John Wiley, 1965).

Expenditure Committee Report on the 1969 Act (London: HMSO, 1975).

Family Law Reports, Special Issue, No, 4 (1987) 269–346.

Farn, K. T. 'Sexual and Other Assaults on Children', *Police Surgeon*, Vol. 8 (1975) 37–58.

Ferguson, H. 'Rethinking Child Protection Practices: A Case for History', in The Violence Against Children Study Group, *Taking Child Abuse Seriously: Contemporary Issues in Child Protection Theory and Practice* (London: Unwin Hyman, 1990).

Ferlie, E. and Judge, K. 'Retrenchment and Rationality in the Personal Social Services', *Policy and Politics*, Vol. 9, No. 3 (1981) 311–30.

Finkelhor, D. *Child Sexual Abuse: New Theory and Research* (New York: Free Press, 1984).

Fischer, J. 'Does Anything Work?', *Journal of Social Science Research*, Vol. 1 (1978) 215–43.

Fisher, M. Marsh, P. and Phillips, D. with E. Sainsbury, *In and Out of Care: The Experience of Children, Parents and Social Workers* (London; Batsford/BAAF, 1986).

Fletcher, H. quoted in 'Too Many One-Parent Children in Care', *Community Care*, No. 247 (18 January 1979) 5.

Floud, J. and Young, W. *Dangerousness and Criminal Justice* (London: Heinemann, 1981).

Forbes, J. and Thomas T. 'Dangerous Classifications', *Community Care*, No. 796 (11 January 1990) 19–21.

Foucault, M. *Discipline and Punish* (London: Allen and Lane, 1977a).

Foucault, M. *The Archaeology of Knowledge* (London: Tavistock, 1977b).

Foucault, M. 'Politics and the Study of Discourse', *Ideology and Consciousness*, No. 3 (Spring 1978a) 7–26.

Foucault, M. 'About the Concept of the "Dangerous Individual" in

19th-Century Legal Psychiatry', *International Journal of Law and Psychiatry*, Vol. 1 (1978b) 1–18.

Foucault, M. *The History of Sexuality, Vol. 1: An Introduction* (London: Allen Lane, 1979).

Foucault M. 'Space, Knowledge and Power', in P. Rabinow (ed.), *The Foucault Reader* (Harmondsworth: Penguin, 1986).

Fowler, N. *Speech to Joint Social Services Annual Conference* (London: DHSS, 27 September 1984).

Fox, L. 'Two Value Positions in Recent Child Care Law and Practice', *British Journal of Social Work*, Vol. 12, No. 3 (1982) 265–290.

Franklin, B. (ed.) *The Rights of Children* (Oxford: Basil Blackwell, 1986).

Franklin, B. 'Wimps and Bullies: Press Reporting of Child Abuse', in P. Carter, T. Jeffs and M. Smith (eds), *Social Work and Social Welfare Yearbook One* (Milton Keynes: Open University Press, 1989).

Franklin, B. and Parton, N. (eds), *Social Work, the Media and Public Relations* (London: Routledge, 1991).

Freeman, M. D. A. *The Rights and Wrongs of Children* (London: Francis Pinter, 1983).

Frost, N. 'Official Intervention and Child Protection: The Relationship Between State and Family in Contemporary Britain', in the Violence Against Children Study Group, *Taking Child Abuse Seriously: Contemporary Issues in Child Protection Theory and Practice* (London: Unwin Hyman, 1990).

Frost, N. and Parton, C. 'Protecting Children – A Critical Assessment' (unpublished, monograph, 1990).

Gamble, A. *The Free Economy and the Strong State: The Politics of Thatcherism* (London: Macmillan, 1988).

Garland, D. 'The Birth of the Welfare Sanction', *British Journal of Law and Society*, Vol. 8, No. 1 (Summer 1981) 29–45.

Garland, D. *Punishment and Welfare: A History of Penal Strategies* (Aldershot: Gower, 1985).

Garland, D. and Young P. (Eds), *The Power to Punish: Contemporary Penality and Social Analysis* (London: Heinemann, 1983).

Gaylin, W. *et al.*, *Doing Good: The Limits of Benevolence* (New York: Pantheon Books, 1978).

Gibb, F. 'Minors have right to expect they won't be left to Suffer', *The Times* (25 November 1988) 4.

Gibbons, T. C. N. and Prince, J. *Child Victims of Sex Offences* (London: Institute for the Study and Treatment of Delinquency, 1963).

Glaser, D. 'Evaluating the Evidence of a Child: The Video-taped Interview and Beyond', *Family Law*, Vol. 19 (December 1989) 487–9.

Gledhill, A. *Who Cares? Children at Risk and Social Services* (London: Centre for Policy Studies, 1989).

Gordon, L. 'Family Violence, Feminism and Social Control', *Feminist Studies*, Vol. 12, No. 2 (Fall, 1986) 452–78.

Gordon, L. *Heroes of their Own Times: The Politics and History of Family Violence* (London: Virago, 1989).

Greenland, C. 'Incest', *British Journal of Delinquency*, Vol. 9, No. 1 (1958) 62–68.

Greenland, C. 'The Prediction and Management of Dangerous Behaviour: Social Policy Issues', *International Journal of Law and Psychiatry*, Vol. 1 (1978) 205–22.

Greenland, C. 'Psychiatry and the Prediction of Dangerousness', *Journal of Psychiatric Treatment and Evaluation*, Vol. 2 (1980a) 97–103.

Greenland, C. 'Lethal Family Situations: An International Comparison of Deaths from Child Abuse', in E. J. Antony and C. Chiland (eds), *The Child and His Family* (New York: Wiley, 1980b).

Greenland, C. 'Preventing Child Abuse and Neglect Deaths: The Identification and Management of High Risk Cases', *Health Visitor*, Vol. 55, No. 7 (July 1986a) 205–6.

Greenland, C. 'Inquiries into Child Abuse and Neglect (CAN) Deaths in the United Kingdom', *British Journal of Criminology*, Vol. 26, No. 2 (April 1986b) 164–73.

Greenland, C. *Preventing CAN Deaths: An International Study of Deaths due to Child Abuse and Neglect* (London: Tavistock Publications, 1987).

Griffiths Report, *Community Care: Agenda for Action* (London: HMSO, 1988).

Hall, P. *Reforming the Welfare: The Politics of Change in the Personal Social Services* (London: Heinemann, 1976).

Hall, P. Land, H. Parker, R. and Webb, A. *Change, Choice and Conflict in Social Policy* (London: Heinemann, 1975).

Hallett, C. 'Child Abuse Inquiries and Public Policy', in O. Stevenson (ed.) *Child Abuse: Public Policy and Professional Practice* (Hemel Hempstead: Harvester-Wheatsheaf, 1989).

Halmos, P. *The Faith of the Counsellors* (London: Constable, 1965).

Hamilton, J. R. 'A Quick Look at the Problems', in J. R. Hamilton and H. Freeman (eds), *Dangerousness – Psychiatric Assessment and Management* (London: Gaskell, 1982).

Handler, J. *The Coercive Social Worker: British Lessons for American Social Services* (Chicago: Rand McNally, 1973).

Harding, J. 'A Child Assessment Order: To Be or Not To Be?', *Community Care*, no. 758 (13 April 1989) p. 6.

Harding, L. 'The Hundred Year Resolution', *The Journal of Child Law*, No. 1 (October–December 1989) 12–17.

Hartley, P. *Child Abuse, Social Work and the Press: Towards the History of a Moral Panic*, Warwick Criticial Studies No. 4 (Department of Applied Social Studies, University of Warwick, 1985).

Held, D. *Models of Democracy* (Cambridge: Polity Press, 1987).

Helfer, R. E and Kempe, C. H. (eds), *Child Abuse and Neglect: The Family and the Community* (Cambridge, Mass.: Ballinger, 1976).

Hewitt, M. 'Bio-Politics and Social Policy: Foucault's Account of Welfare', *Theory, Culture and Society*, Vol. 2, No. 1 (1983) 67–84.

Hey, F. Buchan, P. C. Littlewood, J. M. and Hall, R. I. 'Differential Diagnosis in Child Sexual Abuse', *The Lancet* (31 January 1987) p. 283.

Heywood, J. and Allen, B. *Financial Help in Social Work* (Manchester: Manchester University Press, 1971).

Heywood, J. S. *Children in Care: The Development of the Service for the Deprived Child*, 3rd edn (London: RKP, 1978).

Hilgendorf, L. *Social Workers and Solicitors in Child Care Cases* (London: HMSO, 1981).

Hill, M. and Laing, P. *Social Work and Money* (London: Allen and Unwin, 1979).

Hirst, P. 'Law, Socialism and Rights' in P. Carlen and M. Collinson (eds) *Radical Issues in Criminology* (Oxford: Martin Robertson, 1980).

Hirst, P. 'The Genesis of the Social', *Politics and Power*, No. 3 (1981) 67–82.

Hobbs, C. J. and Wynne, J. M. 'Buggery in Childhood – A Common Symptom of Child Abuse', *The Lancet* (4 October 1986) 792–96.

Hoggett, B. 'Family Law into the 1990s', *Family Law*, Vol. 19 (May 1989) 177–80.

Holman, R. *Inequality in Child Care* (London: CPAG, 1976).

Home Office, *The Investigation of Child Sexual Abuse*, Home Office Circular, 52/1988 (1988).

Horne, M. *Values in Social Work* (Aldershot: Wildwood House, 1987).

Horne, M. 'Is it Social Work?', in The Violence Against Children Study Group, *Taking Child Abuse Seriously: Contemporary Issues in Child Protection Theory and Practice* (London: Unwin Hyman, 1990).

Howarth, V. 'Social Work and the Media: Pitfalls and Possibilities', in B. Franklin and N. Parton (eds), *Social Work, the Media and Public Relations* (London: Routledge, 1991).

Hudson, B. *Justice Through Punishment: A Critique of the 'Justice' Model of Corrections* (London: Macmillan, 1987).

Hutchinson, R. 'The Effect of Inquiries into Cases of Child Abuse upon the Social Work Profession', *British Journal of Criminology*, Vol. 26, No. 2 (April 1986) 178–82.

Ignatieff, M. *A Just Measure of Pain* (New York: Columbia University Press, 1978).

Ignatieff, M. 'State, Civil Society and Total Institutions: A Critique of Recent Social Histories of Punishment', in S. Cohen and A. Scull (eds), *Social Control and the State: Historical and Comparative Essays* (Oxford: Basil Blackwell, 1983).

Illsley, P. *The Drama of Cleveland: A Monitoring Report on Press Coverage of the Sexual Abuse of Children Controversy in Cleveland* (London: Campaign for Press and Broadcasting Freedom, 1989).

Ingleby, D. 'Professionals as Socialisers: the "Psy Complex"', in A. Scull and S. Spitzer (eds), *Research in Law, Deviance and Social Control 7* (New York: Jai Press, 1985).

Jackson, M. P. and Valencia, B. M. *Financial Aid through Social Work* (London: RKP, 1979).

Jenkin, P. *Speech to Social Services Conference* (Bournemouth: 21 November 1980).

Jenkins, W. L. *Policy Analysis: A Political and Organisational Perspective* (London: Martin Robertson, 1978).

Jervis, M. 'Skilful Social Work Can Protect Children at Risk', *Social Work Today*, Vol. 20, No. 50 (24 August 1989) 18–19.

Jervis, M. 'The Lightweight Crusader', *Social Work Today*, Vol. 21, No. 28 (22 March 1990) 16–17.

Jones, B. R. *Children Act 1989 – A Survey of Costs by Questionnaire: A Paper by the Local Authority Associations* (London: AMA, 1990).

Jones, D. N. 'Comment: Framework for a Better Law', *Social Work Today*, Vol. 17, No. 7 (14 October 1985) 2.

Kempe, C. H. Silverman, F. N. Steel, B. F. Droegemueller, W. and Silver, H. K. 'The Battered Child Syndrome', *Journal of the American Medical Association*, No. 181 (1962) 17–24.

Lord Chancellor's Office, *Improvements in the Arrangements for Care Proceedings*, Consultation Paper (August 1988).

La Fontaine, J. *Child Sexual Abuse* (Cambridge: Polity Press, 1990).

Lasche, C. *Haven in a Heartless World* (New York: Basic Books, 1977).

Laurance, J. 'Learning the Lessons', *New Society*, Vol. 74, No. 1197 (1985) 408–9.

Laurance, J. 'The Children's Samaritans', *New Society*, Vol. 81, No. 1280 (10 July 1987) 10–11.

Law Commission, *Family Law: Review of Child Law: Guardianship and Custody*, Law Com. No. 172 (London: HMSO, 1988).

Levitas R. (ed.), *The Ideology of the New Right* (Cambridge: Polity Press, 1986).

London Borough of Brent, *A Child in Trust: Report of the Panel of Inquiry Investigating the Circumstances Surrounding the Death of Jasmine Beckford* (London: Borough of Brent, 1985).

London Borough of Greenwich, *A Child in Mind: Protection of Children in a Responsible Society: Report of the Commission of Inquiry into the Circumstances Surrounding the Death of Kimberley Carlile* (London: London Borough of Greenwich, 1987).

London Borough of Islington, *Liam Johnson Review: Report of Panel of Inquiry* (London: London Borough of Islington, 1989).

London Borough of Lambeth, *Whose Child? The Report of the Panel Appointed to Inquire into the Death of Tyra Henry* (London: London Borough of Lambeth, 1987).

London Borough of Wandsworth, *Report of the Panel of Inquiry into the Death of Stephanie Fox* (London: London Borough of Wandsworth, 1990).

Lowman, J. Menzies, R. J. and Palys, T. S. (eds), *Transcarceration: Essays in the Sociology of Social Control* (Aldershot: Gower, 1987).

Lukes, S. *Power: A Radical View* (London: Macmillan, 1976).

Lyon, C. and de Cruz, S. P. 'Child Sexual Abuse and the Cleveland Report', *Family Law*, vol. 18 (October 1988) 370–378.

McCarthy, M. 'The Personal Social Services' in M. McCarthy (ed.) *The New Politics of Welfare : An Agenda for the 1990s* (London: Macmillan, 1989)

McCron, R and Carter, R. 'Researching Socially Sensitive Subjects – The Case of Child Abuse', in *Annual Review of BBC Broadcasting Research Findings* (London: BBC, 1987).

McGeorge, J. 'Sexual Assaults on Children', *Medicine, Science and the Law*, Vol. 4, No. 4 (October 1964) 245–53.

McMillan, I. 'ADSS Changes Tack on Assessment', *Community Care*, No. 764 (25 May 1989) 1.

Marshall, K. 'In Favour of Child Assessment Orders', *Social Work Today*, Vol. 20, No. 32 (Letters, 20 April 1989) 12.

Mellor, D. 'Learning to Save Our Children', *The Times* (23 December 1988), 12.

Metropolitan Police and Bexley London Borough, *Child Sexual Abuse Joint Investigation Project: Final Report* (London: HMSO, 1987).

Miller, P. *Domination and Power* (London: RKP, 1987).

Miller, P. and Rose, N. 'The Tavistock Programme: The Government of Subjectivity and Social Life', *Sociology*, Vol. 22, No. 2. (1988) 171–92.

Miller, P. and Rose, N. 'Governing Economic Life', *Economy and Society*, Vol. 19, No. 1 (February 1990) 1–31.

Millham, S. Bullock, R. Hosie, K. and Haak, M. *Lost in Care: The Problems of Maintaining Links between Children in Care and their Families*, (Aldershot: Gower, 1986).

Morris, A. Giller, H. Szwed, E. and Geach, H. *Justice for Children* (London: Macmillan, 1980).

Moxon, D. (ed.), *Managing Criminal Justice* (London: HMSO, 1985).

Mrazek, P. B. Lynch, M. and Bentovim, A. 'Recognition of Sexual Abuse in the United Kingdom', in P. B. Mrazek and C. H. Kempe (eds), *Sexually Abused Children and their Families* (Oxford: Pergamon Press, 1981).

Munro, P. 'Can the Courts Cope?', *Community Care* No. 768 (22 June 1989) 26–28.

Murray, I. 'A Ministerial Change of Attitude', *Social Services Insight* (8 November 1989) 8.

National Council for One Parent Families, *Against Natural Justice: A Study of the Procedures used by Local Authorities in taking Parental Rights Resolutions over Children in Voluntary Care* (London: NCOPF, 1982).

National Society for the Prevention of Cruelty to Children, *Child Abuse in 1988: Initial Findings from the NSPCC's Register Research* (London: NSPCC, 1989).

Nava, M. 'Cleveland and the Press: Outrage and Anxiety in the Reporting of Child Sex Abuse', *Feminist Review*, No. 28 (1988) 103–22.

Nelken, D. 'Discipline and Punish: Some Notes on the Margin', *The Howard Journal*, Vol. 28, No. 4 (November 1989) 345–54.

Nelson, S. *Incest: Fact and Myth* (Edinburgh: Stramullion, 1987).

New Society Leader, 'Child Abuse: Finding a Balance', *New Society*, Vol. 81, No. 1279 (1987) 3.

Okell, C and Butcher, C. H. H. 'The Battered Child Syndrome', *Law Society Gazette*, No. 66 (1969) 9.

Osmond, R. 'A Child Assessment Order: To Be or Not To Be?', *Community Care*, No. 758 (13 April 1989a) 7.

Osmond, R. 'Should we have a Child Assessment Order: The Case Against', *Childright*, No. 55 (April 1989b) 14–15.

Osmond, R. 'Lobbying on the Children Bill', *Social Work Today*, Vol. 20, No. 27 (16 March 1989c) 15.

Packman, J. *Child Care: Needs and Numbers* (London: Allen and Unwin, 1968).

Packman, J. *The Child's Generation*, 2nd edn (Oxford: Basil Blackwell and Martin Robertson, 1981).

Packman, J. with J. Randal and N. Jacques, *Who Needs Care? Social Work Decisions about Children* (Oxford: Basil Blackwell, 1986).

Parents Against Injustice, *A Response to Child Abuse – Working Together* (Bishops Stortford, Parents Against Injustice, 1986).

Parker R. (ed.), *Caring for Separated Children: Plans, Procedures and Priorities. A Report by a Working Party Established by the National Children's Bureau* (London: Macmillan, 1980).

Parton, C. 'Women, Gender, Oppression and Child Abuse', in the Violence Against Children Study Group, *Taking Child Abuse Seriously: Contemporary Issues in Child Protection Theory and Practice* (London: Unwin Hyman, 1990).

Parton, C and Parton, N. 'Child Protection: the Law and Dangerousness', in O. Stevenson (ed.), *Child Abuse: Public Policy and Professional Practice* (Hemel Hempstead: Harvester-Wheatsheaf, 1989a).

Parton, C. and Parton, N. 'Women, the Family and Child Protection', *Critical Social Policy*, No. 24 (1989b) 38–49.

Parton, N. 'The Natural History of Child Abuse: A Study in Social Problem Definition', *British Journal of Social Work*, Vol. 9, No. 4, (1979) 431–51.

Parton, N. 'Child Abuse, Social Anxiety and Welfare', *British Journal of Social Work*, Vol. 11, No. 4 (1981) 391–414.

Parton, N. 'Children in Care: Recent Changes and Debates', *Critical Social Policy*, No. 13 (Summer 1985a) 107–17.

Parton, N. *The Politics of Child Abuse* (London: Macmillan, 1985b).

Parton, N. 'The Beckford Report: A Critical Appraisal', *British Journal of Social Work*, Vol. 16, No. 5 (1986) 511–30.

Parton, N. 'Child Abuse', in B. Kahan (ed.), *Child Care Research, Policy and Practice* (London: Hodder and Stoughton, 1989).

Parton, N. 'Taking Child Abuse Seriously', in the Violence Against Children Study Group, *Taking Child Abuse Seriously: Contemporary Issues in Child Protection Theory and Practice* (London: Unwin Hyman, 1990).

Parton, N. and Martin, N. 'Public Inquiries, Legalism and Child Care in England and Wales', *International Journal of Law and the Family*, Vol. 3 (1989) 21–39.

Pearson, G. *The Deviant Imagination* (London: Macmillan, 1975).

Philp, M. 'Notes on the Form of Knowledge in Social Work', *Sociological Review*, Vol. 27, No. 1 (1979) 83–111.

Philp, M. 'Michael Foucault', in Q. Skinner (ed.), *The Return of Grand Theory in Human Sciences* (Cambridge: Cambridge University Press, 1985).

Piachaud, D. 'The Growth of Poverty', in A. Walker and C. Walker (eds), *The Growing Divide: A Social Audit 1979–1987* (London: CPAG, 1987).

Pithers, D. 'A Guide through the Maze of Child Protection', *Social Work Today*, Vol. 20, No. 18 (1989) 18–19.

Rantzen, E. 'Adults' Responses to Childhood Suffering', *The Listener*, Vol. 118, No. 3020 (16 July 1987) 8–9.

Reid, W. J. and Shyne, A. W. *Brief and Extended Casework* (New York: Columbia University Press, 1969).

Rhodes, G. C. *Committees of Inquiry* (London: Allen and Unwin, 1975).

Roberts, R. E. 'Examination of the Anus in Suspected Child Sexual Abuse', *The Lancet* (8 November 1986) 1100.

Robertson, I. 'The Children Bill: Children, Parents and the Local Authority', *Family Law*, Vol. 19 (June 1989) 224–6.

Rodger, J. J. 'Social Work as Social Control Re-Examined: Beyond the Dispersal of Discipline Thesis', *Sociology*, Vol. 22, No. 4 (1988) 563–81.

Rose, N. *The Psychological Complex: Psychology, Politics and Society in England 1869–1939* (London: RKP, 1985).

Rose, N. 'Law Rights and Psychiatry', in P. Miller and N. Rose (eds), *The Power of Psychiatry* (Oxford: Polity Press, 1986).

Rose, N. *Governing the Soul: The Shaping of the Private Self* (London: Routledge, 1990).

Rowe, J. 'Social Work Decisions in Child Care: Implications for Social Workers', in J. McHugh (ed.), *Creative Social Work with Families* (Birmingham: BASW, 1987).

Rowe, J. 'Using Research Effectively', in P. Sills (ed), *Child Abuse: Challenges for Policy and Practice* (Wallington: Reed Business Publishing/ Community Care, 1989).

Rowe, J. Cain, H. Hundleby, M. and Keane, A. *Long Term Foster Care* (London: Batsford/BAAF, 1984).

Rowe, J. and Lambert, L. *Children Who Wait* (London: Association of British Adoption Agencies, 1973).

Ruddock, M. 'The Receptacle of Public Anger', in B. Franklin and N. Parton (eds), *Social Work, the Media and Public Relations* (London: Routledge, 1991).

Rustin, M. 'Social Work and the Family', in N. Parry, M. Rustin and C. Satyamurti (eds), *Social Work, Welfare and the State* (London: Edward Arnold, 1979).

Rutherford, M. 'The Children and Young Persons (Amendment) Act 1986', *The Law Society's Gazette* (17 September 1986) 2741–3.

Satyamurti, C. *Occupational Survival* (Oxford: Basil Blackwell, 1981).

Secretary of State for Social Services, *Report of the Committee of Inquiry into the Care and Supervision Provided in Relation to Maria Colwell* (London: HMSO, 1974).

Secretary of State for Social Services, *Report of the Inquiry into Child Abuse in Cleveland*, Cmnd 412 (London: HMSO, 1988).

Seebohm Committee, *Report of the Committee on Local Authority and Allied Personal Social Services*, Cmnd 3703 (1968).

Sgroi, S. A. *Handbook of Clinical Intervention in Child Sexual Abuse* (Lexington: Lexington Books, 1982).

Sharron, H. 'The Influence of the Patterson Factor', *Social Work Today*, Vol. 18, No. 30 (30 March 1987) 8–9.

Shklar, J. N. *Legalism* (Cambridge, Mass.: Harvard University Press, 1964).

Sinclair, R. *Decision Making in Statutory Reviews on Children in Care* (London: Gower, 1984).

Skinner A and Castle R. *78 Battered Children: A Retrospective Study* (London: NSPCC, 1969).

Smith, P. 'Families in Court – Guilty or Guilty?', *Children and Society*, Vol. 2, No. 2 (1988) 152–64.

Smith, P. 'More Power to their Elbow', *Community Care*, No. 766 (8 June 1989) 20–1.

Smith, P. and Riches, P. 'Rolling Programme of Reform', *Community Care*, No. 773 (27 July 1989) 26–8.

Social Services Committee (HC 360), *Children in Care* (London: HMSO, March 1984).

Social Services Committee Second Report, *Children Bill, House of Commons Paper 178* (London: HMSO, 1989).

Social Services Inspectorate, *Inspection of the Supervision of Social Workers in the Assessment and Monitoring of Cases of Child Abuse when Children, Subject to a Court Order, have been Returned Home* (London: SSI, 1986).

Social Services Inspectorate, *Child Sexual Abuse: Survey. Report on Inter-agency Co-operation in England and Wales* (London: SSI, HMSO, 1988).

Social Services Inspectorate, *A Sense of Direction: Planning in Social Work with Children* (London: SSI, 1989).

Stein, M. and Carey, K. *Leaving Care* (Oxford: Basil Blackwell, 1986).

Stenson, K. *Social Work Discourse and the Social Work Interview* (PhD thesis, Department of Human Sciences, Brunel University, 1989).

Stevenson, O. 'Multi-disciplinary Work in Child Protection', in O. Stevenson (ed.), *Child Abuse: Public Policy and Professional Practice* (Hemel Hempstead: Harvester-Wheatsheaf, 1989).

Stevenson, O. and Smith, J. *The Implementation of Section 56 of the Children Act 1975* (unpublished research report).

Taylor, L. Lacey, R. and Bracken, D. *In Whose Best Interests?* (London: Cobden Trust/Mind, 1980).

Thatcher, M. *Inaugral National Children's Home George Thomas Society Lecture* (London: Cafe Royal, 17 January 1990).

Unsworth, C. The Politics of Mental Health Legislation (Oxford: Oxford University Press 1987).

Van Krieken, R. 'Social Theory and Child Welfare: Beyond Social Control', *Theory and Society*, Vol. 15 (1986) 401–29.

Vernon, J. and Fruin, D. *In Care: A Study of Social Work Decision-Making* (London: National Children's Bureau, 1986).

Von Hirsch, A. *Doing Justice* (New York: Hill & Wang, 1976).

Walker, A. 'Community Care', in M. McCarthy (ed), *The New Politics of Welfare: An Agenda for the 1990s* (London: Macmillan, 1989).

Walker, N. 'Dangerous People', *International Journal of Law and Psychiatry*, No. 1 (1978) 37–49.

Webb, A. and Wistow, G. *Social Work, Social Care and Social Planning: The Personal Social Services since Seebohm* (London: Longman, 1987).

White Paper, *The Law on Child Care and Family Services*, Cmnd 62 (London: HMSO, 1987).

White Paper, *Caring for People*, Cmnd 849 (London: HMSO, 1989).

White, T. 'Running Two Campaigns: Some Changes', in B. Franklin and N. Parton (eds), *Social Work, the Media and Public Relations* (London: Routledge, 1991).

Wells, N. H. 'Sexual Offences as seen by a Woman Police Surgeon', *British Medical Journal*, Vol. 2 (6 December 1958) 1404–8.

Williams, N. H. 'Some Thoughts on Sexual Assault', *Police Surgeon Supplement*, Vol. 5, (1978) 42–8.

Wilson, A. 'Should we have a Child Assessment Order: The Case For', *Childright*, No. 55 (April 1989) 12–13.

Woodcraft, E. 'Child Sexual Abuse and the Law', *Feminist Review*, No. 28 (Spring 1988) 122–30.

Woolgar, S. 'On the Alleged Distinction Between Discourse and Praxis', *Social Studies of Science*, Vol. 16 (1986) 309–17.

Wroe, A. *Social Work, Child Abuse and the Press*, Social Work Monograph 66 (Norwich: University of East Anglia, 1988).

Index

abuse, child
  classification of   129, 204
  co-ordination and assessment
    116–46
  guidelines for diagnosis   219
  high-risk checklist   60–1
  indices of   70
  management   118–46;
    guidelines for   221;
    systematic   128
  as medico-social   18
  prediction of   58, 60–1, 62–3;
    and training   134
  risk and authority   52–78
  as socio-legal   18, 146, 214
  statistics   219
access
  parental   28, 110, 112
  restrictions on   37
  see also entry
accommodation, voluntary
    154–5, 173, 174
accountability   51, 115
  and Beckford   67
  legal   68
  and *Review*   43
  of social workers   97, 98, 152,
    156, 160, 191, 194
  to courts   213
Adcock, M.   26, 34
adolescents   25
ADSS *see* Association of
    Directors of Social Services
agencies
  and assessment   132–3

conflict in Cleveland   81, 83,
    98, 106, 113
  improving cooperation   116–17,
    128–9, 131–2
  of law   106–7
Aldridge, M.   81
allegations of abuse   132
Allen, B.   25
Allen, Denis   28
Allen, F. A.   199
AMA *see* Association of
    Metropolitan Authorities
Amphlett, Steve   94
Amphlett, Sue   94, 95
anal dilatation tests   97, 102, 103,
    136
Area Child Protection
    Committees   133–4, 203
Area Review Committees   71,
    118, 119, 133
Armstrong, D.   91, 101
Armstrong, Hilary   161, 165, 171,
    172
assessment
  and CAO   185–6
  of dangerousness   199
  developmental   73, 181, 186, 187
  medical   212
  multi-disciplinary   132
  and parental rights   138, 145
  principles of   140–1
  social   189–90, 212, 213; and
    sexual abuse   97, 99, 115,
    137–45, 146
  see also family; medical

239

Association of British Adoption
  Agencies (ABAA) 23
Association of County Councils
  (ACC) 167
Association of Directors of Social
  Services (ADSS) 167, 168,
  173, 178, 204
  and CAO 179–80, 182–3,
  184–6
Association of London Authorities
  (ALA) 176
Association of Metropolitan
  Authorities (AMA) 166–7,
  184, 222
authoritarian state and Cleveland
  81
authority
  risk and child abuse 52–78
  use of 141

Bacon, R. 200
Baher, E. 23, 25
Baker, K. 200
balance between state and family
  148, 151–2
Barnardo's 168, 173
Barnes, Rosie 164
BASPCAN 86–7, 220
BASW *see* British Association of
  Social Workers
Battered Babies (DHSS) 118, 120
Beckford, Jasmine/inquiry 54–67,
  89, 125, 217–18
  foster parents of 64–5
  impact of 53, 96, 142
  and intervention 2, 141
  and parental rights 66, 67
  and POSOs 66–7
  predicting abuse 58–9, 62–3
  and public concern 75, 138
  recommendations 52–3, 121–2,
  124, 157, 206
  remit of 54
  right of appeal 109
Beckford, Morris 59–60, 65, 217
Bell, Stuart 81, 93, 114
  on CAO 187, 190
  and Children Act 150, 163–4

criticism of professionals 80,
  82, 104
Bentovim, A. 85, 86, 89–90
Berridge, D. 26
'best interests' 168, 194
Bexley 124
Bishop, M. 67
Bishop, Mr 62–3
Blom-Cooper, L. 52, 53, 69, 199
  on CAO 218
  children of the state 67
  on magistrates 107
Bloxham, R. 124
Bottomley, Virginia 178, 179,
  180, 186
Bottoms, A. E. 17, 142, 199
British Agencies for Adoption and
  Fostering 31, 184, 223
British Association of Social
  Workers (BASW) 121, 122,
  178, 184
Bronfenbrenner, U. 29
Butcher, C. H. H. 22
Butler-Sloss, Lord Justice E.
  105
Butler-Sloss, Mrs Justice/Report
  83, 116, 177, 219
  see also Cleveland
Byrne, K. 124

Campbell, B. 106
Canada 19, 60, 62
CAO *see* Child Assessment Order
care
  growth of numbers in 25
  long-term 25
  orders 49, 213; Beckford
  Report and 67; Carlile
  Report and 74; and
  Cleveland 82, 111; social
  workers' attitudes 56
  research into 26
  short term 40, 41
  social workers view 41
  see also child care system;
  compulsory; leaving care;
  voluntary
Carey, K. 26

Carlile, Kimberley/Report
    68–74, 75–7, 125, 219
  child as client 89
  and intervention 1, 2, 109, 151;
    hierarchy of state 75
  Mellor, David 1, 151, 187
  and parental rights 73
  recommendations of 111, 177,
    178, 186
  on social workers 195
Carlile, Pauline 69
Carter, R. 92
case conferences 118–19, 125,
    126–7, 203
  and parents 130–1
casework and prevention 62
cash assistance 171
Castle, R. 25
centile charts 62
Centre for Policy Studies 163
Channer, Y. 140
Chant, John 53, 179
checklist, high-risk 60–1
Child Abuse DHSS 26
child abuse *see* abuse
Child Assessment Order 151,
    177–81, 182–90, 191, 192, 213
  guidelines 222–3
Child Care Act (1980) 158
child care system 208
  and Carlile case 70–1
  and dangerousness 207
  establishment of 19–20
  and law 17
  original characteristics 21–3
Child Poverty Action Group 205
Child Production Notice 188, 223
child protection
  concept of 3–5, 71
  emergence of 203–8
  as health 13
  reconstructing consensus 150
child/children
  and Children Bill 162–3
  consultation with 141, 144
  in family context 31, 44, 95
  health as sexual abuse 100–6
  homes 26

minders 150, 158, 171
  as primary client 56, 63
  right to see 74, 75
  rights of 117, 141, 145, 148;
    and Short Report 28
  see also abuse
ChildLine 91–3, 196, 204, 220–1
Children Act (1908) 13
Children Act (1948) 21
Children Act (1975) 26
Children Act (1989) 48, 147–92,
    194, 196, 203
  aims of 1–2
  alternative interpretations
    160–6
  amendments 167, 168
  areas of dispute and concern
    170–6
  criticisms 176
  emergency protection 176–90
  identifying risk 198, 208, 212,
    213
  and intervention 209
  lobbying 166–70, 197; impact
    of 192
  principles 11; and structure
    152–60
Children and Young Persons Act
    (1933) 34, 72, 74, 75
Children and Young Persons Act
    (1963) 22
Children and Young Persons Act
    (1969) 23, 34, 66, 107, 111
Children and Young Persons
    (Amendment) Act (1986)
    111, 218
Children's Homes Act (1982) 158
Children's Legal Centre 24, 168,
    184, 188, 197, 223
Children's Rights Movement 196
Children's Society 178
Childwatch 91–3, 196
CIBA Foundation 86–7, 89
  study group members 220
civil liberties 95, 120, 194, 196
civil servants and Children Bill
    169–70
Clarke, J. 12, 15

Clarke, Tom 148
Clayden, G. 90
Cleveland 141, 195
    agencies of law 106–7
    inquiry 83–4
    a new legal framework 107–13
    parents 93–6; lobby 197;
        rights of 79, 107–8, 109–10
    and the private family 79–115
    reasons for crisis 113, 116
    Report: and abuse statistics
        219; on assessment 212; and
        CAO 178–9; and Children
        Act 151; recommendations
        of 108, 159
    social work practice 96–100
co-ordination, management and
    social assessment 116–46
Cohen, S. 7–8, 199, 207, 208
Colwell, Maria 24, 52, 75, 195,
    204
Community Care Bill (1990) 210
Community Care (Griffiths) 117,
    128, 224
community and child protection
    162
compulsory care 25, 41, 50
    and planning 40
    and Review 46–7
concerns in 1970s 23–7
confidentiality 125, 141
Conrad, P. 7
contact order 154
Cooper, J. 19
Corby, B. 204
corporal punishment 162
counselling 22
    lack of 80
Court, J. 22
courts 51
    accountability to 213
    and Beckford case 66
    and care orders 49
    and Children Bill 155–6; power
        to 177
    and EPOs 48
    family 33, 48, 113, 159, 168, 174
    and local authority 33

    role of 32
    and Short Report 31, 32–3
    use of different 158–9
CPAG *see* Child Poverty Action
    Group
Creighton, S. J. 204
Crewdson, R. 90
crime 201
criticism in 1970's 23–7
Croft, J. 201
Cullen, Deborah 167
cultural issues 140
cultural relativism 55–6

Dale, P. 23, 142
dangerousness 15, 142–3, 209,
    212, 213
    assessment of 206
    assessments of 199
    prediction of 60, 207
    prioritisation of 198–203, 208
day care 150, 158, 165, 171
    preventative role 172
de Cruz, S. P. 108
decision-making
    and Beckford inquiry 55
    social work 39–40, 41
delinquency 13, 14, 22
Department of Education
    guidelines 116
Department of Health guidelines
    117, 137, 139, 187, 212
deprivation 205
    and delinquency 13
    and risk of abuse 60, 61,
        164–5
developmental assessment 73,
    181, 186, 187
deviancy 15
Devlin, Tim 80, 81, 82, 149, 150
DHSS
    Battered Babies 118, 120
    Child Abuse 26; *Central Register
        Systems* 120
    Children's Research Liaison
        Group 27
    guidance for doctors 116,
        135–7

guidance for primary care
    team   116, 137
Non-Accidental Inquiry
    118–19, 120
Review of Child Care Law   42,
    43, 47
*Social Services Training
    Support*   117
*Social Work Decisions in Child
    Care*   26, 42
Working Together   141, 203;
    inter-agency co-operation
    116, 121–35, 143
diagnosis, medical   135
Dingwall, R.   12, 13, 55, 57, 62,
    67, 207
disabled children   154
disciplinary society   5–8, 16, 17
    and social order   6–7, 201
disclosure work   89, 96, 98, 137
'disease model'   57–9, 165
doctors, role of   18, 136–7
    see also medical
Dominelli, L.   88
Donzelot, J.   11, 12–13
Douglas, G.   90
Drewry, G.   218
Durkheim, E.   194

Easton, D.   215
Economic and Social Research
    Council   26
Edwards, K.   186
Eekelaar, J.   12, 13
elderly people   210, 211
Eltis, W.   200
emergency protection
    and Children Bill   164, 175,
    176–90, 184
    and *Review*   44, 47
Emergency Protection Order   48,
    153, 157–8, 213
    and appeal   109
    and Carlile Report   74, 75
    and Children Bill   151; and
    CAO   182–90
    and Cleveland Report   111
    and courts   48

entry to premises   73, 74, 75, 111,
    181–3
    and EPO   186, 188–9
EPO *see* Emergency Protection

Faithfull, Lady   168, 170
family
    and assessment   140, 142–5
    autonomy   2, 12, 45
    caring role of   50, 51
    for child rearing   12, 149–50,
    152
    court   33, 48, 113, 159, 168,
    174
    dangerous   142–3, 198
    dysfunctional model   88
    importance of   26, 162
    interactions   140–1
    intervention in   2, 3, 11, 70, 72,
    149, 177
    maintaining links with   26, 40,
    44, 50
    privacy of   172, 197, 204, 214
    and sexual abuse   95, 98–9;
    assessment of   99–100;
    characteristics of   86
    social work and social
    regulation   1–18
    and state agencies   3, 11, 26,
    148
    stress   58, 59
    subjective reality of   11, 212
    support for   45, 46, 51
    undermining of   30, 163
family centres   30, 206, 207
Family Law Review   90
Family Rights Group   24
    and Children Bill   183, 184,
    188, 223
    on parental rights   168, 197
Farn, K. T.   85
feminist view of sexual abuse   88,
    165–6
Ferguson, H.   92
Ferlie, E.   205
financial help as prevention   25
Finkelhor, D.   84
Fischer, J.   24

Fisher, M. 26, 50
Fletcher, H. 24
Floud, J. 199
Forbes, J. 143
Forfar, John 105
foster care 26, 158
  and Beckford case 59, 64, 65
Foucault, M. 3–4, 8, 15, 16,
  142
  on governmentality 9
  on normalisation 5–7
Fowler, Norman 121, 211
Fox, L. 26
Fox, Stephanie 218
Franklin, B. 15, 52, 81, 196
free market society 201
Freeman, M. D. A. 196
Frost, N. 143, 163
Fruin, D. 26
future alternatives 208–12

Gamble, A. 201
Garland, D. 7
Gaylin, W. 201
Gibb, F. 177
Gibbons, T. C. N. 85
Glaser, D. 90
Gledhill, A. 163
GMC 125
Gordon, L. 17, 92
Gorman, Theresa 162–3, 164,
  213
governmentality 9–11
'grave concern' category 129–30,
  207–8
Greenland, C. 60–2, 85, 218
Griffiths Report 117, 128
growth rate charts 62
guardian *ad litem* 168, 174, 185,
  213
  role of 159
Gulbenkian Foundation 24

Hall, Nigel 69–70
Hall, P. 9, 19, 215–16
Hallett, C. 76
Halmos, P. 22
Hamilton, J. R. 142

handicapped children 46, 155,
  174, 210, 211
Handler, J. 25
Harding, Jim 179, 186
Harding, L. 33
Hartley, P. 52
health professionals
  role of 119, 123–4, 136–7
  see also medical
Health and Social Security and
  Social Services (Amendment)
  Act (1983) 34
Held, D. 214
Helfer, R. E. 120
Henry, Tyra 2, 68, 89, 195, 219
  and media 75
Hewitt, M. 9
Hey, F. 90
Heywood, J. S. 21, 25
Higgs, Marietta 80, 101–2,
  104–5, 162, 220
  and police 106
  in Report 97, 114
high risk signs 58, 146
  in sexual abuse 97, 98, 99
Hilgendorf, L. 26
Hill, M. 25
Hinchliffe, David 161, 165, 172,
  190
Hirst, P. 12, 17
Hobbs, C. J. 90–1, 101, 103
Hodgkin, Rachel 167
Hoggett, Brenda 43, 147
Holt, Richard 151, 164
Home Office circular 116, 146
homelessness 170
Horne, M. 15, 99
Howarth, V. 93
Hudson, B. 32
Hughes, Rupert 169–70, 185, 209
Human Rights, European Court
  of 82, 130, 219
Hutchinson, R. 76

Ignatieff, M. 7
Illsley, P. 81
Independent, The 151
individualism, growth of 195, 201

information sharing 125
Ingleby, D. 5, 196
innocent families 94, 95, 100, 164
inquiries, public 25, 76
    and policy change 52
inter-agency cooperation, and
        language 126
interagency practice 124–5
intervention 2
    and civil liberties 196
    and Cleveland 79
    coercive 13, 209
    hierarchy of state 75
    justification for 47
    legitimacy 156
    and magistrates 46–7, 106–7
    and normalisation 20
    parents' challenge 151, 177
    and parents' rights 1
    preventative 13
    and sexual abuse 89
    techniques 10
    therapeutic 22
    see also under family

Jackson, M. P. 25
Jenkin, Patrick 211
Jenkins, Roy 162
Jenkins, W. L. 215
Jervis, M. 163, 178
Johnson, Liam 218
Jones, D. 43, 99
Judge, K. 205
judgement, errors of 57, 68
Justice for Children 24, 197

Kahan, Barbara 28, 36
Kempe, C. H. 57, 120
Kempe, Henry 62, 86, 100
Kempe, Ruth 86
key workers 128, 131
Knight, Jill 149, 162, 164

La Fontaine, J. 91
Labour Group 168, 171
Laing, P. 25
Lambert, L. 31
Lancet, The 90, 97, 103

Land, H. 9, 215–16
Langan, M. 12
language
    of child protection 3, 4, 10, 203
    and inter-agency cooperation
        126
Latey, J. 90
Laurance, J. 53, 93
Law Society 50
law/legal
    accountability 68
    changes in 163–4
    and child care system 17
    clear framework 1, 152
    and Cleveland 107–13
    and discipline 17
    failure to use 65
    responsibility of 159–60
    role in child abuse 18
    sanctions and social order 194
    and sexual abuse 89, 97, 98,
        114
    and social order 6
    and state and family 148
    and welfare 14
see also courts; *Review of Child
    Care Law; and individual Acts*
leaving care 25, 26, 170–1
Lee, P. 12
legalism 209
    in child care 193–8
    emergence of 195
    growth of 203, 213
Lestor, Joan 175
Levitas, R. 200
Liverpool case 112
lobbying, Children Act (1989)
    166–70
local authority 30, 200
    assumption of parental rights
        26, 33, 194
    and courts 33
    homes 26, 158
    legal responsibilities 153, 154,
        155
    role of 163
Local Authority Social Services
    Act (1970) 19

Lord Chancellor   147, 158–60,
  163, 179
  on CAO   180–3
Lorrington, Beverley   59–60, 64,
  65, 217
'love, natural'   55–6
Lowman, J.   17
Lynch, Margaret   85, 86
Lyon, C.   108

McCarthy, M.   211
McCron, R.   92
McGeorge, J.   85
Mackay, Lord   170
McMillan, I.   187
Madden, Max   164
magistrates
  in Cleveland   106–7
  and intervention   46–7
  and POSOs   72
Magistrates Association   35, 50,
  66
male power, abuse of   88, 165–6,
  196
Marshall, K.   184
Martin, C.   90
Mason, Doreen   1, 2, 151, 176,
  183
Meacher, Michael   82
media   52
  and Beckford case   63–4, 67,
    75
  and Carlile case   69
  and Children Bill   151
  Childwatch   91–3, 196
  and Cleveland   79–80, 81,
    103, 113–14, 197
  and Gestapo image   38,
    81
  managing the   135
  and parents lobby   93, 94
  and social workers competence
    63–4
medical
  aspects and sexual abuse   87,
    97
  assessment   212
  diagnosis   135

examination 73–4, 157, 181; in
  Cleveland   95; National
  Children's Bureau   178; and
  POSOs   110, 177
prevention of neglect   62, 63
professionals: in Cleveland   80,
  81, 98, 100–5; role of   119,
  135–7
social problems as   7
Mellor, David   137, 163, 170,
  179
  on abuse statistics   218
  on accommodation   172
  on CAO   186–90
  on consensus   150
  on EPO   153, 186
  on intervention   1, 11, 151, 177,
    183
  and lobbyists   166
  on Southwark   176
Mental Health Act (1983)   36, 73,
  199
Mental Health Review Tribunals
  199
Menzies, R. J.   17
Miller, P.   7, 9–11
Millham, S.   25, 26
moralisation 12–13
Morris, A.   24
Moston, Lord   179
Mottistone, Lord   161, 180–3,
  222–3
Moxon, D.   117
Mrazek, P. B.   85
multi-disciplinary approach   71
  assessment   132
  to sexual abuse   87, 90
  see also agencies
Munro, P.   159
Murray, I.   168
Murray, T.   12

National Association for One
  Parent Families   197
National Children's Bureau   23–4,
  27, 50, 178, 184
  and lobbying   167, 179
  working party members   216

National Children's Home 168, 173, 178
National Council for One Parent Families 34
national efficiency movement 13
National Foster Care Association 173
National Society for the Prevention of Cruelty to Children *see* NSPCC
Nava, M. 81
NCB *see* National Children's Bureau
NCH *see* National Children's Home
Nelken, D. 17
Nelson, S. 88
New Society 83
Newton, Tony 80, 82, 109, 116, 178, 215
NHS Bill (1990) 210
Non-Accidental Injury (DHSS) 118–19, 120
normalisation 5–6, 13, 14, 15
    growth of 16
    and intervention 20
    and 'Review' 49
Noyes, P. 204
NSPCC 161, 178, 203
    on CAO 179, 80, 182–3, 184–6, 188
    early work 22
    registers 204
    review on abuse 85
    role of 123, 126, 128, 130
Nurseries and Child Minders' Regulation Act (1948) 158, 171
'nurturing model' of intervention 22–3

Okell, C. 22
one-parent families *see* single-parent
Osmond, Robin 168, 186

Packman, J. 28, 29, 36–7, 47
    on Children's Departments 21–2, 23

on numbers in care 25, 26
paediatricians 200
    in Cleveland 80, 100–5; and social workers 81
    and parental rights 79
    role of 105–6, 119
PAIN *see* Parents Against INjustice
Palys, T. S. 17
parental rights 110, 114, 117, 153, 196–7
    and assessments 138, 145
    Beckford Report and 66, 67
    and Carlile Report 73
    and Children Bill 177
    and Cleveland 79, 107–8, 109–10
    Resolutions 79, 50, 155, 172; and Short Report 33
    and resources 206
    and Short Report 28
    transference of 26
    in 'Working Together' 122
    see also parents
parents 218
    and case conferences 130–1
    the Cleveland Affair 93–6
    as clients 56
    and decision-making 43–4
    lobby *see* Parents Against INjustice
    and registers 120–1
    response to separation 41
    responsibilities 152, 153, 155, 173, 180
    and sexual abuse 99, 132, 132–3; Cleveland 93–6
    see also parental rights
Parents Against INjustice (PAIN) 94, 184, 197
Parker, R. 9, 24, 195, 215–16
partnership *see* care; family
Parton, Christine 196
    and child protection 122
    male power and abuse 88, 165
    predicting dangerousness 61, 62, 142, 143, 207

Parton, Nigel   *see* abuse; care;
    Children Act; Cleveland;
    family; law/legal; parental;
    social work
Pearson, G.   15
penal policy   199
permanency planning   33
permissiveness   200–1
personal social services
    establishment of   19
    spending on   205
philanthropy   12, 13
Philp, M.   3, 15, 99
Piachaud, D.   205
Pigot, Judge   64, 217
Pithers, D.   139
Place of Safety Orders   37, 50,
    110–11
    appeal against   65–6
    and Beckford case   65–6
    and Carlile case   72
    and Cleveland   67, 80, 96–7,
        98, 99, 102; and magistrates
        106–7
    criticisms of   197
    definition of   34
    guidelines   221–2
    increase in   25, 35, 36
    numbers of   35, 53–4
    and planning   40
    and Short Report   33, 38
police
    in Cleveland   82, 83, 95, 106;
        surgeons   101
    and decision-making   55
    role of   126, 212
    and social workers   119, 146
    and 'working together'   124,
        146
Police   and Criminal Evidence
    Act (1984)   73, 74, 75
policy   210–11, 215
    analysis of   9–10
    changes in   4
political
    concerns   197
    dispute and Children Bill
        170–6

perspectives: changes in   195,
    200–3; and Children Bill
    169–70
POSO *see* Place of Safety Orders
poverty   29, 205
    and risk of abuse   60–1, 164–5
power   7
    abuse of male   165–6, 196
    and governmentality   9
    political   11
    and sexual abuse   97
prediction of abuse *see* abuse
pressure groups   160, 192, 197
    see also lobby
prevention   45, 208
    and high risk checklist   60–2
    and resources   206
    Short Report and   30–1
Prince, J.   85
private children's homes   158
Probert, Mr and Mrs   64–5
prohibited steps order   154
Protecting Children (DoH)   117,
    137, 139, 187, 212
'psy' complex   5–8, 17
psychiatry and sexual abuse
    136–7
public concern/opinion   52, 135
    and inquiries   52, 53
    and sexual abuse   84
    see also media
public inquiries *see* inquiries

Rampton, Tony   23
Rantzen, E.   91–2
Rawstron, Diana   28
reflex and anal dilatation tests
    97, 102, 103, 136
Register Systems DHSS   120
registers 118, 127–30, 203
    management of   120–1
    numbers on   204, 208
    and parents   120–1
    role of   120
rehabilitation   144
Reid, W. J.   24
removal of children   174
    and Carlile Report   74

and Children Bill 184
and high risk 62, 63
and sexual abuse 83
under POSO 36
voluntary 127
research
concerns in 1970s 24–5, 26
role of 50
and sexual abuse 84–5, 92–3
and Short Report 39
residence order 154
resources 205–6, 218
allocation of 138, 206
and Carlile Report 76–7
and Children Bill 171, 175
misdirection of 138
for social work 217
for training 213
respite care 46, 50, 155, 172
Review of Child Care Law 42–9,
109, 169, 208, 209
and Children Act 147, 150,
152, 177, 191
on partnership 155, 173
on POSOs 65, 184
recommendations 43–4, 172
role of research 50
working party 42–3
reviews 26
judicial 31
Richardson, Sue 80, 97, 104, 106,
114
Riches, Peter 159, 167
rights
of children 12
see also parental rights
risk
child abuse and authority
52–78
high risk checklist 60–1
indicators of 58–60, 61
and intervention 47
and registers 129
and removal of children 62, 63
Roberts, R. E. 90
Robertson, I. 160
Rodger, J. J. 17
Rose, N. 5, 9–11, 202, 214

Rowe, Andrew 168
Rowe, J. 26, 31, 40, 42
Ruddock, Martin 69, 70, 71, 76,
77
Rustin, M. 29
Rutherford, M. 218
Ryan, Mary 167, 183

Satyamurti, C. 15
Schneider, J. W. 7
schools 123–4, 133
Scotland 30
Scull, A. 7
Seebohm Report 12, 19, 63, 195
on practice 37, 203
separation of children 24, 40
options 144
sexual abuse
characteristics of families 86,
88
as child health 100–6
and Cleveland 79–115
discovery and nature of 84–91
identification of 90–1, 97, 106,
115, 132
and legal proceedings 86, 89
and male power 88
management of 86–7, 98–9,
102, 115
and parents 93–6, 99, 132–3
physical signs of 90–1, 98, 101,
136
prevalence of 84, 85, 92–3
and removal of children 83
and research 84–5, 92–3
and social assessment 97, 99,
115, 137–45, 146
work with children 89–90
Sgroi, S. A. 89
shared care 45–7, 50, 172
Sharron, H. 95
Shklar, J. N. 194
Short, Clare 165
Short, Renee 27
Short Report 27–39, 65, 77, 208,
209
and Children Act 147, 150,
152, 155, 177

Short Report (*cont.*)
  and children's rights   28
  concerns of   35
  and courts   31, 32–3
  and deprivation   165
  and parental rights   28, 33
  and partnership   173, 174
  and POSOs   33, 38, 171,
    191
  and prevention   30–1
  reasons for   27–8
  recommendations 42
  and research   39
  and Review of Child Care
    Law   42–9
  and role of courts   32
  see also Social Services
    Committee, House of
    Commons
Shyne, A. W.   24
significant harm   156, 177,
  189–90, 207
Sims, Roger   184
Sinclair, R.   26
single-parent families   29–30,
  200–1
Skinner, A.   25
Smith, J.   26
Smith, Peter   159, 167, 168, 174
social assessment   212, 213
  and CAO   189–90
  co-ordination and management
    116–46
  and sexual abuse   97, 99, 115,
    137–45, 146
Social Care Association   168
social control   5–7, 8, 206
  and social work   16
social fund   170
social regulation, social work and
  the family   1–18
Social Services Committee, House
  of Commons   27, 170–1
  see also Short Report
social services departments,
  responsibilities of   211
Social Services Inspectorate   31,
  116, 138

Social Work Decisions in Child Care
  (DHSS)   26, 42
social work/workers
  accountability of   152, 156, 160,
    191, 194; and Cleveland   97,
    98; to courts   213
  attitudes of   54
  and Beckford inquiry   54–5
  characteristics of   14–16
  child care role   17–18, 204
  in Cleveland   95, 96–100, 106
  criticisms of   115, 195, 198, 204
  decline in standards   216
  Gestapo image   38, 81
  growth of   195
  influences upon   26
  lack of knowledge   62–3; and
    media   64
  naivety of   59, 64, 68, 75
  optimism of   55–6, 57, 59
  and police   119, 146
  as powerful   41, 64–5
  practice: bad   76; Cleveland
    affair   96–100; decisions in
    child care   39–42;
    establishment of   11–12
  professional judgements   213,
    214
  responsibility of   57
  role of   54–5, 139, 212; and
    Children Bill   163
  skills   54, 139, 195, 216
  social regulation and the
    family   1–18
  statutory role   68, 69, 75, 77
  strategies and the family   11
  support for   42
  training for   117, 134, 138, 163,
    175
  tutelary complex   11–16
specific issue order   154
state
  and 'best interests'   44–5
  and family   148
  role of   28–9, 202–3
  'strong'   201–3
  see also intervention; local
    authority; social work

Stein, M. 26
Stenson, K. 15
Stevenson, O. 26, 207
strategy discussions 126–7, 131, 203
Supplementary Benefit 30
support 215–16
Suspension Order 48, 49

Taitz, Leonard 59
Taylor, L. 32, 196
teachers 123–4, 133
techniques and intervention 10
Thatcher, M. 163, 176, 200
therapy and sexual abuse 86, 87
Thomas, T. 143
Times, The 169, 176
training and signs of abuse 134
  see also social work
tutelary complex, and social
  work 11–16

unemployment 205
United States 24, 84, 85
Unsworth, C. 196
Utting, Bill 33

Valencia, B. M. 25
Van Krieken, R. 17
Vaz, Keith 149, 188, 223
Vernon, J. 26
violence
  cycle of 60
  in families 196, 197
  see also dangerousness
voluntary care 25, 155, 198, 207
  as accommodation 154–5, 173, 174
  as shared care 45–7
voluntary homes 158
voluntary organisations 124
Von Hirsch, A. 32

Wahlstrom, Gun 59, 217

Walker, A. 210
Walker, N. 199
Walters, Dennis 217
wardship 112, 113, 157, 219
  and Carlile case 73
  and Short Report 31
warrants 157
  and Carlile case 72–3, 74
Webb, A. 9, 206, 215–16
welfare
  element in child care 32
  and free market society 29
  and penalty 7
welfare state 12, 20, 21, 195
Wells, N. H. 85
Westland, Peter 167
White Paper (1987), *Law on Child
  Care and Family Services*
  148ff
White, T. 19
Williams, N. H. 85
Willmore, C. 90
Wilson, A. 179
Wistow, G. 206
women 166
  stress of 165
Woodcraft, E. 90
Woolgar, S. 4
Working Together DHSS 138,
  141, 203
  draft of 122–3, 125, 131, 132, 145
  inter-agency co-operation 116,
  121–35, 143
  parental rights in 122
  and POSOs 123
Wright, Michael 93
Wroe, A. 63–4
Wyatt, Geoffrey 80, 97, 101–5,
  114, 220
Wyld, Nicola 167
Wynne, J. M. 90–1, 101, 103

Young, W. 199